# FOUGHT LIKE A LION

# FOUGHT LIKE A LION

*The Life of an East End Soldier*

PAUL BLUMSOM

Reveille
PRESS

Reveille Press is an imprint of
Tommies Guides Military Booksellers & Publishers

Gemini House
136-140 Old Shoreham Road
Brighton BN3 7BD

First published in Great Britain by
Reveille Press 2025

For more information please visit
www.reveillepress.com

ISBN 978-1-0683111-1-6

Cover design by Reveille Press
Typeset by Vivian Head

Printed in the UK

# *Dedication*

This book is dedicated to the children and step-children of
William Charles Blumsom

My father, George Richard Blumsom 1922–2001

My aunts, Florence Elizabeth Maybank née Blumsom 1926–2019
and Ethel Rose Taylor née Gilbey 1915–1996

My uncles, Charles William Blumsom 1919–2001 and
William George Gilbey 1913–1993

And to the memory of my cousin,
Stephen James Maybank 1951–2024

# CONTENTS

# FAMILY TREE

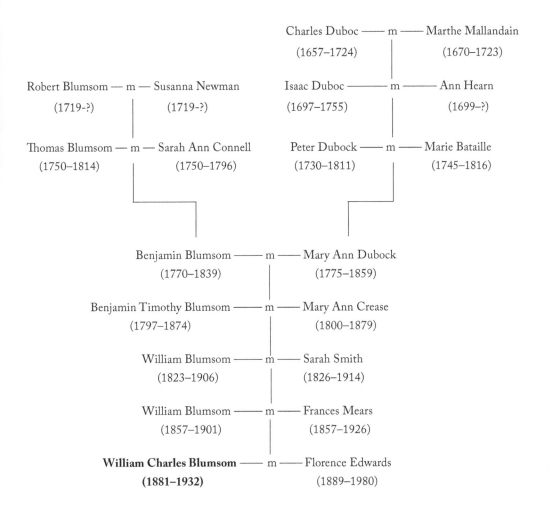

Charles Duboc —— m —— Marthe Mallandain
(1657–1724)                        (1670–1723)

Robert Blumsom — m — Susanna Newman        Isaac Duboc ——————— m ——————— Ann Hearn
(1719-?)                        (1719-?)                        (1697–1755)                        (1699–?)

Thomas Blumsom — m — Sarah Ann Connell        Peter Dubock —— m —— Marie Bataille
(1750–1814)                        (1750–1796)                        (1730–1811)                        (1745–1816)

Benjamin Blumsom —————— m —————— Mary Ann Dubock
(1770–1839)                        (1775–1859)

Benjamin Timothy Blumsom —————— m —————— Mary Ann Crease
(1797–1874)                        (1800–1879)

William Blumsom —————— m —————— Sarah Smith
(1823–1906)                        (1826–1914)

William Blumsom —————— m —————— Frances Mears
(1857–1901)                        (1857–1926)

**William Charles Blumsom** —————— m —————— Florence Edwards
**(1881–1932)**                        (1889–1980)

CHAPTER ONE

# GONE BUT NOT FORGOTTEN

*When you see millions of the mouthless dead*
*Across your dreams in pale battalions go,*
*Say not soft things as other men have said,*
*That you'll remember. For you need not so…*

CHARLES HAMILTON SORLEY,
*When You See Millions of the Mouthless Dead*

I have found him. For over seventy years he has lain here, his grave untended, neglected. But not anymore, for I have found him. His resting place is Nunhead Cemetery, near Peckham, southeast London; grave number 37845, grid reference 106. It's damp, an aptly overcast spring day in May 2005, and the rain falls lightly – a drizzle rather than a downpour. The cemetery is a wilderness; nature has almost reclaimed the land. It is populated with majestic lime, ash, and sycamore trees that grow alongside and amongst the graves; gnarled roots burst from the ground and disappear again, diving through the dead and decaying leaves, through the leaf mould, to return to the depths of the underworld. Headstones stand at crazy angles, knocked askew and flattened by fallen branches. Some appear to have vanished altogether, as if sucked into the ground by subsidence. As I stand by his grave, I can sense the awkwardness of the council graveyard worker behind me, waiting for some sort of response. I say nothing. I am lost in this moment. After an uncomfortable silence, the worker says that he'll leave me to be alone and that he'll see me at the rangers' cabin by the cemetery gates.

I look at the grave, and my heart breaks at the sight of the diminutive stone tablet that serves as his headstone. The inscription reads:

**'In loving memory of my dear husband William Charles Blumsom, Died 18th Febry 1932, Aged 50 years, Gone But Not Forgotten.'**

The tiny headstone is freestanding, mounted on a matching plinth to keep it upright; its innate lack of permanence contrasts with the larger, more impressive gravestones that surround it, which are firmly rooted in the earth. It looks so vulnerable stood in the shadow of its taller fellows, somehow temporary, portable, and liable to be carried off by anyone who cared to. And I confess, the thought crosses my mind to take it for safekeeping, to be venerated, treasured – an act of appropriation born of my protective instinct towards this inanimate object that symbolises so much. Lined up behind it in single file are others, identical in size. This is a common grave; in a bygone time, it would have been known as a pauper's grave. As Siegfried Sassoon's eponymous hero George Sherston observed, 'Life, for the majority of the population, is an unlovely struggle against unfair odds, culminating in a cheap funeral.' The cemetery had strict guidelines as to the size of the tablets used for a common grave: 'No Tablet will be permitted on a Common Grave exceeding twelve inches square and four inches thick', as ordered by the Superintendent, G.H. Gillingham.

The three words that my grandmother had uttered as she stood by his graveside at his funeral come to mind – words that had been relayed to me over seventy years later by my Aunt Florrie, her youngest child. 'It's so deep,' she had said as he was lowered into the ground. The occupants of a common grave were buried in a pragmatically efficient, space-saving way so as to minimise the cost to the public purse. The grave dug to a depth that would accommodate numerous burials, stacked on top of each other and squeezed in wherever room could be found – a subterranean column of forgotten souls. The plot occupied by my grandfather is wedged in between two private graves that are embellished with grand, ornate headstones. Strangers in life, now companions in death, I had no idea who the other occupants of his overpopulated grave were, and neither had he. The one thing they had in common was the poverty that had deprived them of the dignity of a decent burial in their own unique patch of ground where their loved ones could pay their respects.

I place flowers by the stone tablet, bearing my message: 'To a true hero, in awe and admiration, from your grandson Paul.' Eventually, I leave his graveside and make my way through the cemetery to the rangers' cabin. I round a curve in the gravel path and pause at an immaculately kept rectangular plot containing thirty-six graves marked with the unmistakable headstones provided and maintained by the Commonwealth War Graves Commission. Looking back to my initial exploratory visit to the cemetery a couple of months ago during the depths of winter, I might have passed this spot, but such was my intent on finding my grandfather's grave that it didn't register. The headstones, made of white-grey Portland stone, are flawless and elegant in their simplicity and symmetry. They stand in serried ranks like a platoon on parade. It is a sight I would expect to see, on a much larger scale, scattered across the battlefields of Belgium and northern France, but it seems incongruous here in south London.

I feel a pang of jealousy as I gaze at this ordered, peaceful sight, man-made amongst the chaos born of nature surrounding it. My eye is drawn towards the pillar-shaped Stone of Remembrance that commands the plot, inscribed with the phrase taken from Ecclesiasticus 44:14 by Rudyard Kipling in his capacity as literary advisor to the War Graves Commission: 'Their name liveth for evermore.' Unlike my granddad's, I think bitterly. I can't help but compare these immaculate memorials with my grandfather's paltry stone and his space in a crowded grave, so ungenerously provided by an ungrateful state. Lloyd George's so-called 'land fit for heroes'. Like my grandfather, here, too, were buried veterans of the Great War. I have to remind myself that, unlike my grandfather, they didn't survive the war and were denied the chance to see their loved ones again or begin a family as he did. Any one of them would have swapped their pristine headstone for a few more years on this earth.

It gives me great comfort that they are there. That a few hundred yards away, my grandfather has the company of his brothers-in-arms with whom, unlike his fellows in grave number 37845, he shares an *esprit de corps*. I imagine that, as the cemetery gates are locked shut of an evening and as dusk falls, the wraiths of these soldiers will rise from their graves and form up on parade. My grandfather, a corporal, will head his own section, and they will cover off: 'By the left, quick march… left…left…left, right, left.' I can hear the crunch of ghostly boots upon gravel, as if one of Sorley's 'pale battalions' has mobilised, heading for an ethereal front line where no artillery thunders, no machine guns chatter, no mud impedes their progress, and no rats or lice torment them. A front line where peace reigns and the comradeship forged in the fields of Flanders and Picardy, extended to both friend and foe, can be enjoyed for all eternity.

For as far back as I can remember, I have been fascinated by my grandfather's life. I recall as a small boy, sitting cradled in my father's crossed ankles as he relaxed in his armchair, listening enthralled while he spoke about him in such reverential terms that the love and affection that he so obviously felt was transmitted to me. My father described the different sides to his personality; he was a tough man, strong in body and mind, but was gentle and kind as a husband and father. Although he had a real presence, he was not a showy or ostentatious man; rather, he was rational and measured, the one to go to in a crisis. His always-smart appearance and military bearing commanded respect in the south London neighbourhood where he lived.

During my childhood, at some point during the Sixties, I became aware that my grandfather had served in the First World War. During this turbulent decade, the newfound iconoclasm of the age had combined with the cynicism of both the survivors of, and the commentators on, the Great War to produce a generally held perception of needless conflict and the appalling waste of a whole generation. This view was reflected in the arts, led by the stage production and subsequent film *Oh! What a Lovely War* and supported by authors such as the historian A.J.P. Taylor and by the MP Alan Clark in his book *The Donkeys*. The sacrifices and horror of that war described and portrayed were to make a deep impression on me, and the thought that my flesh and blood had served during such wholesale slaughter, let alone survived it, fired my imagination. I was hungry for information about my grandfather, and I pestered my father and his elder brother, my Uncle Charlie, incessantly for details about his life. As they had only been nine and twelve years old, respectively, when he had died, all they could give me were family anecdotes. In common with other survivors of the Great War, whatever 'strange hells' he might have endured remained untold, buried deep in his psyche. I came to hero-worship my grandfather. He had died a quarter of a century before I was born, and distance lends enchantment. That moment when I was introduced to him in Nunhead Cemetery was a watershed moment in my search to find out more about him, to satisfy my need to 'know' him.

When I was a teenager, I read *The First Day on the Somme* by Martin Middlebrook. My grandfather was not involved in the carnage of that particular day, the 1 July 1916; he was bivouacked further north on the Western Front at Locre in Belgium. However, his battalion was transported down to take part in the battle a few weeks later when things weren't going as planned. This book had a profound effect on my understanding of the Great War. The emotional impact was intense. Middlebrook's use of testimonies from survivors of that appalling day was particularly moving. I went on to read Lyn MacDonald's books. She also used the same device, quoting firsthand accounts to great effect. The views expressed by those witnesses appear to support Alan Clark's borrowed description of the generals as 'donkeys'; the way in which the war was prosecuted caused such a profligate waste of life.

Academic work by revisionist historians has made the case for reclaiming the reputations of the generals, particularly that of Field Marshal Douglas Haig, who suffered severe criticism from Lloyd George in his war memoirs published in 1933 up to the present day. The portrayal of Haig as a 'butcher' and/or 'bungler' became the orthodox view throughout much of the mid-to-late twentieth century, but the revisionists pointed to the steep learning curve that the generals had to negotiate in prosecuting a new, industrial-scale form of warfare. In Haig's case, he commanded the largest British force ever put into the field; by the war's end, it numbered 1.8 million men. The logistical challenges presented were enormous. Some saw redemption in the fact that he directed and oversaw the last 'Hundred Days' of the war when the British Army achieved spectacular success through the 'All Arms' approach of bringing together the new technologies of tank warfare and air power with the creeping barrage of the artillery and the 'fire and movement' tactics of the infantry, proving an irresistible force that ultimately brought an end to the conflict. This mitigation put forward by those military historians can be seen as a rational counterbalance to the caricatures portrayed on TV shows such as 'Blackadder'; the overall picture is far more nuanced than either stance. However, it can be said that the lessons learned at the Battle of Loos in 1915 were either not absorbed or acted upon adequately at the Somme in 1916 and at Passchendaele in 1917. The casualty rates were appalling. I am only too aware that my grandfather was fortunate not to have been amongst those who perished.

In early 1988 I finally took my interest further. I wrote to the Ministry of Defence for details of my grandfather's army record. I received a reply dated the 7 March detailing the military service of 'Corporal 28850 William Charles Blumsom MM' and discovered that he had not only served in France and Belgium between 1914 and 1918 but also two other theatres of war: Salonika and the Middle East. He had enlisted on the 5 September 1914 – a month after hostilities began – with the Royal Fusiliers, a London-based regiment who recruited amongst the fertile ground of the slums of the capital. The letter also stated that on the 26 May 1917 he had transferred into the 6th Battalion, Royal Dublin Fusiliers, one of the Irish regiments of the British Army that had existed prior to Home Rule for Ireland in 1922. He was finally demobbed on the 23 February 1919.

The letter lists his medals. He was awarded the Military Medal for gallantry and devotion to duty in action and was mentioned in the *London Gazette* dated the 17 June 1919. As if my admiration for him wasn't already bordering on obsession. The other medals listed were the

1914–1915 Star, the British War Medal, and the Victory Medal. These latter three were campaign medals, the first of which was awarded to troops who had initially served in a theatre of war between the 5 August 1914 and the 31 December 1915. The trio of medals became known as 'Pip, Squeak and Wilfred' after popular comic strip characters that appeared in the *Daily Mirror* after the war. Any soldier serving after the 31 December 1915 was eligible only for the British War Medal and the Victory Medal.

My boyish conversations with Uncle Charlie eventually bore fruit when, two and a half months after I'd received the letter from the MOD, I took delivery of a package from the postman. I knew as soon as I saw the postmark what was within, and I could hardly contain myself as I opened it and read the enclosed letter. My uncle wrote:

> **I decided to let you have my father's medals because you have taken a lot of interest in these things and I know that you will look after them and in any case, I have no boys to leave them to... I have kept my promise and that is the main thing.**

I was deeply moved that he had entrusted me with these treasures and felt honoured that I was the chosen one of my generation to be their custodian. These awards symbolised four years of unimaginable experiences made solid. One by one I removed them almost ceremoniously from the small cardboard box in which he'd packed them, measuring the heft of each in the palm of my hand before arranging them meticulously as they would have been worn on my grandfather's chest. The four medals detailed in the letter from the MOD were unexpectedly accompanied by a fifth, a Queen's South Africa Medal – an award for those who had served in the Boer War – with three clasps for Cape Colony, Orange Free State and Transvaal. Inscribed upon the edge were the details of the recipient, a Private H. Blumsom, regimental number 7535. This was an exciting discovery; I had no knowledge of this family member and could only assume that he was close to my grandfather, maybe a cousin. I wrote again to the MOD, but they held no records under that name and suggested that I contact the Public Records Office at Kew. I decided that I would go there in person at some future date to find out more. It would be many years before I did.

Although my interest has never wavered, the remorseless routine of day-to-day life and the bothersome task of earning a living saw the years roll past, and, as a result, my quest to find out more has been conducted in a random and haphazard fashion, long periods of inaction alternating with the odd sporadic burst of activity throughout adulthood and on into middle age. A catalyst for such a renewed bout of research was the increasing amount of information becoming available on the Internet. The National Archives website drew me in, and discovering that such valuable material was accessible at my fingertips had a galvanising effect, prompting a deep dive into the sources, both digital and analogue.

In the spring of 2004, as a part of this process I visited my Aunt Florrie, my father's younger sister and the sole surviving member of the family who actually knew my grandfather. She lived in Crawley, West Sussex, an 'overspill' town, one of the New Towns created after the Second World War to house those Londoners who had been bombed out or were living in substandard accommodation. Many south Londoners were rehoused here just as east Londoners naturally gravitated to Basildon and Harlow and those from north of the river migrated to Milton Keynes and Stevenage. Here in leafy Sussex could be heard the localised accents of Bermondsey and Brixton, Lambeth and Lewisham, Wandsworth and Woolwich. I have very fond memories of visiting Aunt Florrie; when I was there, the sun would always seem to shine, and her well-tended garden dazzle with colour. This latest visit would be no different.

I opened the front gate and approached the door of the 1950s-built, red-brick, end-of-terrace, ex-council house. She greeted me at the threshold and made a huge fuss. Although seventy-nine years old, Aunt Florrie is slim and sprightly and has inherited my grandfather's fine bone structure. Uncle Jim, her husband, was equally welcoming. We entered her impeccably kept living room and settled down on the sofa with tea.

My aunt was eager to show me the family archive. She was just one day short of her sixth birthday when he died and had always felt a profound sense of loss. This loss was compounded by an eczema-like skin condition that she'd contracted only a few months before his death. She had lost her father, now she was about to lose most of her childhood. As a result of her affliction, she was hospitalised for the greater part of what should have been the most carefree and joyous years of her life, separated from her mother and siblings, she suffered a regime of regular cold baths and full-body dressings (an uncomfortable and restricting mummification process), and was finally discharged over seven years later at the age of thirteen. For the short time that she had with him, her memories were of a kind, gentle and patient man who loved his children unreservedly. She remembers that he would expertly knit socks for the boys, a skill he had learnt in the army, a useful skill to have for an infantryman whose role involved marching for miles on end, essential in protecting his feet. This care became imperative with the advent of trench warfare in the Great War. The low-lying landscape of Flanders would become waterlogged during the rains of winter, and the trenches were constantly saturated due to the high water table. It was crucial for feet to be kept as dry as possible and that socks were changed frequently, and part of an officer's role was to hold regular foot inspections. Soldiers were subjected to disciplinary action if they had neglected their feet. Trench foot was an ever-present threat and gangrene and amputation the worst-case outcome.

As my aunt spoke, I realised that my search had gained a fresh impetus. It was clear that I now had an added responsibility to 'find' him – for her, his youngest child, his little girl, who missed him so dreadfully. She produced her cache of photographs and official-looking papers; irreplaceable artefacts that document a life. She had been left grandfather's army paybook; his Attestation Form; the original certificate for the award of the Military Medal signed by General Rawlinson; and the Army Orders listing the award. To my family, these are holy relics.

According to the Attestation Form, he had originally enlisted on the

4 October 1899 but had lied about his age, declaring that he was a year older than he was. This was intensely exciting; I had had no idea that he'd served prior to the First World War. Clearly, he had joined up as a career choice. (I was to find out subsequently that he had enlisted a year before that, on the 21 October 1898, into the Militia – the forerunner of the Territorial Army – underage, at sixteen years and ten months, and therefore had to perpetuate the lie when he joined the regulars.) His original regimental number detailed on the form was 7535, establishing that the Queen's South Africa Medal sent to me by my uncle was also his; the initial 'H' inscribed on the edge was a red herring. He had joined the Royal Fusiliers, the regiment with which he was also to serve in the Great War, at Dalston Barracks, East London, and his birthplace is shown as Bethnal Green. So, he was an East End boy. The 'H' etched on the medal proved to originate from an oversight on the part of the officer certifying the award, which was confirmed when I eventually accessed the original documents; the Medal Rolls for the Boer War – the 'H' had been written in error rather than 'W'. The officer signing off the awards was none other than Major Guy du Maurier, brother of Gerald, the actor/theatre manager, and uncle of Daphne, the famous author. Du Maurier was my grandfather's commanding officer for the duration of that conflict.

The paybook and Attestation Form revealed the fact that he had served in the Boer War from 1900 to 1902 and subsequently in India from 1904 to 1907, with a home posting back in England in between. He had signed up for a period of twelve years on what was called a short service engagement, which demanded at least seven years' service with the colours and a further five years on reserve. Being a reserve entailed regular bouts of training on return to civilian life and the possibility of a recall to arms when and if needed. His first term of engagement with the army was completed on the 3 October 1911. He could not have imagined that three years later his services would be required again.

The army paybook, issued for his first term of service, is the most precious item in the archive. This is a document of inestimable value containing details of his postings abroad along with the other minutiae of his service; date of enlistment; regimental number; awards; courses passed; record of pay; sickness and injuries suffered; and incorporating a blank Will (for completion by the soldier concerned). Used as a form of identification to be produced to regimental police on demand and, more sombrely, if the bearer happened to be a battlefield casualty, it was incredibly important to both the individual soldier and the army authorities. Everywhere that my grandfather served, including when on active service, it was on his person, at all times. Of his few remaining possessions, this is the one that connects me to him the most. Buttoned safely in his tunic pocket on long, hot days fighting and riding on horseback across the South African veldt during the Boer War and, after that, whilst stationed in Darjeeling with its humid climate, and continually handled by him throughout his first period of service, it is infused with his essence. As I held it, it occurred to me that this was the nearest I could get to shaking his hand. My Great-Uncle James, William's younger brother by two years, died in 1973. If my grandfather had survived to a similar age, he would have seen me reach my teenage years. He never lived long enough to put a reassuring arm around my shoulder or to affectionately tousle my hair. Handling this hundred-year-old paybook was human touch by proxy. I turned it over and over in my hands reverentially and inspected every page painstakingly. I was completely mesmerised.

My aunt had three photographs of him in uniform. Her eyes shone and she radiated pride as she handed them to me, all she had left of the father taken too soon. I had seen them before, but now that I had a context in which to place them, they came alive, practically animating the young fusilier. I studied the images with a fresh pair of eyes, and it dawned on me that he will be forever frozen in time as a soldier, a young man in his early twenties, proud and straight-backed in his uniform. I know of no other photographs of him that survive, and I had to use my imagination to picture him as a civilian and a family man, reaching middle age. To borrow from Laurence Binyon, he 'shall not grow old'. I contacted the National Army Museum and the Imperial War Museum, the staff at both of which examined them and attempted to date them.

The first of these photographs is a head-and-shoulders shot that the National Army Museum stated could have been taken anytime between 1900 and 1914, the uniform corresponding with those worn in both South Africa and India during this period. The Imperial War Museum narrowed it down, concluding that it was an image of a fusilier wearing a style of khaki drill jacket worn from 1896 until 1905.

The second is of a group of soldiers marching in an English country lane. According to the National Army Museum, they are wearing white webbing that dates from the Boer War, but the officer leading them appears to be wearing Service Dress, which was not introduced until 1904. They gave a tentative date of 1904. The Imperial War Museum was able to pinpoint the country lane as being in the village of Runfold in Surrey, near Aldershot. They stated that the group appeared to be on a speed march and estimated the date at circa 1902 to 1908, but definitely predating the First World War. They referred me to a photograph that had appeared in a regimental history titled *Lions of England*. It had been taken from exactly the same viewpoint in 1906, capturing the King's Own Royal Regiment (Lancaster) taking part in the Evelyn Wood Marching Competition, which involved a speed march followed by target shooting. My grandfather and his fellow Royal Fusiliers had been clearly competing for the same trophy, perhaps a year or two previously, that had been originally donated by Field Marshal Evelyn Wood VC in an effort to improve the marksmanship of the rank and file at varying distances.

The third photograph, of a group of five soldiers alternately sitting and standing, taken by the J. Burlington Smith Studio in Darjeeling, India, was dated as circa 1905 by the National Army Museum. They also commented upon the chevrons sported by all five on their left arms. These are good conduct stripes; two chevrons indicate six years' good conduct and three represent twelve years'. My grandfather, sitting on the far left, has two chevrons. His Attestation Form details the year of enlistment as 1899, from which it can be deduced that the image dates from no earlier than 1905 and no later than 1907, when he returned to England. The

Imperial War Museum confirmed that it was taken in India sometime after the Boer War and that the soldier seated on the far right is wearing pantaloons, which indicate he is a member of a mounted infantry troop.

I looked more closely at his Attestation Form and felt an emotional tug inside when I saw his signature. It was written in a copperplate style, but I imagined that I could detect a slight tremulousness in his hand. In my mind's eye I could see him concentrating as he signed it, unused as he was to writing, as he had left school as a thirteen or fourteen year old. The form lists his trade as 'Labourer'. The life of a labourer in the late nineteenth century could be a very insecure one. Without a skilled trade, a labourer lived in a precarious state, on the precipice of poverty. Unable to rely on permanent employment, earnings could be intermittent, the fear of being laid off ever-present. Many labourers were casually hired on a piecework basis; in the East End, 'casuals' would assemble at the dock gates to the riverside wharves in the early morning for the 'call-on' in the hope of earning a day's pay. This process was repeated at lunchtime for an afternoon's work, if any were available.

Hundreds were disappointed every day and left, dejected, to return to their overcrowded, inadequate homes wondering how they were to feed their families that night. Still in its infancy, the trade union movement, even with the uptake of membership following the success of the London Dock Strike in 1889, was nowhere near powerful enough to challenge these working practices; universal subscription was a distant ideal. Trade union membership amongst the population of London had shrunk to only three and a half per cent by 1897 after the employers had gained the upper hand earlier in the decade, and even then, the labourers weren't represented to the extent that skilled and semi-skilled tradesmen were; they were the lowest ranked of all workers. Nationally, on the eve of the new century, only twenty per cent of the whole male workforce and far fewer of their female counterparts belonged to a union. In that signature, I imagined I could see encapsulated the whole insecurity and lack of self-confidence of the working class.

It became obvious that there was so much about his life that was unknown to the rest of the family. The seed of an idea was planted in my head; here was a story crying out to be told, from the cradle to the grave, a written narrative that would commemorate his life, which might otherwise have passed unremembered. It also occurred to me that there must be many others like him. How many other veterans who survived the Great War are lying forgotten and neglected in cemeteries around the country, with stories that deserve to be told? At the cessation of hostilities, waves of demobilised soldiers returned to the UK. Those that were disabled or disturbed had precious little to look forward to. But those that were apparently able-bodied or considered of sound mind had uncertain futures, too. Disillusioned and disenfranchised, many of them were to some degree psychologically affected by the experiences and privations of the previous four years. Many veterans couldn't bring themselves to speak to their families about the horrors they'd seen and endured. Most had problems readjusting to civilian life. After all, what did they have in common with those who had remained at home? For all of the awfulness they'd undergone, some missed the camaraderie and close bonds formed with their fellows, under extreme circumstances, that civilians in no way could relate to. Sassoon articulates the veterans' collective experience in *They*:

> *'We're none of us the same!' the boys reply.*
> *'For George lost both his legs, and Bill's stone blind;*
> *'Poor Jim's shot through the lungs and like to die;*
> *'And Bert's gone syphilitic: you'll not find*
> *'A chap who's served that hasn't found some change.'*
> *And the Bishop said: 'The ways of God are strange!'*

The promises from the politicians proved predictably empty. Heroes were forgotten with indecent haste. Bemedalled beggars on street corners were a common sight. In some cases, ex-commissioned officers along with demobbed men from the other ranks were reduced to selling matches to scrape a living. My grandfather, with a new family to support, was fortunate in that he was able to secure regular employment upon demobilisation, and although he was insulated to a certain extent from the privations suffered by the jobless, he would nevertheless face financial challenges. His burial in a common grave is proof that he was not immune to the prevailing economic climate; traditionally, it was a matter of honour for the working class, however poor, to make provision for a good 'send-off'. He died during the depths of the Great Depression of the early Thirties, and the disastrous effects of the global economic situation were catastrophic for those lower down the social scale.

The suffering of the surviving war veterans, compounded by the Depression, led me to reconsider the whole concept of a 'Lost Generation'. From everything I'd read up until this point, my understanding of the Lost Generation was of an officer class – an elite – made up of the brightest and best, the great and the good, who had died serving King and Country. The nation had been robbed of those public school and Oxbridge-educated subalterns who were destined for greater things. Vera Brittain famously expressed this notion in *Testament of Youth*, which details the tragic loss of her fiancé, brother and two close friends in the conflict. The deaths of the war poets Rupert Brooke, Wilfred Owen, Charles Hamilton Sorley and Edward Thomas reinforced this view; such talent could not be replaced. The Lost Generation, as far as I could see, was (a) upper-middle class, and (b) dead. But my assumption was challenged by Ernest Hemingway, who had served as an ambulance driver on the Italian front during the war and had a different take on the Lost Generation, one that predated my interpretation. In the 1920s Hemingway lived in Paris where he enjoyed a friendship with fellow ex-pat Gertrude Stein. Stein expressed this alternative view to Hemingway: 'That's what you are. That's what you all are. All of you young people who served in the war. You are a Lost Generation.'

Hemingway replied, 'Really?'

Stein said, 'You are. You have no respect for anything. You drink yourselves to death.'

Not that my grandfather had resorted to drink after the war – he embraced the security and stability of family life. After serving in the army for the best part of seventeen years, on and off, stationed around the globe in various outposts of the British Empire, his wanderlust satisfied, he became a family man. But this alternative reading resonates, and it has shown me that the Lost Generation can be perceived in other ways, redefined to include the living as well as the dead. And also, to include the working class, not just the upper middle class; artisans as well as artists; labourers, miners, dockers and farmhands as well as poets, politicians and future captains of industry. As Sassoon so effectively writes, these men were profoundly altered by the war, whether physically or psychologically. For many of the survivors, they came back as different people, 'lost' to their families and loved ones. I wondered how my grandfather might have been affected. Although already a battle-hardened veteran of the Boer War, had this subsequent, greater and more awful war damaged him in any way? Was he also one of the Lost Generation?

His story is one of many, of countless others laid to rest in graveyards across the country and whose exploits remain unrecorded. They, too, deserve recognition and remembrance. Those vast armies of men who never spoke about their experiences, who came home and quietly got on with their lives, wrestling with their demons in private. For there are such stories to be told – that need to be told. Stories that will leave us, their descendants, wide-eyed in wonder, marvelling at the stoicism, humanity, good humour and sheer courage displayed by these remarkable men. Awe-struck in admiration at the part that our ancestors played in one of the most tragic periods of history that the world has ever known. And my grandfather's story will, I hope, in addition to commemorating his life, bring to mind all of these ordinary soldiers who had survived but have been forgotten. But how ordinary were they? It has been said that these were ordinary men who did extraordinary things. Not so to the generations that were born after the Second World War: the 'Baby Boomers' and even more so, 'Generation X' and the 'Millennials'. To us, these men *are* extraordinary; their sense of duty and willingness to sacrifice their lives for a perceived 'greater good' is alien to many today, some of whom question the need for armed conflict and require greater justification for going to war in our more sceptical age; deference to our so-called 'betters' no longer exists. As L.P. Hartley memorably wrote: 'The past is a foreign country; they do things differently there.'

The plight of these forgotten men is perfectly expressed by Private John McCauley of the 2nd Border Regiment, who was one of them:

> **In the two minutes' silence I see great hosts of khaki-clad figures, phantom figures, the ghosts of yesterday. The long line of soldier comrades, such noble comrades they were, march before my blurred vision. I see them in battalions, brigades, divisions, army corps, and I distinctly hear their cry: 'In honouring the dead, forget not the living. Remember us, but remember too, those who survived.'**

So, remember those 'ordinary' soldiers whose stories will never be told. Those who did not pay the ultimate price but had suffered in other ways, physically, psychologically, emotionally, socially and economically. Those without elaborate headstones, family vaults and mausoleums; those who lie unremembered like my grandfather had been. And it was this; this need for remembrance, that drove me on. My path ahead having cleared before me, my search now began in earnest.

CHAPTER TWO

# THE SEARCH

*Your suggestion that I should write history, has often been made,*
*for a good many people have given me the same advice. I like the*
*idea: not that I feel at all sure of being successful – it would be*
*rash in an amateur – but because the saving of those who deserve*
*immortality from sinking into oblivion and spreading the fame*
*of others along with one's own, seem to me a particularly splen-*
*did achievement [...] and the philosophers say that it is an ex-*
*cellent thing to follow in the footsteps of one's forebears, provided*
*that they trod an honest path.*

PLINY THE YOUNGER, *Letter to Titinius Capito*

The challenge I had in attempting to tell my grandfather's tale was that, in common with many other soldiers of his rank and class, he had left no correspondence or diaries detailing his experiences. As observed by Richard Price, author of *An Imperial War and the British Working Class*, 'It is well known that working men were not and are not in the habit of committing their thoughts to paper.' This is in stark contrast to the abundance of material generated by officers involved in the Great War, who were so much more literate than the average 'Tommy' and not subjected to the same level of censorship. There were precious few accounts in existence by the 'men' or other ranks, as Price further points out 'there is very little manuscript material to which one can turn and find what the working class thought about particular events and episodes'. In lieu of my grandfather's own voice, I needed to establish what documentation was available that could help me to construct a meaningful narrative of his life – what Price describes as 'indirect evidence to build up a composite picture'. And so, the most intense phase of my search began. Throughout 2004 and into 2005, I was to undertake the bulk of my research into army records.

This entailed numerous visits to the National Archives in Kew. Built in 1977 to accommodate the ever-growing collection of official state papers and court records, it supplanted the Public Record Office at its Chancery Lane site, which had reached full capacity long before. In a curious instance of synchronicity, it inhabits the former location of a First World War hospital. Upon arrival, the first impression of the building is that of a massive fortress or giant bunker. Indented windows run the length and breadth of each of the top three floors in a continuous narrow strip, resembling the slit-shaped openings of the enormous concrete gun emplacements built as coastal defences during the Second World War. These windows are not designed with a view to appeal aesthetically; these floors are where the actual records are stored, and ultraviolet light contamination has to be kept to a minimum in order to preserve these hugely important historical documents. The artificial water feature in front of the building along with the later additions of the glass-clad atrium that serves as the entrance and the more conventionally glazed section of the wing that flanks it are more akin to a modern university campus, but they are overshadowed by the brutalist storage block. Awe-inspiring both in its physical appearance and in the concept of its function, the building is a repository of a thousand years of documented British history. Contained within is the collective memory of the nation. The security is tight; obtaining a reader's ticket entails a rigorous vetting process. The reading rooms are partitioned and are virtually sterile areas; bags are to be checked into lockers; no pens, food or drink are allowed to pass the threshold.

Having pre-ordered the war diaries of the battalions in which he'd served, I arrived at the counter and was provided with the relevant files. I took them to a desk and opened the first file. I felt a thrill as I studied these original documents, nearly a hundred years old and completed by commissioned officers under whom William would have served, in the Royal Fusiliers and the Royal Dublin Fusiliers on the Western Front, Macedonia and the Middle East. I felt a distinct connection across the years, privileged to be handling these documents as they had handled them, composed whilst on active service and within the sound and range of artillery fire. As I worked my way through them, it became clear that the amount of information that could be gleaned varied, and was totally dependent upon the officer completing them. Every day was itemised, but the records varied from single-line entries to whole passages. This could have been due to the conditions under which they were written, how much time the author's other duties allowed him, or how diligent he was. Casualties were generally well recorded and, in the main, only officers were named; the men or 'other ranks' were usually expressed in numbers. However, I did find that the early diaries of the Royal Fusiliers were an exception in that some privates and NCOs were actually identified.

On subsequent visits to Kew, I sought out other records, including the campaign medal index cards and the British Army pension records 1914–1920, the latter proving invaluable. Around 2004-5 when I carried out this research, the pension records were still being stored on microfiche film in ranks of metal cabinets filed alphabetically. Once I'd located the relevant reel, I loaded it into a reader and started scrolling through the images. I scanned these records with an acute sense of anticipation. It was by no means certain that my grandfather's was amongst them, two-thirds of the six and a half million paper records having been destroyed in September 1940 during the Blitz. The surviving documents were known as the 'burnt documents' due to the charred and water-damaged state they were left in. The burnt edges were clearly visible on the microfiche images; some pages were more damaged than others, with only parts of the remaining text legible. I felt a huge sense of relief combined with excitement when I found his record. And it became immediately clear that the information provided to me by the MOD back in 1988 had not only been extracted from these records but also that these documents contained even more granular detail, which would be essential in reconstructing his life.

I then looked further back, retrieving Boer War records. There was no central index cross-matching the records of soldiers who had served in both conflicts with a break in service in the interim. In my grandfather's case, as in those of others I have found, no attempt had been made to marry the records of his separate periods of engagement. Following one soldier's career across two wars requires a painstaking and forensic approach to examining the various records and files available and an ability to interpret said records, including idiosyncratic handwriting by army officials, misspellings and human error, to establish a complete narrative. Despite this challenge the meticulous record-keeping and bureaucracy of the British Army became my greatest ally. Thanks to the archives, for the most part, I knew exactly where he was on any particular day during the First World War and what events his battalion were involved in. My research widened, and I became a voracious reader of Great War literature, scouring second-hand bookshops, hunting down copies of books that made any mention of the units with which he'd served and actions that he'd been involved in.

I had to formulate a strategy. I interwove facts gleaned from the war diaries and official records with the contemporaneous accounts of other troops along with my informed imaginings of his personal experience. In the first instance, the testimony of soldiers who'd served in either of his respective battalions would be invaluable. The battalion, consisting of a thousand men at full strength, is the most meaningful unit to follow when retracing a particular soldier's steps. One could be more certain than not that the individual concerned had played his part in the recorded activities of such a battalion. Therefore, by necessity, my grandfather's story was told by others. Where published accounts were not available from those serving in the same battalion, I sought out any that were in existence from soldiers who had served in other battalions belonging to the same brigade or division. The most valuable of these was a diary published under the title *Stand To*, kept by Captain F.C. Hitchcock MC of the 2nd Leinster Regiment, which belonged to the 17th Brigade and 6th Division alongside the 1st Royal Fusiliers.

A division consists of three brigades, each of which, in turn, is made up of four battalions. These units' records chronicle his experience through a panoramic lens, but they do have some worth, as these formations will have occupied the trenches alongside his battalion and fought shoulder-to-shoulder with him in many of their actions. As most of this material, whether official records, personal diaries, or published prose, was composed by those of a different social class – with one notable exception – the narrative was lacking in the views of a working-class soldier. But this doesn't detract from their usefulness; they provide context and document the same events that the working-class soldier witnessed and experienced. As a result, this story became an exploration of the times in which my grandfather lived. The perceptions of those providing testimony inevitably impinged on his story, which became to a greater or lesser degree a story about *them*; detours were taken in the telling that reveal the attitudes of the age. These accounts should be seen as parallel to and in conjunction with my grandfather's experience; informing his biography but not eclipsing it, although relying so heavily on such sources requires the application of imagination and interpretation to extrapolate his story. So, their value cannot be discounted on the grounds of class and rank: they were fellow combatants and eyewitnesses, and, certainly in the case of du Maurier, my grandfather was directly under the command of some of them. This mix of personal testimony and official records sits within an historical narrative that teases out the relationship between seismic international events – the Boer War, the First World War and the Great Depression – and the common man. The social, economic, political and cultural climate that impacted and directed the path of an East End boy whose way of life would change forever as he grew into a man in this new world order. The whole work is formed of three main strands: first and foremost, my grandfather's story; secondly, my journey in 'finding' him; and, finally, a narrative of the times in which he lived. The parallel journeys that my grandfather and I took provide the *warp* and the contextualising history supplies the *weft*; it is a history viewed through the prism of the working-class soldier, juxtaposing the macrocosm of these great movements in world affairs with the microcosms of his family, community and army battalion.

The battalion was the basic building block of the British Army. Each regiment typically had an establishment of two battalions. Prior to the

Great War, one battalion would be posted on overseas service to some far-flung outpost of the Empire, the other on home service, often supplying reinforcements to its sister battalion abroad. These could be exchanged and sometimes were. The Royal Fusiliers were one of several regiments to become exceptions to this rule due to army reforms. In the spring of 1898, a third battalion was formed, and in early 1900, a fourth. With the advent of the Great War and the accompanying massive recruitment drive, regiments formed subsequent 'service' battalions for the duration. During the conflict, battalion numbers fluctuated dramatically depending on casualties sustained. At full strength, a battalion consisted of four companies, each with over two hundred soldiers and headed by a major or captain; each company was subdivided into four platoons of just over fifty troops, led by a lieutenant or second lieutenant; and each platoon comprised four sections of twelve men under a sergeant or corporal.

I was to discover two invaluable sources of information. The first came to my attention when my research threw up the fact that the medical officer of the 1st Royal Fusiliers was a Captain Charles Wilson, later Lord Moran, who was to become Winston Churchill's personal physician during the Second World War and thereafter. He had kept a journal during the Great War and had subsequently published extracts in his book *The Anatomy of Courage*. Captain Wilson would undoubtedly have been involved in the treatment of my grandfather and the subsequent decision to send him back to England when he was wounded on the Somme during the action at Guillemont. The fact that the man who would become the personal physician of a Prime Minister of Great Britain had also treated my grandfather was an incongruity that fascinated me. Wilson's writings were archived at the Wellcome Library for the History and Understanding of Medicine on the Euston Road. His papers were an essential resource in attempting to chronicle my grandfather's service with the Royal Fusiliers in the Great War.

Studying Wilson's journal became my priority. I obtained a Wellcome Library reader's card and made my way to central London. Ascending the stairs from Euston Underground Station to street level, it was but a short walk along one of London's main east-west arterial routes, through the exhaust fumes from the nose-to-tail traffic, before arriving at the grand neoclassical edifice at number 183. Housing the Wellcome Collection, it is a world-renowned centre for the study of medical science and history. Designed by Septimus Warwick, the architect of Lambeth Town Hall, the building was completed in 1932, the year my grandfather died, and is constructed of the same Portland stone used for the Commonwealth War Graves Commission headstones.

I entered the main entrance underneath an imposing pediment supported by four Ionic columns, its size and scale echoing the glories of ancient Greece and Rome. From the reception I was directed to a reading room and presented with a slightly larger than shoebox-sized container made of heavy-duty cardboard. Inside I found photocopies of Wilson's contemporaneous notebooks completed whilst he served on the Western Front, including during the Battle of the Somme. His family retains the originals. They are written in an 8 x 5½ inch field notebook consisting of graph-paper pages. Considering the conditions under which they were written, the handwriting is neat and formal, although his idiosyncratic style makes some words illegible. The information he records is invaluable to the historian or biographer, a primary source expressing a personal view that complements the official war diaries. I arranged to have a copy made of Wilson's notebook, which was subsequently mailed to me.

The second significant source of information emerged when I found that an officer from the 6th Battalion Royal Dublin Fusiliers – the battalion to which my grandfather had been transferred following his convalescence and recovery from his injury sustained at the Somme – had kept a detailed diary of his time with them. His name was Captain Noel Drury. Born and bred in Dublin and immensely proud of his regiment, his writings covered the battalion's service in Salonika, the Middle East and subsequent deployment to France in the final days of the war. These writings are stored at the National Army Museum in Chelsea.

Sometime after my visits to Kew and Euston Road, whilst on holiday in Cornwall, I came across a small but well-stocked bookshop named

Bookends in Fowey. Fowey is forever linked with the du Maurier family. They owned a house on the river, named Ferryside, which they had purchased in 1926, and it is still owned by the family today. Daphne wrote her first novel, *The Loving Spirit*, there. Bookends specialises in works written by and about the du Mauriers. The owner, Ann Willmore, who was something of an expert on the family, showed me a rare volume, her personal copy of Guy du Maurier's published letters written during the early years of the Great War before he was killed in action. This opened up a new line of enquiry for me. Du Maurier was clearly a prolific letter-writer, and I wondered if there existed any correspondence from his service in the Boer War throughout the period he commanded my grandfather's battalion there. Ann was aware of other letters he'd written but not specifically any that had been composed during the campaign in South Africa. She provided details of institutions that held du Maurier archives, including Harvard University and the University of Exeter, and individuals, including the writer Andrew Birkin, author of *J.M. Barrie and the Lost Boys: The Real Story Behind Peter Pan*, who would possibly be able to help. Her advice was to prove invaluable.

I corresponded with both Harvard and Exeter, the archives of both of which contained some of his letters but none written during 1901–1902, the period in question. I then contacted Andrew Birkin and struck gold. He recalled having obtained copies of the relevant letters some time ago, and he generously went to some trouble to retrieve them for me. He transferred the letters – originally xeroxed and thirty pages in total – on to compact disc and sent them to me. The letters include a linking narrative by Peter Llewellyn Davies, who, with his siblings, was the inspiration behind Barrie's 'Boy Who Wouldn't Grow Up'. Guy du Maurier had been appointed as one of the guardians of Peter and his brothers after they had been orphaned in 1910, when Peter was thirteen. Llewellyn Davies had been collating family papers, including du Maurier's letters, into a collection that he labelled the *Family Morgue*, when he committed suicide at the age of 63 in 1960. Andrew had obtained this material from Peter's younger brother Nico whilst researching for a TV script that would develop into his book. The letters were composed by du Maurier both on the voyage out to South Africa and then whilst on active service there. It was a priceless discovery, and I devoured the correspondence greedily. The letters provided a unique insight into the conditions my grandfather had faced during the Boer War.

These discoveries brought home to me how dependent I was on these sources – without any primary source material from my grandfather, no first-person account that tells us of his own experience, these writings were crucial in reconstructing what he went through. I was able to piece together his life. It was like putting the pieces of a jigsaw puzzle in place, the only segment missing being the central piece, that which his own hand would have produced. I had to metaphorically walk in his footsteps, retracing his movements. It was the closest I could get to knowing him.

But to produce a more rounded picture of his experience, I needed to look also at his life outside the army. Although he spent a substantial amount of his adult life as a soldier, I sought out information about his experience as a civilian to see if I could find out anything about his early days and upbringing and whether there was a specific family culture that informed his attitudes and behaviour. I started to travel backwards in time, using census, school, and birth, marriage and death records, accessing the National Archives resources at Kew, and cross-referencing my findings with those of other members of my extended family previously unknown to me who were also tracing the Blumsom lineage.

This research revealed that the family had lived in the East End of London for most of the eighteenth and nineteenth centuries. For the last two generations, however, our particular branch of the family had lived in south London; my grandfather had moved there after the war when he married my grandmother. He was born at home in 1881 at 7 West Street, Bethnal Green, and this gave me another potential avenue for research. In 1902 a wealthy shipping magnate from Liverpool named Charles Booth published a social inquiry into the lives of the inhabitants of London, focusing initially on the East End, titled *Life and Labour of the People in London.* Therein, he systematically recorded data collected by his researchers, who had visited the streets of the East End, mostly accompanied by police officers for safety.

This data revealed that the level of poverty exceeded the estimates. Booth's book was published at a time when there was great concern amongst parliamentarians and social commentators regarding the widespread privation suffered by the residents of the East End. *Life and Labour* would be used as an instrument for social reform, and its contents are a valuable source for social historians and researchers to this day. Booth compiled street maps and devised a colour-coded system to classify social status and levels of poverty:

> **Black**  Lowest class. Vicious, semi-criminal.
> **Dark Blue**  Very poor, casual. Chronic want.
> **Light Blue**  Poor. 18s. to 21s. a week for a moderate family.
> **Purple: Mixed**  Some comfortable, others poor.
> **Pink**  Fairly comfortable. Good ordinary earnings.
> **Red**  Middle class. Well-to-do.
> **Yellow**  Upper-middle and upper classes. Wealthy.

By cross-referencing data harvested from census returns and birth certificates with Booth's records, I was able to reconstruct an accurate picture of the quality of life experienced by my ancestors in the streets where they'd lived. It also explained how the Army had been so successful in recruiting from the East End. Many poor, working-class boys and men were unable to resist the lure of new boots, a smart uniform and the promise of three square meals a day, who otherwise only had a life of mind-numbing drudgery, back-breaking labour, vagrancy, or the workhouse in front of them.

This brought to mind my father's own experience. Just as his father had done before him, he enlisted in the armed forces shortly before the nation was plunged into war. He joined the Royal Marines on the 11 July 1939, short of two months before the onset of the Second World War.

Aunt Florrie still recalls the shock of him coming home and suddenly announcing to her and my grandmother what he'd done, as he had not discussed his plans with anyone. Like my grandfather, he served for the duration of his war and was also wounded in action. When my father passed away in 2001 at the age of seventy-nine, it prompted me to re-examine our relationship. In my grief, I thought deeply about him and what he meant to me. He was a mainstay in my life, a stabilising influence, and there was no finer role model for a son to look up to. His qualities of stoicism, resilience, calmness under pressure and a fiercely protective instinct where his family were concerned were, I came to understand, inherited from *his* father. The poet Kahlil Gibran wrote: 'You are the bows from which your children as living arrows are sent forth.' My grandfather was the bow to my father's arrow. These traits formed part of a legacy passed from father to son through nature and nurture, via the genes and by example. It was a revelatory moment, a realisation that, by knowing my father, I would also know my grandfather.

During my father's later years, I had asked him where Granddad was buried. He could tell me no more than that it was in Nunhead Cemetery. I formed the impression that the grave had rarely been visited since his death in 1932. This was not through any lack of feeling or respect; I know, from my father and uncles and aunts, how well loved he was. It was probably more the case that the cemetery was some distance from the family home in Bermondsey, and, as a widow raising and keeping her brood fed and clothed, my grandmother had her hands full. It would have been both impractical and too expensive on public transport for her to travel there on a regular basis.

The very first time I had visited Nunhead Cemetery, some time before that fateful day when I was shown his grave, was in the dying days of the winter of 2005. I turned up at the main north entrance of the burial ground in Linden Grove and parked the car. I paused to take in the sight of the imposing gates designed by James Bunstone Bunning, an architect who had also worked on Highgate Cemetery, before walking through into a wide, gravel-paved avenue lined with mature lime trees. Prior to my visit, in my mind's eye I had expected to see an ordered graveyard with neat symmetrical rows of headstones in well-tended lawns. I had assumed that the authority managing the cemetery would hold some kind of record of burials, but I wanted to carry out the painstaking task of walking and inspecting every row, with no foreknowledge, and with fresh eyes, in a methodical fashion until I found him; I wanted that moment of discovery when I first saw his name on a headstone.

It quickly became obvious that this would be impossible. As I walked along the path, I could see that beyond the lines of lime trees was an almost impenetrable thicket of ash, oak and sycamore trees that had obviously grown uncultivated. Unlike the limes, these trees had not been planted to any pattern or design; they had taken root naturally, organically. The foliage disguised most of the graves, which were hidden from sight beyond a veil of green. It was apparent that, for a considerable period of time, this cemetery had been neglected and left untended, and had undergone a natural rewilding. It was, though, strikingly atmospheric – not in a macabre way but as a triumph of new life over death; nature had taken back its territory from man's manufactured attempt to shape this particular landscape.

I followed the gravel path to an impressive Gothic chapel. As I got closer, I could see it was a roofless shell. The path split into two branches at right angles in front of the chapel. I stood there waiting expectantly, as if my grandfather might call to me from beyond the grave, as though his spirit would lead me to where he lay. I decided to turn left and hadn't walked far when the path forked again, curving away in opposing directions. I took the right fork, scanning from side to side as I walked, all the time attempting the practically impossible task of identifying his headstone while trying not to veer off the path. Peering into the undergrowth shadowed by the towering trees, I realised that I needed to focus my search.

I would later find out, however, that I hadn't been that far from his grave. Considering the huge size of the cemetery, all of fifty-two acres, I had somehow been within a stone's throw of finding him. If I had taken the left fork, I would have passed a few feet away from him, just off the path. But even then, I wouldn't have seen the small stone tablet that serves as his headstone. I eventually returned to the main gates and looked at a notice board, hoping to glean more information. I left disappointed and resolved to come back better prepared.

I subsequently discovered that the cemetery had been abandoned by the London Cemetery Company in 1969. It had also suffered from bomb damage during the Second World War. It was originally lawned; however, with the passage of time and lack of attention, the lawn had given way to meadow and eventually woodland. Originally a privately owned cemetery, it was opened in 1840 and was one of the London cemeteries, including Highgate Cemetery, known as 'the magnificent seven', all of them commercial enterprises. Built between 1837 and 1841 as a solution to the inadequacy of local parish grounds to cope with London's dead. Southwark Council purchased the derelict cemetery in 1975 for the nominal sum of one pound. Most of the cemetery has now been given over for wildlife and has been designated a nature reserve, although some areas are reserved for burials.

I eventually returned to the cemetery armed with the date of my grandfather's death and spoke to a graveyard worker stationed in the rangers' cabin at the Limesford Road entrance. I was advised to make enquiries at the Camberwell New Cemetery where all the records were now kept.

The day I went there it was late afternoon, somewhere between half past four and a quarter to five, on my way home from work. I entered the office through the archway of the administrative block and spoke to a member of staff. He had an anaemic pallor and an air of torpor about him that seemed apt for an official involved in the bureaucracy of death. I sensed a reluctance on his part to engage with me, as if he was hoping his attitude would put me off. His lack of enthusiasm and curt responses to my questions were clearly in reaction to my arrival so near to closing time, which I understood and almost sympathised with, but the determined investigator in me would not be denied. He briskly warned me that the chances of finding an intact grave were minimal. That due to bomb damage, subsidence and natural plant growth, it was unlikely the tablet that had served as his headstone would have survived.

He took me to a side room where the records were kept, the walls furnished by floor-to-ceiling shelves containing huge leather-bound volumes. It was positively Dickensian; they looked like ledgers straight out of Scrooge's counting house. I told him the date of death and he retrieved the corresponding volume. He opened the book at the relevant section, and I saw the entry almost immediately. It was amongst a list of burials that had been painstakingly entered in a florid, archaic script. Alongside his name was listed the date of burial, the grave number, a square number that clearly related to a grid pattern and the fact that it was a common grave. I was told that a burial would have taken place and then the grave would have been temporarily sealed until the next interment. Many years later, I wrote to Southwark Council and received a response revealing that twelve other souls shared my grandfather's grave, which had been dug to a depth of 21 feet. The occupants had been cremated and buried in a 'Remains Casket'; clearly, space being at a premium they were interred in the most efficient way. I found that the final interment in the plot had taken place on the 10 March 1932, nearly two weeks after my grandfather's burial, after which it was permanently sealed.

The clerk at Camberwell New Cemetery told me to return to Nunhead and supply the graveyard workers on site with the grave and square number, and they would attempt to locate it. When I did I was pleased to find that the graveyard workers (or park rangers as they were known) were enthusiastic and eager to help and that they would work on it the following week. However, on the day of the attempt it was considered too dangerous due to the strong winds that brought branches crashing down from the trees. They were successful on a second occasion, and gave me the welcome news that my grandfather's headstone had survived all that nature and the Luftwaffe had thrown at it.

This brought me to the cemetery on that fateful day in May 2005. As I approached his resting place that day, it was obvious to me that the rangers had cleared a path, found a number of surviving tablets bearing the names of other occupants of the grave, and cleaned them all, lining them up in single file, removing the surrounding undergrowth, and placing my grandfather's at the front. Although seemingly unconnected, the symbolic significance of the Commonwealth War Graves Commission (CWGC) plot nearby came to mind. It became inextricably linked with my quest and my need to honour my grandfather's memory; it was a convergence of the Great War, remembrance, memorialisation and fallen soldiers. It contained the graves of soldiers from the Commonwealth, consisting of Canadians, South Africans, and New Zealanders. These were troops who'd been wounded on the Western Front and had been evacuated to hospitals in England, including King's College Hospital in nearby Denmark Hill, but who, sadly, having made it to safety, had lost the battle for their lives. Further along towards the Limesford Road gate, there was another CWGC plot about half the size consisting of graves of Australian soldiers only. And adjacent to the gate was a memorial to about 500 other Great War casualties.

Standing by my grandfather's grave on that wet spring day was a watershed moment in my journey. It was an emotional moment, and I reached for the reasons why it was that his life had obsessed me so much and why I had embarked on this search; to what end? Certainly, it was a search to 'find' him; not just where his remains lay – although that became part of it – but also the essence of the man. But was it just a vain attempt to form a relationship with a man beyond my reach and to whom I had attributed legendary status – a man whom I could never know personally? My initial motivation had been the desire to bridge the chasm between life and death, to restore his humanity, and get close to him. At times he felt so near. Just one generation from me, just my father's life spanning the void between us; frustratingly, maddeningly, almost near enough to touch but just out of reach. At other times he seemed to be so far away, and the Battle of the Somme may as well have been Waterloo, or even Agincourt.

There were other, obvious reasons. To remember him, to commemorate his achievements, to celebrate his life, to prove that it meant something.

And from all that I had learned, I felt that there was something noble in the way that he had lived, some dignity that transcended class, social status or honours. Something that needed to be acknowledged. This quest, this process, was an act of validation, of authentication. It was also an expression of my pride in him and in the bloodline. I was standing in his shadow, his reflected glory washing over me, hoping to absorb some of it and become half the man that he was.

I walked away realising that I'd come a long way in tracing his earthly life through existing records from birth to death. I now had to make some sense of it all. But this was not the end of the quest. Although I'd reached the end of the paper trail, there was still something missing. Later that year, I travelled to the battlefields of Belgium and northern France, the first trip of what became an annual pilgrimage. Chasing the ghost of my grandfather.

This, then, is the story of William Charles Blumsom. Of a soldier who took part in what has been described as the last British imperial war, and the first truly technological, industrialised 'total war'. Who had lived through the turn of the last century; an age of seismic shifts in social and class consciousness, when the old barriers began to break down; of the final flowering of the British Empire that contained the seeds of its decline; and of the long struggle of suffrage for women. Whose life ended during the Great Depression of the early Thirties. A life that began in the slums of the East End and ended a short hop away across the Thames in south London. From Bethnal Green to Bermondsey via the veldt of South Africa, the uplands of northeast India, the cloying mud of France and Belgium, the mosquito-infested borderlands of Bulgaria, Greece and Serbia and the dry, dusty deserts of Egypt and Palestine. A life reconstructed through the testimony of contemporary witnesses including Major Guy du Maurier, Captain Charles Wilson, Captain Noel Drury and Captain Francis Clere Hitchcock, men from a different class and rank. A life of duty done; a life well lived, in adversity, with dignity and gallantry, not only throughout his military life but also in his heroic struggle to provide for his family. A life ended, not by the Boer, German, Bulgar or Turk, but by his own body, which finally failed him. Ravaged by bullet wounds and other service-related injuries and illnesses, having endured extremes of climate, the heat of the deserts of the Middle East and the cold of the winter on the Western Front. He'd come through it all to be cheated of the chance to see his children grow up.

But I had found him, and I wasn't going to allow him to be forgotten. I would place him alongside those who had died during the conflict, who are in our thoughts every Remembrance Day, and who have had their names engraved on memorials in every town and village throughout Britain and had consequently achieved a kind of immortality. I would make certain it would survive in perpetuity, etched in the minds of his family, if not carved in wood on a gilded panel or in stone on a monolithic memorial. I would write his life: the life of William Charles Blumsom, MM, dead at 50, buried in a pauper's grave; the grandfather I never knew; so that he should not be forgotten, so that his memory would live on.

# CHAPTER THREE

# FAMILY HISTORY: SILK WEAVERS, HUGUENOTS & BOOTMAKERS

*'Twas August, and the fierce sun overhead*
*Smote on the squalid streets of Bethnal Green,*
*And the pale weaver, through his windows seen*
*In Spitalfields, looked thrice dispirited…*

MATTHEW ARNOLD, from East London

It's the 22 June 1815. The church bells are ringing at the news of the Duke of Wellington's triumph over Napoleon at the Battle of Waterloo. The taverns are full, and the streets are alive with the populace celebrating the narrow victory over 'Boney' by the Iron Duke, 'the nearest run thing you ever saw in your life' in the words of the latter. The general festivities and merrymaking indulged in by his fellow citizens on that glorious day would not be something that Benjamin Blumsom would enjoy over the coming weeks and months; he would look disconsolately out of his windows in Bethnal Green with a sense of hopelessness. With the end of the Napoleonic Wars came a catastrophic downturn in his livelihood. Benjamin is a journeyman silk weaver. He is also William's great-great-grandfather.

Benjamin's fortunes were inextricably tied to the inexorable decline of the silk weaving trade in Britain. The British silk industry had suffered a troubled and turbulent history throughout its existence. The trade was vulnerable to fashion and cyclical trends, inconsistent and uncertain supply streams of raw materials, and competition from cheaper imports from abroad. It was largely a case of feast and famine, boom and bust, as short-lived periods of growth were inevitably followed by and interspersed with downturns, the latter proving more persistent in an overall downward trajectory for the trade. For a while, there had been an upturn – from 1798, the French Revolution and the Napoleonic Wars had disrupted and diminished the import of silk goods from the continent – but it proved to be a false dawn. The fall of Bonaparte's empire and the restoration of the French monarchy marked the resumption of the long, tortuous descent of the silk weaving industry in the East End, causing the sufferings of the Spitalfields weavers to be described as 'far more extensive and severe' than ever before. On the 26 November 1816, a public meeting was held at the Mansion House in the City of London. The subject was the relief of the Spitalfields weavers. It was stated that the majority, at least two-thirds, were unemployed and with no visible means of support. William Page, in Volume 2 of his *History of the County of Middlesex* recounts that 'some had deserted their houses in despair unable to endure the sight of their starving families, and many pined under languishing diseases brought on by the want of food and clothing.'

Sir Thomas Fowell Buxton, owner of the Truman, Hanbury, Buxton and Company brewery in Brick Lane, Spitalfields, an abolitionist and social reformer, described the appalling state of the silk weaving community as so profound that 'it partook of the nature of a pestilence that spreads its contagion around and devastates an entire district.' The Blumsom family suffered as much as any; at the age of forty-four, with a wife and six children, these were desperate times for Benjamin.

In the 1820s, the Jacquard loom was introduced into the silk industry in England. Joseph-Marie Jacquard, a Lyons-based manufacturer of straw hats, had invented a loom in 1804–5 that could produce the kind of figured silks and elaborate brocades that previously only the most skilful and painstaking of weavers could have made. This clearly benefited the masters, who could use this new technology in their factories and employ ordinary craftsmen to produce silks of the highest quality without needing any more effort or skill than was needed for the plainer silks. This innovation led to increased profits, but it was to the detriment of the 'single-hand' or 'outside' weavers, those highly skilled artisan home workers of the East End whose labour was now considered too expensive and uncompetitive. It set the 'outside' weaver against the factory or 'inside' weaver, causing resentment and conflict. Clearly, it was no coincidence that the spiralling downward slide of the trade in Bethnal Green and Spitalfields corresponded with the mechanisation of manufacturing that was part and parcel of the Industrial Revolution.

With the passing of the Poor Law Amendment Act in 1834, the weavers worked in the shadow of the dreaded workhouse. Prior to this enactment, each parish had been responsible for ensuring that the wealthier members of their community were taxed (via the 'poor rate') in accordance with legislation dating as far back as the Poor Relief Act of 1601, thus providing for the needy by ensuring that they had at least a basic standard of shelter and clothing and had enough to eat. This aid had been distributed predominantly through the system of 'out-relief', or payment in cash or kind, as opposed to that of 'indoor relief', admission to the workhouse. The origins of the workhouse (or poorhouse) system also date back to the seventeenth century, but the preferred option was the provision of a weekly pension, or one-off amounts for essential items such as clothes and footwear, or the donation of food staples such as bread, flour, and rice. The scheme also included supplementary payments from the funds collected through the poor rate to top up the starvation wages paid to their workers by employers, masters, and mistresses. (A parallel can be drawn here with the present-day benefits system of Universal Credit for the working poor.) This altruistic impulse, enshrined in law, was about to change. Admission to the workhouse was to become the default position.

The 1834 Act reflected a rising and more uncompromising change in attitude toward the poor by their 'betters'. This was partly due to the rising expense of providing for the poor, but it is also believed by some historians to have been influenced by the recent enlargement of the franchise to include middle-class men, which was a direct result of the passing of the 1832 Reform Act. There were ideological reasons for this change in attitude. Some believed that the system of poor relief distorted the free market economy. There was also a perception that the existing system was being widely abused by 'idlers'; this belief was encapsulated in the concept of the 'deserving' and the 'undeserving' poor. It was generally accepted and tolerated that the poor could not be lifted out of poverty; it was the natural order of things. And so the poor were divided into these two categories, the *deserving* and the *undeserving*, as if it were a lifestyle choice to be one or the other. A slavish adherence to free market ideology blinded the ruling classes to the direct causal link between laissez-faire economics and the poverty endemic within the working class. It simply hadn't occurred to the political economists, along with the newly enfranchised 'un-landed' middle class, that the free market policies so aggressively pursued by many of them might be instrumental in perpetuating casual working, starvation wages, sweated labour and frequent unemployment – all conditions that contributed to the impoverishment of the labouring classes.

It is clear that the poor had no control over their own destinies and that far greater forces were at work – those of laissez-faire economics. No matter how hard or how long they worked, they could never beat the market and, as a consequence, were sacrificed on the altar of free trade. In her novel *Out of Work*, the late-Victorian radical writer Margaret Harkness satirises the system thus: 'There, then, he fell out of the ranks of the great army that goes marching on, heedless of stragglers, whose commander-in-chief is laissez-faire, upon whose banners "Grab who can" and "Let the devil take the hindermost," are written in large letters [...] for drink and crime follow close on the steps of laissez-faire's army'.

This sentiment had been expressed as early as the 26 April 1773, when a handbill was reportedly distributed among silk weavers at a meeting at Moorfields in the City: 'Suffer yourselves no longer to be persecuted by a set of miscreants, whose way to riches and power lays through your families and by every attempt to starve and enslave you.'

The post-1834 workhouse, then, was intended to be a deterrent, a last resort barely preferable to being homeless (indeed, some preferred vagrancy); consequently, the living conditions, including accommodation and diet, were basic. And the work harsh and mind-numbingly repetitive, such as stone-breaking and picking oakum – recycling old hemp ropes by teasing out the strands so they could be mixed with tar and used as a sealant for the wooden hulls of ships. This was to be the fate of many destitute silk weavers, and, as will be seen, the Blumsom family was not immune.

The East End was a well-established centre for the manufacture of silk goods, and Spitalfields, in particular, was the nucleus of the industry, especially so after the influx of French Protestant refugees, many of whom were skilled in the craft. They came in two main waves. The first, following the St. Bartholomew's Day massacre of 1572, ordered by the French King Charles IX, consisted mainly of Calvinists fleeing to England from France (joining a smaller number that had come from the Low Countries in the 1560s). The environment created by Henry VIII's English Reformation and built upon by Elizabeth's Protestant rule made for a natural safe haven for those fleeing atrocities such as those committed during the Inquisition and the 1572 massacre in Paris, which also spread to Lyons, Toulouse, Bordeaux, Rouen, and elsewhere.

The second wave, part of a greater diaspora, included an estimated 40,000 to 50,000 souls bound for England and came about as a result of the revocation of the Edict of Nantes in 1685 by Louis XIV, following a long period of tolerance and freedom of religious expression. It was nothing less than the faith-based persecution by the Catholic majority of these refugees (known as Huguenots), which had its origins in the French Wars of Religion dating back to 1562. The term 'Huguenot', applied to Protestant believers by Catholics, possibly stems from the Flemish 'Huisgenooten', meaning house fellows, merged with the German 'Eidgenossen', meaning confederates. The occupation by the émigrés of Spitalfields would spill over into Bethnal Green, Shoreditch, Whitechapel, and Mile End New Town. Many of the refugees were skilled silk weavers from centres of the industry such as Lyons and Tours, who set up their trade and went about teaching the natives of Spitalfields the workings of their craft. In time, their cockney apprentices were able to produce silk goods that equalled those of their tutors and, in some cases, surpassed them.

Many journeymen weavers practised their craft at home as part of a 'putting-out' system – a cottage industry in the East End – whereby master weavers would effectively subcontract work to these artisans. Weavers' houses needed light, and lots of it, in order to ply their trade. The unique quality of the windows of weavers' houses in Bethnal Green was noted by Dr Hector Gavin: 'The houses of the weavers generally consist of two rooms on the ground floor and a workroom above. The workroom always has a large window for the admission of light during their long hours of sedentary labour. Whole streets of such houses abound in Bethnal Green, and a great part of the population is made up of weavers.'

Gavin, a lecturer in forensic medicine at Charing Cross Hospital, carried out a survey in the Bethnal Green area in the mid-nineteenth century and found there was a twenty-two per cent infant mortality rate (death before their first birthday) amongst children born in 1847. This high infant mortality rate produced a skewed average life expectancy of just sixteen years for the labouring classes.

The trade was passed from father to son, mother to daughter – the whole family involved in the production of silk goods. In general, a weaver had two looms, one each for his wife and himself, but it was not uncommon for a family to operate four looms. Children as young as six or seven would be put to work winding silk using a quill or bobbin, and at nine or ten, they would progress to picking silk. At twelve or thirteen, if the child was physically capable, they would graduate to weaving, working the looms.

This would undoubtedly have been the case with Benjamin's children. His three boys and three girls were born between 1797 and 1811 from his marriage to Mary Ann Dubock. (They had wed on the 8 August 1795 at St. Dunstan's, Stepney.) Mary Ann was born the same year as Jane Austen, whose novels bring to mind the challenges facing daughters of the minor gentry in landing moneyed husbands and the whirl of Regency balls that they attended – a very different world to that experienced by an impoverished East End silk weaver's wife.

Mary Ann, born in England and christened on the 29 September 1775 at St. Matthew's Bethnal Green, was of Huguenot descent. Her great-grandfather, Charles Dubock, fled France in the second wave of immigration after 1685. Charles abandoned his home at Houquetot in the Pays de Caux, Normandy, as part of a large exodus leaving the surrounding département of Seine Maritime, a region bounded by Dieppe, Le Havre, and Rouen. Robin Gwynn, in his *Huguenot Heritage: The History and Contribution of the Huguenots in Britain,* has established that 'ninety per cent of the largest single monthly influx of newcomers reaching the French Church of London in May 1687' came from that region. The journey to England for these refugees was a perilous one. Gwynn details the experience of the de Robillard family's escape that year in his book, *The Huguenots of London.* Theirs was an experience typical of so many families, and from this account, it can be assumed that William's five times great-grandfather Charles underwent a similar ordeal when he fled France. To have undertaken such a dangerous journey reveals how intolerable life had become for the Huguenots. Louis XIV's *Dragonnades* policy, whereby dragoons were quartered in towns and billeted in the homes of Protestant families, where they would employ a regime of threats and intimidation in an effort to force them to convert to Catholicism. Soldiers would muscle their way into their homes, waving billeting orders and demanding meals and other comforts with menaces. Goods were seized, and houses were ruined. Clearly, those who chose to flee rather than sign away their rights to worship in accordance with their beliefs were highly principled, to an extraordinary degree.

Small boats were engaged for hefty fees. The captains of these vessels risked losing everything if caught assisting their passage, and it had to be made worth their while. Likewise, those outcasts caught attempting the crossing to England faced punishment, undoubtedly imprisonment. Thus, they were engaged in a game of cat and mouse with the authorities.

Fleeing in the dead of night with whatever possessions they could carry, leaving behind most of their material wealth, the Huguenots faced many challenges. Apart from the official punishments of imprisonment and confiscation of property, they ran the risk of being robbed of their remaining chattels by brigands who knew perfectly well that, due to their victims' status as outlaws, they would face no legal repercussions.

The refugees lived rough whilst awaiting an opportunity to sail. When one presented itself at low tide, the crew would carry their outcast passengers to their vessel, where they would be manhandled through a small trapdoor into the bilge, below the waterline. There, in anticipation of two or more separate inspections by officials, the refugees would keep their heads directly under the beams supporting the deck. That way, they could avoid being injured when the inspectors thrust their swords between the wooden planks. They would keep perfectly still, and quiet their young ones in wet, cramped, and extremely uncomfortable conditions. All this before making the hazardous crossing.

Charles set up home initially in Canterbury, which was, outside of London, the largest Huguenot ghetto. Canterbury was the natural destination for these recent arrivals from the continent. A Protestant community had been established there by the Walloons from the Low Countries, who had settled there during Elizabeth I's reign, having also sought refuge from religious persecution. Charles and his wife Marthe (née Mallandain) baptised their offspring at the Walloon, or French Protestant, Church in Canterbury, including their son Isaac, who was born on the 14 March 1697 and christened seven days later.

The Dubocks' followed a well-trodden path to London. Records show that Isaac was living in the East End when he married Ann Hearn at St. Dunstan and All Saints, Stepney, on the 19 March 1720. This church became an important institution in the history of the Dubock family. The parish registers of births, marriages, and burials at St. Dunstan's chronicle the family's milestone moments from cradle to grave, including Charles's death at the age of fifty-four on the 28 May 1724 and the baptisms of Isaac's and Ann's children.

Their son Peter was christened in July 1730. He grew up and followed in his father's trade as a weaver, marrying four times: Anne Judith Lebeau on the 5 November 1751, Anne Bodwine on the 16 July 1760, Ann Larken on the 28 June 1768, and, for the last time, and as a three-times widower, to Marie Bataille (the name later anglicised to Mary Batail), a wet nurse, on the 29 September 1770. His first three wives had died in 1759, 1767, and 1769, respectively. Surviving records indicate he had three children from his first marriage, three from his second, and one from his third. To modern eyes, it might seem that Peter had an indiscriminate or casual approach to marriage, but there were sound economic and social reasons why marriages for the labouring classes were pragmatic decisions as much as romantic ones. As the provider for his ever-growing brood, he would have been unable to earn a living without the support of a spouse to care for the children. And it was an arrangement that would have suited both parties. The life of a single woman in impoverished circumstances, whether a spinster, abandoned wife, or widow, had a very bleak outlook: either poorly paid piecework such as assembling matchboxes, taking in laundry, or other sweated trades – working excessive hours from early morning until late at night – or a one-way ticket to the workhouse. A marriage of convenience it might have been, but it was a fruitful one; the records indicate that Marie and Peter went on to have seven children, although some might have died in infancy.

Thus, their third child, Mary Ann Dubock, was fourth-generation immigrant stock. Gwynn asserts that the assimilation of an ethnic minority into a host society takes at least three or four generations. There are a number of ways that the assimilation of the Huguenot refugees can be measured, one of which is the degree to which the English language was adopted. During Elizabeth I's reign, which ended in 1603, the early French Protestant refugees had only meant to stay as long as the atmosphere in France was hostile to them. Hopeful that the religious and political climate would come to accommodate or at least tolerate their form of worship, they intended to return at the first opportunity. During these turbulent times, the congregation at Rye, Sussex, fluctuated as events unfolded during the French Wars of Religion between 1562 and 1598 and Huguenots shuttled to and fro across the Channel. Under such circumstances, speaking the English language then was not a priority.

The later waves of Huguenots in 1685 and after were also, at least initially, resistant to learning or speaking English, and they persisted in using French to worship in their churches. The acceptance of their permanent status as refugees building a new life in a foreign country was sealed by events on the continent. The Treaty of Utrecht signed in 1713 made no allowance for the Protestant cause, thereby killing off any hopes of a return to their native lands for the foreseeable future. It was not until 1787, seventy-four years later, that the signing of the Edict of Versailles by Louis XVI gave the Protestants the freedom and legal rights to practise their faith. By this time, partly due to the requirement for second-, third-, and fourth-generation immigrants to swear their loyalty to England during periods of conflict between their adopted country and France, the process of assimilation had run its course.

Intermarriage between the immigrant community and the host population is, in Gwynn's estimation, 'probably the best criterion' of this process. The Anglicisation of names is another, for example, Pierre to Peter and Marie to Mary, or, in the case of surnames, Blanc to White and De La Neuvemaison to Newhouse. Another reliable indicator of assimilation is the history of the rise and fall in the number of French' churches. These numbered twenty-eight in London and the surrounding areas in 1700, reducing to eight in 1800 and only three in 1900. Attendance at these churches also mirrored this decline. The Threadneedle Street church's congregation numbered 7,000 during the late seventeenth century and early eighteenth century but had declined to around one to two hundred by the early nineteenth century, the period when Gwynn states that 'the process of assimilation is virtually completed'. In the case of William's ancestors, this is best illustrated by the change of attendance from the traditional Huguenot places of worship, such as the Walloon Church at Canterbury and L'Eglise de l'Hôpital in Spitalfields, to joining the Anglican congregations at St. Dunstan's in Stepney and St. Matthew's

Bethnal Green. Mary Ann meets all of the above criteria and can be said to be the first of the line to have completely assimilated.

The transition from Huguenot to Cockney was complete. Or was it? Was there any evidence, other than the intangible, but observable, family trait of an inherited aspirational and industrious work ethic (which is common to East End immigrants of all backgrounds and from every age, whether Huguenot, Jewish, or Bangladeshi), of our French heritage? An incident came back to me from my past that, perhaps, reveals that the slightest trace, a barely noticeable homeopathic drop, remains proof of our Gallic ancestry. As a younger man, before I'd looked into the origins of our surname and established its (likeliest) English provenance as an evolved version of the place name Bluntisham in Huntingdonshire (from De Bluntisham to Bluntsham to Blunsom to its modern-day variants of Blumsom and Blumson), I had idly asked my father where it had come from. After all, it was a fairly unusual name, not least with the suffix 'som' rather than 'son'. My assumption had been that maybe it was Germanic in origin, deriving from Blum, a surname that comes from the Middle High German for 'flower' and is related to the Old Norse 'Blom' of the thirteenth century that entered the English language as Bloom. I was taken aback when he told me he believed it had originated in France; at that time, neither he nor I had any idea of our Huguenot bloodline. My first reaction was that this could not be right, but, although we were both mistaken as to the name's etymology – it was neither French nor German in origin – my father's reference to our family's origins had not been plucked out of the ether. It was the last remaining link, surely passed down by word of mouth and just about visible through the fog of time – a fragment of an oral and unwritten working-class history.

Marriage between the Blumsom family and Huguenot families was not uncommon. Mary Ann Dubock and Benjamin Blumsom's marriage on the 8 August 1795 was not the first union between the respective families; Mary Ann's brother William Dubock had married Benjamin's sister Susanna nine months earlier, on the 2 November 1794, in the same church. Other Blumsom relatives married into the Nay and Vandome families, both of Huguenot origin. This Huguenot ancestry paid dividends for Mary Ann and Benjamin's youngest son, Henry (1811–1891), and their grandson George (1826–1898), when they were admitted as patients to the French Hospital in Hackney in need of medical attention (the hospital was funded by a charity to treat and care for Huguenots and their descendants).

It wasn't until May 2018 that I eventually decided to walk the ground of what remains of French Protestant east London in search of my Huguenot roots. One of the earliest places of worship for the refugees was established in 1550 in Threadneedle Street in the City of London, in a building previously occupied by the chapel of the Hospital of St. Anthony. The original building had been destroyed in the Great Fire of 1666 and had been swiftly rebuilt, making it one of the first structures to rise from the ashes. The twelve-year-old Edward VI, son of Henry VIII, had granted the Huguenots freedom of worship by means of a Royal Charter. It was a tolerant move by the young King, for there were liturgical differences between the manner of worship preferred by the Calvinistic Huguenots and the state's Anglican model.

Today, nothing remains of the second manifestation of the church; it was demolished in 1840 to facilitate the development of the Royal Exchange. The only sign that the church once existed there is the installation of a commemorative blue plaque on the wall of the current building on the site. Made of glazed clay and designed in an ornate Victorian style, these rectangular tablet-shaped memorials are unique to the square mile of the City of London (not to be confused with the 'official' blue plaque scheme administered by English Heritage). Although the plaque is eye-catchingly decorative, today's pedestrians are oblivious to the significance of this place. The perambulating, plugged-in workers of the financial markets are totally obsessed with their smart phones and devices and can be overheard in shouted conversations, revealing that work has already started for the day prior to their arrival at the office.

Others nod their heads to their playlists tailored specifically for the daily commute. Now numbered 53 Threadneedle Street, the building where the church once stood is occupied by an asset management company and is flanked by a surf and turf–themed restaurant frequented by expense account cardholders and a branch of an upmarket chain of outfitters of formal office wear. It takes an immense leap of imagination to picture Charles Dubock and his family at the doors of the church, one of the first ports of call in London for the refugees, upon their arrival from Canterbury in the late seventeenth century.

Leaving Threadneedle Street, I continue walking east before joining Bishopsgate and heading north. After passing Liverpool Street railway station on my left, I turn right into Artillery Lane. At the junction with Sandys Row, I arrive at the present-day synagogue that occupies the building that used to house L'Eglise d'Artillerie, a French Huguenot church that had been established in 1766 but had merged with the London Walloon church in 1786. It seems appropriate that the building was subsequently occupied by poor Ashkenazi Jewish immigrants from the Netherlands, whose founding of their own place of worship was publicly disowned by the Chief Rabbi. Just as the original Huguenots had been viewed by some in the established Anglican church as dissenters, the Ashkenazi Jews were not only outsiders to the existing local inhabitants but also to some of their own faith community.

With a jolt, I am dragged from the eighteenth century back to the present day when I scan the window of the estate agents adjacent to the synagogue. The current stratospheric property prices displayed are evidence of the desirability of an area outside the City walls that was once labelled 'Outcast London'. Penthouse apartments are advertised for rent at eye-watering prices, and relatively modest houses in E1 are listed for sale for seven-figure sums.

I head north along Fort Street, then turn east onto Brushfield Street. Crossing Commercial Street into Fournier Street, I find the Brick Lane Jamme Masjid on the corner with Brick Lane. It is a mosque that was also originally a Huguenot chapel known as L'Eglise de l'Hôpital, which was built in 1743 as an annexe to the Threadneedle Street church. It replaced a wooden structure that had stood on the site for sixty years (and in which my five times great-grandmother Marie Bataille was baptised on the 2 December 1739). The existing building has housed all three of the great Abrahamic faiths: Christianity, Judaism, and Islam. If there is such a thing as spiritual capital, this place is overflowing with it. Looking at the south face of the building, the pediment is adorned with a sundial and the Latin motto *Umbra Sumus* ('We are shadows') – a reference to the fleeting nature of life and also an apt phrase in relation to a sundial. But this phrase can be interpreted in another way. The Huguenots, in common with refugees and asylum-seekers anywhere and at any time in history, could be described as 'shadows' – often treated as non-persons, belonging neither here nor there, exiled from their native land but not wholly accepted by their host country, and outsiders to both.

A short walk northwards along Brick Lane, followed by a left turn into Hanbury Street, brings me to another Huguenot place of worship that was founded in 1719 and would become La Patente Church. Now named Hanbury Hall, its present-day use as an events hub – hosting exhibitions of art and photography, small-scale music concerts, providing party and reception facilities, and a café – belies its remarkable history. After the original Huguenots, a succession of various Christian denominations worshipped here; the building was occupied by Lutherans, Baptists, and Methodists before being purchased as a church hall for Nicholas Hawksmoor's Christ Church, the Anglican colossus around the corner. Charles Dickens spoke here. The building also has great significance in the evolution of trade unionism. In 1888, Annie Besant and Eleanor Marx addressed the 'Matchgirls' here during the strike action at the Bryant and May factory in nearby Bow.

The entrance to Hanbury Hall is flanked by an informative elliptical blue plaque on one side and an installation of twenty Delft Blue tiles on the other. The tiles portray aspects of Huguenot life, including the trading of silk. These three places of worship – L'Eglise d'Artillerie, L'Eglise de l'Hôpital, and La Patente Church – founded by the French outsiders, were overshadowed by Christ Church Spitalfields in nearby Commercial Street, an edifice of almost cathedral-like proportions. Dominating the skyline, it was built during the reign of Queen Anne as a show of Anglican authority over the Huguenots – a demonstration of power by the established church.

I wander through Fournier Street, Elder Street, Fleur de Lis Street, Blossom Street, and Folgate Street, amongst the preserved and restored four-storeyed Georgian terraced townhouses once occupied by the master weavers of Spitalfields and Norton Folgate. I pause outside Dennis Severs' House at 18 Folgate Street – a 1724 house purchased derelict in 1979 and refurbished by Severs' as a fanciful imagining of the lifestyle of a wealthy Huguenot family – and I picture my ancestors at the doors of elegant buildings like this, delivering the fruits of their labours to the master weavers. Although also part of French Protestant London, these houses bear no resemblance to the modest two-storeyed or even smaller premises consisting of one or two rooms, some little more than hovels, lived and worked in by the artisan weavers in Bethnal Green.

During my personalised tour, within the space of a few minutes and the confines of a few streets, I came across no fewer than three separate organised walking tours. Groups of sightseers led by their guides, each a confident orator brandishing an umbrella, walking stick, or sheets of prompts above their heads as a beacon for their entourage to follow. This is a thriving industry in touristic Whitechapel. I tarry awhile on the fringes of these gatherings and overhear snatches of well-rehearsed spiel. Tales of large-scale Jewish immigration to Britain caused by the pogroms in late-nineteenth century Russia blended with the particular sites of Jack the Ripper's killing spree and the earlier diaspora of the Huguenots, all conflated in a whistle-stop excursion through Outcast London.

I make my way back through the Old Spitalfields Market, weaving my way through the City workers queuing up for lunch at the street food stalls. Too many appetising options to choose from: fusion, traditional or modern dishes, and produce from every continent – Jamaican or Japanese, Taiwanese or Turkish. More tourists, vacationers, and the merely curious work their way through the clothes shops and stalls in search of the authentic. Business is booming. I can't help but feel that the silk workers from yesteryear would have found their own demographic within this climate of consumerism. The demand for artisan-made and handcrafted textiles grows, and the pursuit of vintage and retro clothing likewise, providing a ready-made market for the weavers.

The silk trade was crucial to the local East End economy in the nineteenth century. Evidence presented in 1831–32 to a House of Commons committee on the trade concluded that, of the 100,000 residents in the weavers' catchment area of the greater Spitalfields district, half were totally dependent on the manufacture of silk and the remainder, to a greater or lesser degree, were indirectly dependent. A total of 14,000 to 17,000 looms were employed in the trade, 4,000 to 5,000 of which would lie idle in times of hardship or depressed trade. Taking into account the employment of children, it was estimated that 10,000 to 15,000 workers were without income and suffering severe poverty and privation during such times. Charles Greville, in his diary entry dated the 17 February 1832, noted:

> A man came yesterday from Bethnal Green with an account of that district. They are all weavers, forming a sort of separate community; there they are born, there they live and labour, and there they die. They neither migrate nor change their occupation; they can do nothing else. They have increased in a ratio at variance with any principles of population, having nearly tripled in twenty years, from 22,000 to 62,000. They are, for the most part, out of employment and can get none. 1,100 are crammed into the poor house, five or six in a bed; 6,000 receive parochial relief. The parish is in debt; every day adds to the number of paupers.

He goes on to state that 'the district is in a complete state of insolvency and hopeless poverty, yet they multiply, and while the people look squalid and dejected, as if borne down by their wretchedness and destitution, the children thrive and are healthy.'

But it would be wrong to view the silk weavers simply as passive victims of the free market. They had a long tradition of militant action in defence of their livelihood dating back to the Civil War, during which they supported the Levellers. This was based on a strong radical impulse amongst the weavers, and their rights have been championed through history by such diverse individuals as John Lilburne, John Wilkes, and Daniel Defoe. Apart from public demonstrations and petitions, the weavers resorted at various times to breaking into the premises of master weavers to destroy their silks and smash their looms.

The smashing of looms by the weavers of the East End predated by at least forty years the more famous smashing of mechanised looms by the Luddites. A law was passed in 1765 that declared it to be a felony and punishable with death to break into any house or shop with malicious intent to damage or destroy any silk goods in the process of manufacture. Iorwerth Prothero, in his *Artisans and Politics in Early Nineteenth-Century London*, details a violent demonstration on the 9 November 1830 where 'thousands gathered in the Strand, mostly East Enders, especially half-famished Spitalfields weavers' who went on to break the Duke of Wellington's windows at Apsley House before attacking the recently formed Metropolitan Police or 'Peel's bloody gang' in the evening, showering them with rocks and other missiles.

Despite the straitened circumstances that affected Benjamin throughout his life, he managed almost to reach his allotted three score years and ten. He died at the age of sixty-nine on the 21st of January 1839, at 1 Mape Street, Bethnal Green, in the presence of his youngest son, Henry. Benjamin's children, including William's great-grandfather, Benjamin Timothy, carried on the family trade of silk weaving.

Benjamin Timothy Blumsom was born in 1797 at Grants Yard, Shoreditch, and christened on the 20 September at St. Leonard's Church. He was married in the same church on Christmas Day, 1820, to Mary Ann Crease, also a silk weaver. The census of 1841 shows him living in Sweet Apple Court, Old Castle Street, Bethnal Green, with

Mary and their children, seven in number at that time, probably in one room. Dr Hector Gavin describes Bethnal Green in 1848 thus:

> The houses built by the French refugees are all several storied, and have large rooms on each floor, with a common staircase; the houses are, without exception, let out in rooms; each room contains a family, with a bed common to all; generally it is a workroom as well as a dwelling-room … The poor inhabitants generally prefer any kind of abode to the workhouse. The occupations of the inhabitants are chiefly weaving and shoemaking; hawkers, toymakers, and cabinetmakers, abound here, and the women wind silk and cotton. Those small manufactures which are carried on here are chiefly prepared in the prospect of being sold to the ready-money shops, or on speculation. The earnings of the population of this district are very low and precarious.

Gavin actually visited Sweet Apple Court that year, seven years after the younger Benjamin and his family were recorded as residing there, and gave a detailed account:

> The gutter in the centre of this court was very filthy; garbage was strewn about, the privies were quite full and dilapidated. Each house has water supplied to it, but by a [stop] cock let through the wall; and as the house is parcelled out, whenever the person who inhabits the first floor is from home, and the door therefore locked, no one can procure water. This may happen when the water is on, and a great difficulty in obtaining it may thence arise. From the dripping of the water-pipe the place had become damp, and on opening the door, a horrid odour of nastiness, like putrid paste, was found to pervade the room.

The section of the 1841 census that features Benjamin's family records eighteen families as residing in Sweet Apple Court, as well as individual lodgers: a total of ninety-three persons, most of whom were silk weavers or otherwise connected to the silk trade. Ed Glinert, in his *East End Chronicles*, focuses on this area as typical of those colonised by the silk weavers: 'The Weavers, who comprised the majority of the local silk workers, lived in cramped cottages on what were then still semi-rural lanes – Fleur de Lys Street, Greenwood Alley, Sweet Apple Court. As the industry grew, the weavers' cottages spread further out, to Brick Lane and Bethnal Green.'

By this time, Benjamin's mother, Mary Ann, widowed for two years, was in dire straits. Her slide into extreme poverty, occasioned by the death of her husband, is documented by the census of 1841, where she is listed as 'Mary Blumsom, Silk Weaver', and is shown as lodging, on her own, at premises in what was then Church Street – now the western section of the Bethnal Green Road. Church Street formed the southern boundary of the notorious Old Nichol (also traditionally known as Friar's Mount – a slum district or rookery of around thirty streets bordering Shoreditch), which was considered a den of depravity and a haunt of criminals and ruffians. The precinct's limits extended to Hackney Road to the north, Mount Street to the east, and Boundary Street to the west.

The *Poor Law Removal & Settlement Records*, dated 22 November 1847, show Mary Blumsom residing at 6 Friar's Mount. The writer Sarah Wise observes that a disproportionately high number of women were recorded as heads of households in the nineteenth century in the Old Nichol, including widows, abandoned wives, and victims of domestic violence – the very poorest of the poor. By the last quarter of the nineteenth century, it was estimated that 6,000 people were crammed into the dilapidated and decrepit houses that made up the district. Arthur Morrison's novel *A Child of the Jago* is set in the 'Jago' or the 'Old Jago', a thinly disguised Old Nichol, which he describes as 'the Jago, for one hundred years the blackest pit in London.' Morrison's map of the fictional Jago was lifted street for street from that of the actual Old Nichol.

It has to be said that Morrison's depiction of the area as a hotbed of crime and depravity was a crude and possibly sensationalist generalisation, as there were many law-abiding and hard-working occupants struggling to survive against the odds. To traduce all of the residents of the Old Nichol as thieves and gangsters purely on account of where they lived is grossly unfair and untrue. Sarah Wise points out that five policemen lived within the precinct in the late nineteenth century, and respectable tradesmen such as cabinetmakers, French polishers, ivory and wood turners, japanners and marble masons were listed as the main breadwinners of some of the families living there. But it is clear that poverty was particularly endemic; the mortality rate of the Old Nichol was practically twice that of Bethnal Green as a whole. For some, living there was but a staging post in the hopeless descent towards complete destitution.

And so it was for Mary. Four years later, things have got as bad as they could be. 'Mary Blumsom, Widow, 76, Weaveress', is recorded in the 1851 census as an inmate in the Bethnal Green Workhouse. This was the workhouse built at Bonner's Hall Fields in 1840–42 by the same James Bunstone Bunning who built Nunhead Cemetery around the same time; the synchronicity is striking.

A three-storey brick-built complex, the workhouse's official capacity was 1,016, and the initial intention was to house the different categories of inmates in separate sections of the building. The sick, the infirm, and the insane were to go into the north wing of the long rectangular block and an annexe to the northeast; the vagrants were allocated a block to the northwest; and the able-bodied were to reside in the south wing. The centre of the workhouse was given over to a chapel and a large dining hall. But this original conception was corrupted by a blend of inefficiency, incompetence, underfunding, and neglect. An article published in *The Lancet* in January 1866 listed numerous deficiencies in the management of the Bethnal Green Workhouse, including overcrowding, insufficient toilet facilities, little or no thought given to the composition of wards, with 'imbeciles' and 'foul cases' billeted with able-bodied inmates, poor diet, and untrained staff, the most notable of which was an unqualified male pauper and former weaver charged with the care of the insane, who were housed in airless, unlit, confined rooms. It is a measure of how poor conditions were in the workhouse system as a whole that, despite the shortcomings detailed in *The Lancet*, Bethnal Green was rated in the highest of three categories for care of the ill and infirm.

But records suggest that Mary's story did not end there in the workhouse. The 1859 burial register for Victoria Park, Hackney, shows a 'Mary Blumston [*sic*], George Street, Bethnal Green, [*aged*] 84', interred there on the 9 July. 59 George Street is where her son Benjamin lived, having left the overcrowded and insanitary Sweet Apple Court by the time of the 1851 census. He is still there ten years later, according to the 1861 census, as confirmed by the electoral registers in the intervening decade; it appears he rescued his mother from a miserable death in the workhouse.

Benjamin lived eight years longer than his father, reaching seventy-seven, but had fared no better than him as the silk-weaving industry had continued to wither on the vine. His second son, William, born in 1823, nevertheless followed in his father's and his forebears' footsteps. In 1851, aged twenty-seven, William is living with his new wife Sarah. The young couple started their married life together, lodging at 15 George Street, having wed the year before on the 19 May 1850, at St. Johns, Hoxton.

Life was not any easier for him than it was for his father and grandfather. Just over a decade after William and Sarah had tied the knot, John Hollingshead sets out the state of the trade in his *Ragged London in 1861*. He describes the male populace of Bethnal Green as comprising 'mainly poor dock labourers, poor costermongers, poorer silk weavers clinging hopelessly to a withering handicraft'. He tours the district with a guide for this report, entering many dwellings. Overcrowded, insanitary, and badly maintained, the houses that he encounters are obviously not fit for human habitation, even by the standards of the day. In one house, which he describes as 'of greater height, with a close, black, uneven staircase, almost perpendicular' and lived in by a large number of families, he estimates that about fifty people live there. At the top of the house, he comes across a weaver's workroom containing two inactive looms. He describes the diamond panes of the two long windows. He finds there a 'sickly woman, almost sinking with anxiety, if not from want'. Her husband is engaged on a fruitless mission in the silk market, looking for work in competition with countless other weavers.

Although changes in fashion were a contributory factor to this parlous state of affairs, without any doubt the greatest blow to the Spitalfields silk-weaving industry was the treaty struck with France in 1860 allowing for the duty-free importation of French silks. British weavers were unable to compete, and the treaty was the death knell for the trade. The industry swiftly diminished to a moribund state, devastating an already poverty-stricken area. Many of these highly skilled workers knew no other means of earning a living, and those few that were able to continue weaving found their wages reduced to pathetic levels. Hollingshead goes on to observe that:

> The statistics of silk weaving show a melancholy decline. In 1824 there were 25,000 looms in and about Spitalfields, now there are only 8,000. In 1835 wages were lower by thirty per cent, than in 1824, and they did not average more than eight or nine shillings a week. Now they cannot be higher than seven shillings, or seven shillings and sixpence a week, on an average; and there are only from twenty-five to thirty master weavers. Perhaps, 20,000 working weavers are now struggling against this decay of their handicraft, and many of them, in despair, are taking to street hawking. The Rev. Mr. Trevitt has set up many of these skilled labourers in this rough calling, with a capital of a few shillings.

The effect of such a drop in wages for those already on an income barely above subsistence levels must have been catastrophic. Hollingshead details a letter dated the 2 February 1861, addressed to the editor of *The Penny Newsman* that calculates the expenditure of a working man with a wife and one child on a wage of eighteen shillings a week as follows:

| Consumable | Shillings | Pence |
|---|---|---|
| Bread | 4 | 0 |
| Beer | 1 | 2 |
| Meat & Potatoes | 3 | 6 |
| Butter & Cheese | 1 | 6 |
| Tea & Milk | 1 | 0 |
| Candles & Firewood | 0 | 6 |
| Coals | 1 | 0 |
| Clothes & Shoes | 2 | 6 |
| Rent | 2 | 0 |
| Soap & Cleansing materials | 0 | 10 |
| **Total** | **18** | **0** |

The letter writer goes on to state that although the London labourers' standing wages are, indeed, eighteen shillings a week, many have to make do on fifteen or sixteen shillings a week. Using the Retail Price Index, eighteen shillings in 1861 equate to £99.69 of relative purchasing power in 2022. Compare this with Hollingshead's estimated seven shillings and sixpence average weekly wage (equivalent to £41.54) that a silk weaver earns, and one can see it is a starvation wage. And Hollingshead's calculation of expenditure was for a family of three. Such a small family would have been atypical of a working-class household; the families that relied on the wage earner were often much larger. This was certainly the case with William; the 1861 census shows him living at 6 Great George Street, Bethnal Green, with Sarah and their four children. How they managed to feed and clothe their brood is beyond knowledge or understanding.

But even in the dire circumstances in which they lived, it appears that the weaver managed to maintain an air of respectability in comparison to his fellow residents. An article in *The Illustrated London News* dated the 24 October 1863, states:

**It may be remarked that the worst parts of Bethnal Green are not those inhabited by weavers, and that wherever the weaver is found his personal cleanliness and the tidiness of his poor room**

offer a striking contrast to those of many of his neighbours. His work requires a 'long light' or leaden casement, so that he most frequently occupies garrets originally designed for his trade. Poor, suffering, nearly starved, and living in a house which shares with the rest the evils of bad or no drainage and insufficient water supply, his business requires at least some amount of personal cleanliness, or the delicate fabrics on which he is employed could never come out unsullied from the touch of coarser hands.

John Marriot observes that the:

> …Huguenots brought a distinct culture to East London, one remote from the carnivalesque pursuits of the largely unskilled and uneducated labouring population: serious, intellectually vigorous and virtuous, it remained an important presence until the decline of silk weaving in the first half of the nineteenth century. In the longer term, Huguenot culture helped define the cultural pursuits of the respectable indigenous working class.

And the good reputation of the weavers continued regardless, even as the trade dwindled towards its demise in the early twentieth century. In December 1898, Inspector Pearn of the Metropolitan Police, one of the officers assigned as an escort and guide to Booth's researchers in their survey of London, described them as 'a quiet, respectable set of people'.

By the time of the 1871 census, William is still living at 6 George Street, now with five children, and he is still clinging on to his trade; his occupation is listed as a velvet and silk weaver. His eldest son, born in 1857 and also named William after his father, is shown as a shoe binder, aged fourteen. After generations during which the family had made (or scraped) their living in the silk weaving trade, it was clear that it was no longer sustainable. The transition from weaver to shoemaker was a natural one, and many made the same switch. Henry Mayhew, in his *London Labour and the London Poor*, quotes one such weaver-turned-shoemaker:

> I took it up because my wife's father was in the trade, and taught me. I was a weaver originally, but it is a bad business, and I have been in this trade seventeen years. Then I had only my wife and myself able to work. At that time my wife and I, by hard work, could earn 1 pound a week; on the same work we could not now earn 12 shillings a week. As soon as the children grew old enough the falling off in the wages compelled us to put them to work one by one – as soon as a child could make threads. One began to do that between eight and nine. I have had a large family, and with very hard work too. We have had to lie on straw oft enough.

The father would then have to ply his trade on foot, peddling his wares to wholesalers and shopkeepers in the hope he could make a sale in order to put bread on the table for his hungry brood. Mayhew's shoemaker recounts such an instance:

> About two years ago I travelled from Thomas Street, Bethnal Green, to Oxford Street, on the hawk. I then positively had nothing in my inside, and in Holborn I had to lean against a house, through weakness from hunger. I was compelled, as I could sell nothing at that end of town, to walk down to Whitechapel at ten at night. I went into a shop near Mile End turnpike, and the same articles that I received 8s a dozen for from the wholesale houses, I was compelled to sell to the shopkeeper for 6s 6d.

It can be seen that the manual dexterity required for working silk could be readily transferable to that of cutting and stitching leather. Similarly, as detailed by Mayhew's subject, the work was performed at home with the family all involved as outworkers. Alan Fox, author of *A History of the National Union of Boot and Shoe Operatives*, documents the experience of a Croydon shoemaker's great uncle: 'An out worker … his wife and daughter were closers; all the work was done in the kitchen, and the meals were cooked during working time. Many other members of the family were in the industry either as managers, pattern cutters … clickers, skivers, and closers. Nearly all families were more or less connected by marriage.' This description of a shoemaker's domestic work arrangements closely resembles that of a silk weaver. The older William eventually caved in to the inevitable and followed his son into the shoemaking trade. Ten years later, the 1881 census shows his occupation as 'Boot Finisher' and him residing at 7 West Street, Bethnal Green, aged 57. The younger William is now aged 24 and is shown, with his wife, living with his parents. He had married Frances Mears, the daughter of a neighbour named Charles Mears, on the 8 October 1877, whilst the family was still living at 6 George Street. It appears that Frances was about three months pregnant with their daughter Elizabeth when they wed. Their baby was born in 1878, followed by another daughter, Sarah, in 1880.

In 1881, the younger William was employed as a boot riveter, and this was his principal source of income in providing for his young family. But the adoption of boot and shoemaking to make a living was unlikely to bring an upturn in the family's fortunes. As with silk weaving, boot and shoemaking in the East End was structured along pre-Industrial Revolution lines: each stage of the production process was parcelled out amongst specialists working from home. The masters kept labour costs low in an attempt to compete with larger manufacturers. But no matter how low the pay or how long the hours they worked, the outworkers could not rival the economy and productivity of the mechanised factories. History was repeating itself. As with silk weaving, boot and shoe manufacture would eventually be relocated to the provinces, with Leicester and Northampton being amongst the principal beneficiaries. Thus, the next generation would need to find another way of earning a living. For one of them, this would be to take the Queen's Shilling – to become a soldier; to follow the way of the warrior.

# CHAPTER FOUR

# THE LIE

*He told a lie to get his way,*
*To march, a man with men, and fight*
*While other boys are still at play.*
*A gallant lie your heart will say.*

EVA DOBELL, *Pluck*

On the 21 November 1881, my grandfather was born at 7 West Street, Bethnal Green. As was customary, being the eldest boy, he was named William after his father. He joined his elder sisters, Elizabeth and Sarah. His birth was followed by his brother James' in 1883 and two further sisters, Ada and Florry, in 1885 and 1887, respectively, who completed the family. During this period, from 1877 to 1890, the family moved frequently. Birth, marriage, census, and school records show them living successively at eight addresses in Bethnal Green and finally settling at 59 Russia Lane. There could have been any number of reasons for moving so often. The growing family could have needed more space. Conversely, it could have been that, with more hungry mouths to feed, money was tight and the need for lower rent was the motivation. But this nomadic pattern of behaviour could also have been an indicator of severe money troubles.

Paying the rent was a perennial challenge for many of the labouring classes of the East End. A fifth of all dwellings consisted of only one room, and rents almost doubled in the 1890s. London's high housing costs, casual work, low wages, unemployment, and an unsympathetic economy were factors both individually and collectively that would lead to families falling into arrears, to the point where either landlords lost patience and evicted these unfortunates or the families took matters into their own hands and would 'do a bunk' – a moonlight flit. A subject interviewed as part of research carried out by the University of Essex on the *Family Life and Work before 1918* project stated:

> We had so many addresses. We couldn't ... pay the rent. We had to keep moving. And we came home from school and find ... bits and pieces slung out on the road; or passed over ... the wall to the next bloke to look after, and while ... the landlord came in he found nothing there. And you was in the next garden, see. He looked after 'em until we found a place.

It is striking that all of the addresses where the family lived during this period are neighbouring streets in the same locality, concentrated within a few hundred metres clustered around Cambridge Heath railway station. Clearly, they had a strong bond with the area and had no wish to move further afield. Maud Pember Reeves, in her survey *Round About a Pound a Week* (1913), provides a compelling reason why this would be so:

> A family who have lived for years on one street are recognised up and down the length of that street as people to be helped in time of trouble... A family which moves two miles away is completely lost to view. They never write, there is no time and money for visiting. Neighbours forget them. It was not mere personal liking which united them; it was a kind of mutual respect in the face of trouble.

Each street was a community in its own right, a distinct 'village' adjoining and surrounded by others, forming a constituent part of a precinct or subdistrict such as Cambridge Heath, Victoria Park, or Globe Town, the streets clustered around Old Bethnal Green Road, and those further west around Brick Lane, all subsumed within the greater Bethnal Green area. The district as a whole cannot be looked at as an amorphous mass; it was composed of these individual microcosms.

The tight-knit East End communities provided support structures for families in need. Whatever little resources the neighbours had, whether in the form of food, possessions, or simply their moral support, they were willing to share. There is evidence of this informal network in a description supplied by an East Ender quoted in Gilda O'Neill's *My East End* (1999):

> There was a neighbourliness and a readiness to help those in need, from the simple cup of sugar to helping a family who had lost their home because of a fire. Many times I have seen a family being turned out of their home when getting behind with the rent. But neighbours never let them suffer for long. With temporary shelter found for them somewhere in the street, their bits and pieces of furniture looked after until they found another home, they got through.

But the generosity of neighbours was not the only factor, or even the major one, in helping a family that had fallen on hard times. Kinship was crucial; relatives living in neighbouring streets, turnings, alleys, and courts would form a network extending into their own circle of friends, which could be relied upon. Another of O'Neill's contributors provides an insightful observation: 'We all lived within a few streets. Nan and Granddad, from Mum's side, all her brothers and sisters and their kids, and all the brothers and sisters, cousins and that, on Dad's side.' Inspector Pearn of the Metropolitan Police maintained that Bethnal Green itself changed very little. Generations of the same family would take on the tenancies of the same houses – only lodgers migrated, and that was just confined to neighbouring streets. He saw the district as inhabited by 'great family parties'.

I examined the census records of 1881 and 1891 to see if the Blumsom family had conformed to this ready-made support system. During this period encompassing the two censuses, when William's nuclear family had moved so often, it became clear that they had. Cousins, aunts, uncles, great-aunts, and great-uncles lived in Alma Road, Charles Terrace, Daniel Street, Green Street, Hackney Road, Old Bethnal Green Road, and Sewardstone Road nearby. The family spilled over into the greater

East End, to the west in Commercial Street in Spitalfields, to the east in Kenilworth Road in Bow, to the south in Hanbury Street in Mile End New Town, and to the north in Church Road, Hackney.

In their seminal work *Family and Kinship in East London*, Michael Young and Peter Wilmott found that:

> **When a person has relatives in the borough, as most people do, each of these relatives is a go-between with other people in the district. His brother's friends are his acquaintances, if not his friends; his grandmother's neighbours so well known as almost to be his own. The kindred are, if we understand their function aright, a bridge between the individual and the community.**

If it were the case that my great-grandparents William and Frances had fallen on hard times, they could call on the extended Blumsom family, not only in Bethnal Green but also in the surrounding districts, to see them through.

The Blumsom family had colonised Bethnal Green in the late 1700s, having relocated from Putney. My French ancestors, the Dubocks, had arrived in the East End even earlier; my sixth great-grandfather, Isaac, is shown as marrying at St. Dunstan and All Saints Church in Stepney in 1720. I had 'walked the ground' in search of my Huguenot heritage; now I needed to explore my cockney roots in Bethnal Green – the Blumsom heartlands – specifically those intimately connected to William. I was looking for a sense of place that would evoke something incorporeal, an impression, a feeling, or trace of the essence of my grandfather. To experience a personal and emotional reaction to a geographical location – perhaps a lesser version of what I had felt in Nunhead Cemetery at his graveside thirteen years earlier. I had no preconceptions as to how I would achieve this aim. By breathing the Bethnal Green air? Walking the streets that he had walked? Or by finding something physical, architectural, although I knew that none of the houses where he had lived would have survived the Blitz or the slum clearance programmes of the early to mid-twentieth century. But I still hoped to find some vestige of the Victorian East End in which my grandfather had grown up.

On the day of my tour, emerging to street level from the Bethnal Green underground station via the exit on the west side of the Cambridge Heath Road, I turned to head north. Straightaway, I was reminded of the ephemeral nature of things and of how easily the past is erased, particularly relevant to my trip that day. A familiar landmark, Nico's Café, at number 299, which I had expected to see sitting immediately adjacent to the station entrance, had gone. It had been replaced by a branch of one of the largest multinational coffee shop chains. The previous tenants had obviously been a casualty of the generic gentrification of the area. I had occasionally enjoyed a full English breakfast at Nico's when work brought me to the area; the café's unique selling point has been that it serves a portion of chips with every breakfast, whether or not you'd ordered it. In contrast to my previous work-related visits as a sporadic bit-part player on the Bethnal Green stage, making cameo appearances in the café amongst the early-morning regulars – the builders, tradesmen, and locals – this time, I was a tourist, an observer, engaged on a field trip, and viewing the landscape through a different lens. My first observation was framed by this recent transformation of the traditional café into a corporate franchise, and my hopes of finding the East End that my grandfather would recognise were rapidly diminishing.

Reassuringly, the Salmon and Ball pub at the junction with the Bethnal Green Road remains a building largely unchanged since the nineteenth century. It was at this very place, on the 6 December 1769, that two silk weavers named John Doyle (or D'Oyle) and John Valine were executed by hanging, having been found guilty of an offence of riotous behaviour on the questionable testimony of two fellow weavers, Thomas and Mary Poor, who, it was alleged, were paid to do so by a master weaver named Lewis Chauvet. The place of execution was cynically chosen by the authorities to make an example of the unfortunate Doyle and Valine. The execution would traditionally have taken place at Tyburn gallows (now the site of Marble Arch), the official destination for those sentenced to death. John Doyle's last words were:

**I John Doyle do hereby declare, as my last dying words in the presence of my Almighty God, that I am as innocent of the fact I am now to die for as the child unborn. Let my blood lie to that wicked man who has purchased it with gold, and them notorious wretches who swore it falsely away.**

Two bodies hanging from a gibbet in the weavers' own territory would have sent out a clear and brutal message that any collective action taken by the silk workers would not be tolerated by the masters. The displays of organised protest by the weavers in defence of their livelihoods that had provoked this ruthless retribution were a precursor to the founding of the trade unions, the establishment of which was anathema to the employers.

I took a slight detour into Paradise Row, still heading northwards, with the chorus of the famous music hall ditty *On Mother Kelly's Doorstep* name-checking the street in my mind ('On Mother Kelly's doorstep / Down Paradise Row …'). The clothes worn by the subject of the song, Nelly, suggest her social class and deprived background:

> *She'd got a little hole in her frock*
> *Hole in her shoe*
> *Hole in her sock*
> *Where her toe peeped through*

The poverty implicit in the lyrics is belied by the row of handsome three-storey Georgian townhouses that remain. Grade II listed, they would sit just as prettily in Bloomsbury as in Bethnal Green. Beyond this elegant terrace, I came across a bar fashioned as a New York-style tap room set back from the road under the arches of the Great Eastern Railway and, predictably, named Mother Kelly's after the song. The beer menu listed a bewildering selection of ales and lagers to choose from.

I returned to the main drag, then turned west beneath the rumbling railway tracks into Poyser Street, the first on my tour of the streets that were inhabited by my forefathers. One hundred and twenty years before, on the 31 March 1898, one of Charles Booth's researchers, George Duckworth, carried out the self-same walk for the *Life and Labour of the People in London* survey. Duckworth was the writer Virginia Woolf's half-brother and was to become a noted public servant. He was to be rewarded with a knighthood in 1927. For local knowledge and safety, he was accompanied on his walks by officers from the Metropolitan Police and, on this occasion, by Inspector Barker. Barker was forty-five years old at the time and had served in the force for twenty years. Duckworth describes the policeman as of 'middle height, moustache, squash black felt hat. Not like a policeman to look at. Has been 4 years in the subdivision, is now a Sub divisional Inspector. Rather timorous.'

Poyser Street, previously named George Street, is coloured light blue on Booth's maps, thus categorising the general condition of the residents as *Poor. 18 to 21 shillings a week for a moderate family.* My great-grandparents were living at 6 George Street in 1877, four years prior to William's birth. Today, no dwellings remain in Poyser Street, which is bordered by the walls of Beatrice Tate School to the west and hugs the start-ups and small businesses nestled under the railway arches to the east (including yet another microbrewery, symptomatic of the 'Shoreditch effect' on the area).

I carried on to nearby Clarkson Street, where William's older sister Sarah was born at number 7 in 1880. Duckworth records the houses here as 'all two storey', and the street is coloured pink on the map: *Fairly comfortable. Good ordinary earnings.* Standing here now are a number of architecturally uninspired blocks of flats adjacent to a green square and an asphalt basketball court.

On into Old Bethnal Green Road, where I walked the length of the street, studying the numbering system in an effort to determine where number 87 might have stood in 1883 – where my great-uncle James was born. Duckworth described the street as a 'very mixed road, some pink, some purple (*Mixed. Some comfortable, other poor*); others light blue'. By my calculation, the Minerva housing estate now occupies the site where the terraced rows of houses were previously situated. This estate was the first postwar development of flats by the London County Council, with construction commencing in 1946. (The area had already been earmarked for redevelopment before the war.) The small two-storeyed houses that had stood on the site, including the former Blumsom house, had been compulsorily purchased from 1938 onwards. The Luftwaffe assisted in the demolition process during the Second World War, unwitting subcontractors for the LCC.

I had studied a facsimile of the 1893 edition of the Ordnance Survey map of the area prior to my research trip. The houses, including the one in which my family had lived, had been painstakingly depicted by the cartographers; each of the individual terraced houses had been reproduced to scale in minute detail, but they were unnumbered. Tracing these illustrations with my finger, I had wondered which of these tiny boxes was theirs. Now, tracking these roads, squares, courts and alleys in person, I saw proof, though none was needed, that although the street plan remained more or less the same as that of the late-Victorian period, the building fabric had changed beyond all recognition.

I headed east, traversing back underneath the railway again, and crossed the Cambridge Heath Road into Parmiter Street (formerly Gloster or Gloucester Street), where my family were recorded as living at number 5 in 1885 and 1887. Rated as purple to pink on Booth's map, Parmiter Street is described by Duckworth as consisting of 'two-storey houses, two families in each, respectable working class.' Today, yet another block of flats stands here and runs most of the length of the street. Ironically, it's named Jacquard Court. There's a dissonance created by the presence of a modern building bearing the name of the inventor of the loom that had so adversely affected the Blumsom family's fortunes in a bygone age and the surrounding streets where their descendants were born and bred. I walked the whole perimeter. The building is directly bordered on three sides by such streets: by Parmiter Street to the south; by Russia Lane to the east (where the family lived from 1889 onwards); and running at right angles to the north is Mowlem Street (formerly West Street), where William was born at number 7 and educated at the elementary school that had been founded further along the same road in 1887. Mowlem Street is described on the 31 December 1897 by Duckworth as 'two-storey cottages, flush with street, poor, light blue as map'. Russia Lane, where the family finally settled at number 59, was reported as 'respectable and purple at the north end, two-storey houses, built 1852, some lately done up. Map gives it light blue. Lower down where there is a nursery marked on the map it is much worse.' Referring to Booth's notebooks, it can be seen that the family managed to maintain at least some degree of respectability: all of the streets where they lived range from *poor* to *fairly comfortable* on the scale. It gives me some comfort that they were never reduced to living in streets rated dark blue *(Very poor. Casual, chronic want)* or even worse, black *(Lowest class, Vicious, semi-criminal)*.

I imagined this block of flats, Jacquard Court, bordered as it is by the streets lived, worked, and played in by the family, as under siege, haunted by the successors of Benjamin Blumsom, their ghosts unable to rest whilst the impersonal, inhuman, ruthless march of technological progress continues to be celebrated – in the form of the building's name – to the present day in the hinterland of the silk weavers. Whatever I was looking for, I didn't find it there in those reconstructed streets.

I continued eastwards along Bishops Way and on through the Bonner Gate across the canal bridge into Victoria Park, the green lungs of the East End, where my grandfather had spent a large part of his childhood. The park had been established in 1845 for the health and amusement of the people of east London and was frequented by the working classes. As a younger man, I had played rugby here, at that time completely unaware that I was virtually following in William's footsteps, my leisure pursuits synchronising with his across the years.

I walked through the park and exited from the north side onto Wetherell Road, entering the borough of Hackney, my next destination harking back to my Huguenot roots. I reached the junction with Victoria Park Road, and there before me was the imposing Victorian edifice now occupied by the Mossbourne Victoria Park Academy. Built in a Gothic Revival style and opened in 1865 to house the French Protestant Hospital, replacing the previous building in Finsbury just north of Old Street, this is where my four-times great-uncle Henry Blumsom (d. 1891) and my three-times great-uncle George Blumsom (d. 1898) were patients towards the end of their lives. The hospital was originally established by a wealthy Huguenot named Jacques de Gastigny, who had risen to the position of Master of the Hounds to William III, and subsequently funded by other benefactors of his ilk. It provided a level of care and treatment that would have been well beyond Henry's and George's means were it not for their Huguenot bloodline.

I retraced my steps through the park, back to Bethnal Green. My last port of call was Mowlem School, formerly Mowlem Street School, where William and his siblings would have learned to read and write. Just south of the Regent's Canal and Victoria Park, it was opened in 1887 with a capacity for 360 girls and 360 boys. Looking through the heavy security gates, it was clear that the building they would have been taught in had been demolished. In its place was a 1971-built, generic, single-storey structure. However, I noticed an aged brick building bordering the playground that was obviously an original annexe that had survived the dismantling of the main structure. Through the intercom at the school gates, I made contact with a member of staff and explained the reason for my visit. I was advised to arrange a meeting with Jackie Cloves, a senior administration officer at the school who had a keen interest in its history.

Several weeks later, I met Jackie and she talked me through the school's history. Her knowledge and insight are invaluable, and she is rightly proud of the school's traditions. She told me that the school had featured in the long-running *Up* series of TV documentary programmes, the first of which, titled *Seven Up!*, had been broadcast in 1964 and followed up at seven-year intervals thereafter. The *Up* programmes followed the fortunes of fourteen seven-year-old children from differing socioeconomic backgrounds. One of the children chosen was a pupil at Mowlem Street named Tony Walker. Tony initially trained as a jockey, competing against Lester Piggott on one occasion, before becoming a London black cab driver.

My initial disappointment at seeing the modern reincarnation of the school premises when I first looked through the security gates turned into a sense of eager anticipation. This discovery gave me an unexpected opportunity: by watching footage of the programme posted online, I would be able to see the original school building largely unchanged from when my grandfather had been a pupil there.

Jackie then produced a handsome leather-bound, gold-embossed volume: the school's roll of honour listing former pupils that had served in the Great War. Their names are written in an ornate calligraphic hand similar to that used in a religious illuminated text. To me, this *was* a sacred manuscript, for there he was on the page, my grandfather, his name in all its glory.

It was a fruitful visit. After I bade Jackie goodbye, there was one more thing I had to do. I walked through the playground to the Victorian outbuilding and placed my hand against the brickwork, as if the wall might impart to me a retained memory of my grandfather. And in a sense, it did, by prompting me to create one. I pictured him as a child, full of energy and mischief, careering around the playground with his pals. The interior of the outbuilding known as 'the Annexe' has been refurbished, and it is now used for breakfast club, music lessons, meetings, and other extracurricular activities. But the exterior is just as it had been when my grandfather played here as a child a hundred and thirty years ago. And during the rough and tumble of playground games, he had surely touched this very wall, just as I was touching it. I walked away and realised I was smiling as I thought of his carefree existence as a child in this place.

For a poor, working-class family, the role of children in adding to the family income was a vital one. They would be expected to obtain employment as soon as they were physically able to supplement their parents' earnings. Benjamin Seebohm Rowntree, in *Poverty: A Study of Town Life*, reports that 'The importance attached to the earnings of the children in the families of the poor, reminds us how great must be the temptation to take children away from school at the earliest possible moment, in order that they may begin to earn.' This was the challenge that had faced those in favour of a national system of elementary education. In the run-up to the enabling of the Education Act 1870, Matthew Arnold, who supported a national system of schooling and was acutely aware of this pressure placed by parents on their offspring to contribute financially, felt that the employers who recruited children should be targeted: '…a law of direct compulsion on the parent and child would … probably every day be violated in practice; and so long as this is the case, to a law levelled at the parent and child a law levelled at the employer is preferable'.

From existing records, it is clear that my great-grandparents, William and Frances, were content for all of their children to attend school. The likelihood is, from the official documents available, that William Charles and his siblings were the first functionally literate generation of our Blumsom line (there had been the odd individual, including Benjamin, who had signed his marriage certificate to Mary Ann Dubock back in 1795). Most of their forebears had 'made their mark' with an X on birth and marriage certificates and other documents.

Education for the working classes at this time was elementary – in the truest sense of the word – concentrating on the three Rs: reading, 'riting, and 'rithmetic. A few schools added some history, geography, and science to the curriculum. Great attention was paid to handwriting; the copperplate style was the standard in Victorian times. Certainly, there is evidence of this education on a 1911 census form completed by William in an accomplished, neat hand when he was twenty-nine.

My grandfather was nearly seven years old when the body of Mary Ann Nichols was discovered in the neighbouring district of Whitechapel. It was the first of the five savage murders thought to have been the work of one man between the 31 August and the 9 November 1888. The fact that he had lived through such appallingly murderous times and so near to these gruesome events is horribly compelling. The suspect became known as 'Jack the Ripper' following the publication in a newspaper of a letter purportedly written by the murderer. Unprecedented worldwide media coverage, much of it sensationalist, contributed to the shadow that fell over the East End. It attracted the attention of social commentators, churchmen, and politicians, who linked the depravity of the murders with the degradation and abject poverty of the residents of Whitechapel, Spitalfields, Bethnal Green, Shoreditch, and the surrounding areas.

The conjunction of these events with Charles Booth's groundbreaking study, *Life and Labour of the People in London,* first published the following year, was soon followed by slum clearance programmes, including the demolition of the infamous Old Nichol. The area was ripe for development, and in 1890 the model Boundary Street estate began to rise phoenix-like out of its rubble (literally as hardcore for the raised bandstand in Arnold Circus). It provided new, clean accommodation for the 'respectable' working class. The 'Ripper' murders were, in all probability, a causative factor in setting in train these events.

William would have been only too aware of the monster stalking the East End. And it wasn't only the children of East London who were conscious of the Ripper's gruesome attacks. The well-to-do kids from 'up west' were just as afraid; a terrified Compton Mackenzie, the future writer, political activist, and commentator, who was only four years old at the time, recounts:

> It was Jack the Ripper who first made the prospect of going to bed almost unendurable…. it would have been bad enough if I had only heard the talk about him… Talk about Jack the Ripper was small talk compared with the hoarse voices of men selling editions of the Star or the Echo as half a dozen of them, with posters flapping in front of them like aprons, would come shouting along the street the news of another murder in Whitechapel. 'Murder, Murder! Another horrible murder in Whitechapel. Another woman cut up to pieces in Whitechapel!' Whitechapel became a word of dread,

**and I can recall the horror of reading 'Whitechapel' at the bottom of the list of fares at the far end inside an omnibus. Suppose the omnibus should refuse to stop at Kensington High Street and go on with its passengers to Whitechapel?**

The hysteria whipped up by the media had an indelible effect on children. The grisly coverage was consumed by the newly literate working-class young as much as it was by the adults, and it terrified them to the extent that many refused to attend school. The Ripper became the most fearsome bogeyman of them all. And my grandfather was more familiar with the murders than most of his schoolmates. His older cousin and namesake, William Blumsom, aged forty-seven, was the landlord of the Commercial Tavern, 142 Commercial Street, directly opposite Commercial Street Police Station, where the investigating officers were based, and within a few hundred metres of where Annie Chapman, in Hanbury Street, and Mary Jane Kelly, in Dorset Street, were murdered. It was a convenient watering hole for the investigating officers to enjoy an off-duty drink or two; Cousin William may have even served the great Ripper-hunter himself, Inspector Frederick Abberline, with a well-earned pint. Indeed, the possibility exists that the Ripper himself, along with his prey, might have enjoyed Cousin William's hospitality. All five 'canonical' victims were known to have had a drink problem, and on their constant quests for sustenance, whether facilitated by sweated work, begging, stealing, or borrowing, the fruits of their endeavours would be spent in the local hostelries.

Adjacent to the pub, at 136 Commercial Street, was the Royal Cambridge Music Hall. The Commercial Tavern would doubtless have enjoyed a roaring pre- and post-show trade from the theatregoers, who, again, might have included the killer himself. Leaving aside whether the Ripper's victims had frequented the pub, it is entirely possible, if not likely, that Cousin William knew them by sight; he had previously lived at number 106 Hanbury Street, a matter of yards from where Annie Chapman was murdered at number 29, and which was within the stamping ground of all of the victims, and their paths might have crossed on any number of occasions.

Apart from school, my grandfather's childhood would largely have been spent outside on the streets, playing rudimentary football or cricket, or games such as follow-my-leader, leapfrog, or 'knock down ginger' – the classic knock-and-run childhood prank that dates back to at least the nineteenth century. Children had to make their own entertainment, and in order to avoid getting under their mothers' feet whilst they maintained and ran homes that were invariably too small for the typically large families of the working class (sometimes just one or two rooms), the streets became their playground. A rope thrown over a streetlamp standard served as an improvised swing. Other attractions included the Regent's Canal and the Thames, where cockney scamps could strip off and take a dip when the weather was warm enough, although sometimes with tragic results. Boys were allowed more licence than girls and could be out until dusk (as late as ten o'clock during the summer months). William lived a stone's throw from Victoria Park, perhaps the greatest attraction of all for mischievous children. Another one of Gilda O'Neill's sources recollects their excursions to Victoria Park:

> We would go along Hackney Road, then across Cambridge Heath Road into Bishop's Way, which led to the main park entrance, [then] over the canal bridge, stopping to see if there were any barges being towed along by horses, then turn left to the pens where they kept the guinea pigs, rabbits and wallabies, then have a look at all the different birds in the aviary, and, just round the corner from there, the playground with swings, slides, sandpit and other things to ride on. After playing there for a while, we would go a bit further round on to the island with the Chinese pagoda and have a look at that before going on to see the deer.

My grandfather is statistically likely to have left school at the age of thirteen, almost certainly not later than fourteen, and possibly as young as twelve. The Liberal MP Leo George Chiozza Money, in his book *Things That Matter*, states that '…when visiting our elementary schools, I have obtained permission to ask the scholars in the highest classes who have attained the age of 14 years to rise in their places. The test always gives the same result. Of a class of sixty or more children, only some five or six are found to have passed their thirteenth year.' and Money himself then goes on to quote statistics obtained from schools on the Register of Public Elementary Schools from the 1906/7 school year. The number of pupils aged twelve who are still at school totals 596,759; for thirteen, it drops to 408,341. 'And then comes the great stampede. At fourteen years of age the scholars drop to 67,811, a decline of 340,000!'

As the son of a bootmaker, William had no family tradition of an apprenticed or viable 'recognised' craft to inherit. Therefore, he'll have either followed in his father's footsteps or entered the world of work as a labourer.

He grew up steeped in an identifiable 'cockney' culture comprising a support network of community and strong family values allied with a native wit – a resourceful and inventive spirit born of necessity. The ability to make do and mend, maximise opportunities, and eke out meagre resources was essential for survival. Within this cultural milieu, were distinct family characteristics that can be traced back to his Huguenot ancestors. For example, a strong work ethic informed by the refugee mindset of making a success of a new life in a foreign land, many of them having fled penniless from their countries of birth. The highly skilled immigrants, including silk weavers, watchmakers, goldsmiths, silversmiths, printers, and bookbinders, contributed enormously to the artistic, scientific, and manufacturing potential of their host country. These traits – hard-working, aspirational – passed down through generations are part of a value system that places the family in what is patronisingly known as the 'respectable working class'. They are traits that are recognisable to this day.

Despite being a deprived area, the East End was full of life. The soot-stained blackness of the buildings contrasted starkly with the vivid colours of the flower market in Columbia Road and the noise and hubbub of the live animal market at Club Row, both legacies of the Huguenots. Walking along the Bethnal Green Road or the Roman Road on a market day, assailed by the shouts of the costermongers, barrow boys, and hawkers, the music of the barrel organ players, and the sights and the smells, would have been a sensory extravaganza. Practically anything and everything was sold and consumed here, including oysters, hot eels, pea soup, fried fish, pies and puddings, sheep's trotters, pickled whelks, gingerbread, baked potatoes, crumpets, cough drops, street-ices, ginger beer, cocoa, and peppermint water, as well as clothes, second-hand musical instruments, books, live birds, and even birds' nests. Henry Mayhew's study *London Labour and the London Poor* (1851) lists the commonly used cries of the market sellers and stall holders hawking their produce:

[Fish] *Ni-ew mackerel, 6 a shilling; Buy a pair of live soles, 3 pair for 6d; Plaice alive, alive, cheap; Salmon alive, 6d. a pound; Cod alive, 2d. a pound; Real Yarmouth bloaters, 2 a penny; New herrings alive, 16 a groat; Eels, 3lbs. a shilling, large live eels 3lbs. a shilling; All large and alive-O, new sprats, O, 1d. a plate.*

[Shellfish] *Buy a pound crab, cheap; Mussels a penny a quart; Oysters, a penny a lot.*

[Fruit and nuts] *Pine-apples, ½d. a slice; Oranges, 2 a penny; Cherry ripe, 2d. a pound; Fine ripe plums, 1d. a pint; All new nuts, 1d. Half-pint.*

[Vegetables] *Penny a bunch turnips* [the same for greens, cabbages, etc.]; *Ing-uns* [Onions], *a penny a quart.*

[Cheap meat] *Wi-ild Hampshire rabbits, 2 a shilling.*

This was the East End that William grew up in – poverty-stricken for sure – but noisy, vibrant, and full of characters. A distinct and unique working-class community of shared values, surrounded by an altruistic network of family and friendly neighbours, united in adversity. This was what shaped him.

And so it was that, in September 1898, two months short of his seventeenth birthday, my grandfather was working as a labourer for Edwin Atkins, furniture-makers in Church Row off Bethnal Green Road, when he enlisted with the militia as a part-time soldier in the 5th Battalion Royal Fusiliers. With no firsthand account to rely on, I don't know what motivated him to join up. Generally, boys and men of the poor, urban, working class were attracted to the armed services by regular rations, a bed at night, and a uniform. But this class was also the most malnourished and underdeveloped, and many would not have passed the requisite medical examination. Only the strongest and fittest passed muster, as Jack London observed in his social polemic *The People of the Abyss*: 'Wherever a man of vigour and stature manages to grow up, he is haled forthwith into the army.' Charles Booth advances a number of reasons why the working class enlists, including relationship breakups or affairs of the heart and the lack of paid employment. The latter is the most common, especially in London, and recruiting is most fruitful during the winter months. Indeed, winter was known as the 'recruiting season', clearly linked to the period of highest unemployment, especially among the building trades.

But as he was joining the part-time militia whilst also holding down a job, this doesn't appear to be the case for my grandfather. He had joined the militia at the first opportunity, albeit he was underage, and clearly he already had an eye on joining the regular army in the future. If my grandfather was not joining due to a lack of work, perhaps it was for a chance to experience life free of the confines of a routine working-class existence. The experience of a contemporary of his may shed light on the possible explanation for his joining the militia rather than the regulars. Frank Richards, born in Wales in 1883, underwent a similar working-class experience to my grandfather, albeit from a mining community rather than an urban one. There are remarkable parallels between my grandfather's and Richards's experiences in the army as a whole. Both served in India in the early twentieth century, and their paths did eventually cross for a short period in the Great War; their career trajectories were almost identical and all but correlated chronologically. The writer Robert Graves, who during the Great War was an officer in Richards's regiment, the Royal Welch Fusiliers, helped him publish his memoirs. The resulting books, *Old Soldier Sahib* and *Old Soldiers Never Die*, were unusual in that they gave a voice to a ranker from the trenches. They are, therefore, a very useful resource in extrapolating my grandfather's story and will feature in this narrative accordingly, especially so with regard to his time in India.

Richards left school at the age of twelve and worked in a colliery prior to enlisting. He tried to join up in 1900 at the age of sixteen, lying about his age, but he was turned away due to his obviously adolescent physique and told to 'pack twelve months dinners in my belly'. The phenomenon of underage working-class boys falsely representing themselves in order to join up is closely linked to the Great War, but the experiences of both my grandfather and Frank Richards predate that conflict, showing that 'Twas ever thus'; it has always been one of the few career options for the underprivileged who crave adventure or escape from a life of either frequent unemployment or backbreaking, repetitive, low-paid work.

When Frank Richards presented himself for the second time at seventeen and a half – still underage – the doctor examining him mentioned that although he was well built, he looked 'extremely youthful'. Richards was bent on succeeding on this occasion, and decided that:

> …instead of putting six months [in order to present himself as eighteen years old] on to my age I had put on eighteen months [instead posing as a nineteen year old]: I was determined this time that if I was big enough I would also be old enough. The recruiting-sergeant never questioned my age and no birth certificate was required. If I had only been big enough the first recruiting-

sergeant would not have questioned my age either: he would have been only too glad to pocket the fee that recruiting-sergeants received for each man they enlisted who passed the doctor.

Could it be that William had attempted to join the regular army at the age of sixteen years and ten months but was, instead of being told to build himself up with 'twelve months dinners' and come back a year hence, advised by the recruiting sergeant to join the militia, whose programme of training (which included forty-nine days of drill throughout the year) would achieve a similar physical transformation? He was obviously determined to enlist; just over a year later, on the 4 October 1899, he joined the regular army with the Royal Fusiliers at Dalston barracks. The lie he'd told a year earlier was perpetuated; he would go on to experience active service and see combat whilst still a teenager.

I like to think that his desire to serve was due to an adventurous spirit, a wanderlust, a deep-seated need to break out from the poverty and drudgery of a life in the East End that wasn't for him. William was on the threshold of a great adventure that would take him far, far away from Bethnal Green, to experiences beyond his imagination.

CHAPTER FIVE

# SOUTH AFRICA

*What has your country done for you,*
*Child of a city slum,*
*That you should answer her ringing call*
*To man the gap and keep the wall*
*And hold the field though a thousand fall*
*And help be slow to come?*

EMILY ORR, *A Recruit from the Slums*

It was not long before William's wish for adventure was granted. A week after he enlisted with the regular army, war broke out on the 11 October 1899 between Great Britain and the two Boer republics of Transvaal and Orange Free State in South Africa. These fiercely independent nation-states were populated by Dutch-speaking descendants of those settlers who had colonised Cape Town and its coastal environs beginning in 1652. For nearly 150 years, the Cape Colony had been administered by the Dutch East India Company until the British arrived during the Napoleonic Wars and seized power in order to control the strategically important staging post on the route to India and prevent France from making any inroads into the subcontinent. The relationship between these two disparate European peoples – the British and the Boers – deteriorated further as a result of the liberal, more enlightened policies of the governing British. The Empire's abolition of slavery in 1834 and the subsequent emancipation and granting of certain rights for the black African population were unacceptable to the Boers, prompting their 'Great Trek' inland to eventually found the two republics, thus leaving the Cape Colony to the British.

The Boers ('Boer' is Dutch for 'farmer') settled these interior lands with farming communities connected by wagon trails. They were a tough breed, possessing superb horsemanship and shooting skills that would serve them well in times of conflict. The British formally recognised the Boer republics of Transvaal and Orange Free State in 1852 and 1854, respectively, but this was not to last. The imperialistic impulse could not be contained, and it was manifested in an attempt to create a South African confederation under British supervision by the annexation of Transvaal in 1877. The Boers resisted this move, peacefully at first, but subsequently by taking up arms in December 1880. In what was to become known as the First Boer War, the Boers won a decisive victory at Majuba, following which the British negotiated an armistice at the Pretoria Convention in August 1881 whereby a largely independent Boer state was restored but with British control of foreign policy and legislation protecting the black population. It was the desire to exploit the mineral wealth of the region that precipitated the second, greater conflict. With its origins in the diamond rush of 1870 at Kimberley on the border of Cape Colony with the Orange Free State, later followed by the gold rush of 1886 in the Witwatersrand in Transvaal, the prospect of such riches to be had attracted the interest of investors, speculators, and empire builders, none more so than Cecil Rhodes, a vicar's son from Bishop's Stortford, who would make his fortune off the back of the diamond mining industry. Rhodes's disastrous attempt to prompt the British expatriate workers in the Transvaal to revolt against the Boer government in 1895, an escapade known as the 'Jameson Raid', was instrumental in the breakout of the second Boer War. Relations deteriorated between Great Britain and the Transvaal government: the latter swiftly formed an alliance in 1897 with their brethren in the Orange Free State. The stage was set for war.

The Boer republics did not maintain a conventional standing army but were able to mobilise a mounted force – estimated at 50,000 strong initially – comprising smaller regimental units, each formed as a 'commando' (a body of fighting men; the British would adopt the term in the Second World War for the special forces units recruited from the ranks of the Royal Marines and the Army), utilising the marksmanship and riding ability of these hardy outdoorsmen and reinforcing them with existing police units and artillery pieces that they'd stockpiled in anticipation. Even so, this was a real David and Goliath situation, as the Boers couldn't mobilise anything like the number of troops that the British Army had at their disposal. But the imperial forces were scattered around the globe and at home in the UK; it would take time to put them in the field. Initially, the South Africans outnumbered Queen Victoria's soldiers by somewhere between three and four to one. They had to strike fast before the British could muster their superior forces and energise the Dutch-speaking population to rise up against the might of the Empire in order to seize territory and achieve the most advantageous terms, including some degree of independence, in any future peace negotiations.

Within days of the outbreak of war, the Boers had laid siege to the garrison border towns of Mafeking and Kimberley; Cecil Rhodes had moved into the latter just before the onset of the blockade and was trapped for the duration of the siege. A few weeks later, they also besieged Ladysmith.

To add to the embarrassment, the British suffered a disastrous period, known as 'Black Week', from the 10 to 17 December 1899, when the army lost three battles at Stormberg, Magersfontein, and Colenso, sustaining the highest casualty rate since the Napoleonic wars. The British senior command did not cover itself with glory. Frequently deploying conventional frontal assaults by lines of infantry, often in close order, against the greater mobility of the Boer-mounted units, who fired from cover to great effect, was a recipe for disaster. The Boers were able to exploit the terrain to their own advantage. In what was a foreshadowing of the shortcomings of the generals in the Great War (the 'Donkeys' as Alan Clark would have it), the British were taught, in Rudyard Kipling's words, 'no end of a lesson'. Kipling highlights the strategic and tactical mistakes of the high command by pointing out what, in hindsight, is blindingly obvious:

**We have spent two hundred million pounds to**

prove the fact once more,
That horses are quicker than men afoot, since two and
two make four;
And horses have four legs, and men have two legs,
and two into four goes twice,
And nothing over except our lesson – and very cheap at the price.
(The Lesson)

General Redvers Buller, commander-in-chief of the British forces, paid the price. He was relieved of his command and replaced in December 1899 by Lord Frederick Roberts, whose chief of staff, Horatio Herbert Kitchener, would become the poster boy of the Great War.

The British army already had a mounted infantry (MI) capability, but it was clear that it would have to be expanded exponentially if the Boers were to be subdued. The MI was quite distinct from and performed a different role from the cavalry, fourteen regiments of which were already in South Africa. The difference between the two corps came down to how they utilised their mounts in a combat situation. The cavalry actually *fought* on horseback (traditionally with sword and lance; more recently with short-barrelled carbines), whereas the MI used the horses to move around the battlefield in flying columns to dismount, deploy, and engage the enemy on foot – ideal tactics for outflanking manoeuvres. But the MI was not a permanent fixture like the cavalry. A unit would be drawn together as and when needed from a pool of trained horsemen serving with various regiments of foot. To qualify as a mounted infantryman, a prospective candidate had to go through a selection process, having already achieved marksman status, before receiving instruction, including horsemanship and stablehand duties; mounted drill practising marching formation in single rank; and rapid deployment in combat as a flying squadron, involving mounting and dismounting swiftly and firing at will. Captain Stratford St. Leger, a company commander of the 1st Mounted Infantry (and eventually to be killed in action at the Somme in 1916), describes in his book *Mounted Infantry at War* how his battalion was composed of soldiers from eighteen separate parent regiments. Two companies would form a unit roughly a third the size of a battalion of foot. The MI was a hybrid of regular infantry and cavalry, combining these roles to respond effectively to fast-moving situations in mobile columns.

Troops answering the call of the Mother Country poured into South Africa, including large contingents from Australia, Canada, and New Zealand. The tide started to turn in late February 1900. Kimberley was relieved on the 15 February, Ladysmith on the 28th. It took until the 17 May to liberate Mafeking, sparking celebration at home, thereby creating a new verb, 'to Maffick' or 'Mafficking about' ('to rejoice in a boisterous manner'). Many Boers laid down their arms, and as the British had all but won the 'conventional' war, those still fighting were forced to revert to guerrilla tactics. The perennial problem of defeating a 'citizen army' – as would be faced by the US in Vietnam and the Russians in Afghanistan much later in the century – confronted the British. A Boer commando could melt away after a skirmish or campaign, the men returning to their farms for rest and resupply.

Kitchener devised a strategy that involved establishing a network of blockhouses. They were built initially to guard bridges and railway lines but were then expanded to cover main roads and other strategic points. Linked by barbed wire, they were manned by troops and functioned as garrisons that were erected at roughly 1,000 yards apart, a spacing that made it almost impossible for the Boers to pass between them unobserved. The connected blockhouses, in tandem with the increase in Mounted Infantry battalions, would enable the British to sweep the countryside in a series of 'drives', corralling their prey and forcing an inchmeal surrender.

About 8,000 blockhouses were built, covering 31,000 square miles of the two Boer republics. They were manned by 50,000 British soldiers and 16,000 Africans. This network of blockhouses and connecting wire formed a grid-like system of huge pens. Along with this, Lord Roberts operated a scorched earth policy of evicting the Boer women and children, burning down their farmhouses, and escorting them to newly constructed internment camps for the duration of the conflict. The menfolk who surrendered would also be detained there. The British troops carrying out these duties did so without any appetite for this sort of work; it was not what they had joined up for. An officer who served alongside my grandfather in the 20th Mounted Infantry battalion, Lieutenant Ralph Verney, wrote an account of such an eviction in a letter to his mother on the 16 December 1901:

> Since I wrote the last page, we have been on a patrol to clear some farms, and bring in all the women who were living in them. We started at 10am yesterday morning and we reached the farms about 1pm. I had to take two wagons and collect the women from two farms a little distant from the others. I found a Dutch woman with 3 daughters in one farm. They were rather angry with me when I had explained that they had to pack up at once and get on the wagon, and come away with me. I told off six of my men to take what things they wanted out of the house and load them up on the wagon. I then hoisted the mother and daughters on top of their furniture in the wagon and set fire to the house.
>
> I went on to the second farm and found a woman with 5 small children. I soon made friends with them and they rather enjoyed being lifted on to the wagon with all their chairs and tables, but the mother did not like it at all, especially when she saw her house in flames. I did not enjoy having to do this job much, but it had to be done, as the Boers were known to sleep in these farms.

Verney goes on to describe how they rounded up the menfolk of these farms. Hearing that the Boers were hiding nearby in a *kloof* (a deep, wooded ravine), they disguised their intentions by pretending that they were returning to camp five miles back, turning the wagons around, and giving the impression that they had left the area completely, away from the burning homesteads. However, having travelled far enough to be out of sight, they halted in some thick bushland, where they found cover and lay in wait until nightfall. The feint worked perfectly. At midnight, they crept back to the *kloof*. Small detachments of men were deployed, quartering the ravine methodically. An officer named Sanderson and his fifteen men covered the centre, with similar-sized detachments positioned on the left and right. As the sun began to rise at 4 o'clock, Verney made his way with twenty men to the bottom of the valley by a circuitous descent in order to close in on the Boers. My grandfather might have been one of these men, stalking his prey under the blood-red sky of a South African dawn, some 6,000 miles away from the grey, drab, labouring life in Bethnal Green, away from the factories and docks, the sweatshops and workhouses of the East End; in his element, enjoying the greatest adventure of his young life.

Verney and his troops then stealthily scoured the *kloof*, ascending towards the top of the ravine, where they were to link up with Sanderson. It was slow-going. The dense subtropical undergrowth impeded their advance, necessitating a single-file formation led by the guide, who was fearful of being shot by the Boers. They had gone so far when the scout suddenly dropped to his haunches and whispered, 'Dutchmen'. Verney stealthily made his way forward and espied eight armed Boers sitting in a group. He crept up to the clearing and sprang to his feet with a surge of adrenaline, wielding his carbine and bellowing, 'Hands up!' He swiftly realised he had only two men close enough to assist him in a firefight, and there was a brief moment where he was in danger of losing his life. Fortunately, the guide came to his rescue. He had recognised that one of the group was his brother, and he called to him in Dutch to surrender. The Boers laid down their arms and held their hands in the air. The game was up. They were destined for the internment camp.

Although these were built as 'refugee camps' for avowedly humanitarian reasons, they became overcrowded and insanitary. These were ideal conditions for diseases such as measles and typhoid to flourish, and the army could not cope with the logistical problems presented by the numbers involved, including shortages of food. Twenty-eight thousand

Boer men, women, and children perished; the young being affected the worst. Less attention has been paid to the blacks who were also interned (according to research, 115,000, of whom an estimated 20,000 died).

The internment camps were termed 'concentration camps', a name adopted from the Spanish *reconcentrado* camps; such establishments had not yet assumed the horrific connotation with which we now associate them. The causes of this catastrophe were maladministration and neglect rather than malice, thus differentiating these camps from those used in the Holocaust. And the army simply wasn't set up or well enough resourced to service these facilities. Although the tragic fatalities caused by the epidemics and hunger were not intended, the camps attracted fierce international criticism. And domestically, too, David Lloyd George was a vociferous opponent of these tactics, and Emily Hobhouse, the humanitarian daughter of a former Archdeacon of Bodmin, campaigned passionately against the camps, even travelling out to visit them during the war. Whatever moral high ground the British may have held for their insistence on voting rights for the black African population, it was undermined by the deaths of 20,000 of the potential beneficiaries of this policy as victims of the disease and starvation that ravaged the camps.

Kitchener was initially against Roberts's scorched-earth policy but was forced to change his mind when he became commander-in-chief upon Roberts's return to Britain in late 1900. He saw it as the most effective solution to the Boers' tactic of using the farms to regroup and take on supplies. Although Roberts had initiated these tactics, it was Kitchener's reputation that would suffer as a result of their implementation. The Boers demonised him. The irony is that Kitchener had striven to make peace within a few months of taking command and had been prepared to make major concessions in a conference with Louis Botha on the 28 February 1901, at Middleburg. The Boers would not yield with regard to the British policy of giving the vote to the black African peoples, and Kitchener indicated that this policy could be put in abeyance. It seemed the war was nearing its end. But Kitchener did not have the backing of the powers that be, especially that of Alfred Milner, High

Commissioner of Southern Africa, who would not accept anything less than unconditional surrender. Thus, the war was to last another thirteen months.

On the 30 January 1900, a year and a month before Kitchener's failed peace conference at Middleburg, Captain Guy du Maurier of the 3rd Battalion Royal Fusiliers had been ordered to return home from his posting in Gibraltar to form a 4th Battalion in Dover. Accompanying him was one of his subalterns, a second lieutenant named F. Moore. Some five weeks later, on the 8 March 1900, my grandfather was posted to this newly formed battalion. He was destined for South Africa, but it would be a year before he saw action. With the urgent need for trained horsemen, a company from the 4th Battalion was earmarked to become a constituent part of the 20th Mounted Infantry. William was one of those chosen. He subsequently passed the Mounted Infantry course at Shorncliffe Army Camp (near Folkestone in Kent) with the highest possible grading; his MI Certificate signed off by Lieutenant Moore.

The 16 March 1901 dawns grey and dismal at the Southampton Docks. The HMS *Kildonan Castle* is berthed at the quayside. Trains have been arriving continually from Aldershot all morning, transporting active service companies from regiments hailing from the length and breadth of the country, including the Derbyshire, Hampshire, Liverpool, Norfolk, Royal Sussex, Suffolk, Warwickshire, West Kent, West Surrey, and York and Lancaster Regiments, and the King's Royal Rifle Corps, Lancashire Fusiliers, as well as the Yorkshire Light Infantry. Also arriving from Shorncliffe is William's Mounted Infantry contingent.

The dockside teems with masses of troops awaiting embarkation. Although the day is dreary with occasional rainfall, that does not dampen the mood of the men; the air is alive with a sense of excitement and anticipation. A press correspondent reports that 'not since 1st Army Corps left England has such scenes been witnessed here as was the case this morning ... the men were in high spirits, and cheerfully went about their work in carrying their kit and baggage aboard.' One thousand five hundred troops file up the gangplank, and amongst them are the 41 officers and 282 men of the Mounted Infantry, including William with his draft of Royal Fusiliers, along with their new commanding officer Guy du Maurier, now promoted to major.

The ship proceeded to Queenstown, Ireland, where further drafts of troops were boarded, bringing the total embarked to nearly two thousand, before departing at 4 o'clock in the afternoon on the 18 March. The vessel was also laden with five railway-wagon loads of explosives and camp equipment weighing forty tons. They stopped off at Madeira on Friday, the 22nd, before continuing their voyage. Whilst on board, du Maurier wrote to his mother, Emma, '...I shan't be away long, and I'm only going to one of the healthiest places in the world. And the war is so much over I'm rather sorry to say there isn't any danger of accidents … the joy of getting away from it all is very great.'

Major du Maurier, clearly sharing the general perception that the war had been won, assumed that they were to be engaged in a swift mopping-up operation. He hadn't taken into account the determination of a hard core of Boers to fight on; in fact, the war had not reached the halfway stage. He would soon find that there was still some soldiering to be done. Three weeks after leaving the UK, the 20th Mounted Infantry arrived in South Africa on the 7 April 1901.

He soon came up against harsh reality. The 20th MI took part in their first action only a month after their arrival. Du Maurier wrote to his mother on the 6 May:

> …Well, I've had my baptism of fire, and I don't live in hopes, as the song says.… It's not the jolliest thing in the world and I guess I can do with very little of it – I'm too highly wrought, and the sense of responsibility is too much developed in me. The feeling that I have got the men out of it and the knowledge that they are looking to me to straighten things out is very painful – I think I

should enjoy it more as a private soldier...

In this letter, du Maurier displays his natural propensity for self-deprecation. He was a career soldier whose service would end with his tragic death in the Great War. Within his correspondence, one finds humanity, intelligence, and a well-developed sense of humour – attributes that would earn the affection and respect of those he served with. It is clear that he took responsibility for those serving under him seriously. At this time, he was a few days short of his thirty-sixth birthday. He had a paternalistic concern for his men, some of whom he would have viewed as barely more than boys. My grandfather was nineteen years old, and many of his comrades were of a similar age. The self-doubt expressed here shows du Maurier to be a perceptive and sensitive officer, capable of self-reflection, a quality that could only improve him as a leader of men. He was to lead his battalion through some dangerous and fraught situations, testament to his courage and duty of care to the Tommies in his charge. Continuing in this vein, two days later he writes, 'But I don't hunger after more than a year of this. It means being under fire two days out of three as far as I can see and I didn't bargain for that.'

Although he hadn't expected this level of enemy action, having assumed that the war was petering out, du Maurier was to prove his worth in the face of enemy fire. An illustration of this was chronicled in a further letter dated the 23 June 1901. Written from Middlefontein, du Maurier goes into great detail with regard to a skirmish with a Boer force that resulted in the death of one of his young subalterns:

An exciting day and a sad one. Poor little Besley was killed literally at my side. We marched out of Modder Nek at 8 a.m. and McMicking sent me a long and circuitous route with my company to try and cut some burghers off and get them between me and himself with the main column. I had a most damnable nasty pass to go through which I got through successfully, then began to circle round to the right and enclose the Boers. However, the wily Burgher was not to be caught and made a dash to get round me and secure me before the column hove in sight. To our left was a long ridge or kopje [a small, isolated hill], very thickly wooded.

As the Boers turned and made for it. I turned to the left and did likewise – luckily they got off and opened fire on us, which gave us some time. They simply rained bullets on us, but only a horse or two was hit, and we scattered in the trees, dismounted and made for the kopje. We found it was already held by some of the enemy. The wood was pretty thick, and I lost sight of every man, and found it was no good attempting to give any orders, so I just turned myself into a private soldier and went on. I found young Besley and Howlett both sticking to me and we dashed for the top. I was much excited and bullets were fizzing all round and from pretty close quarters which, I own, I didn't absolutely love. Then quite close to the top we all three halted and looked for something to shoot at, but the Boer is an adept at taking cover and we saw nothing. Then suddenly, about 10 yards to our front, we saw three of them. The nearest one fired and poor little Besley fell back and crawled away groaning. Then I saw scarlet, and I stood and took the most careful shot I ever took in my life and fired – I aimed at his throat and hit him there and had the satisfaction of hearing his groan. Then I saw another to the right just creeping away and I got him. All this time a devil of a fire had been going on and it gradually stopped. There I stood – wondering what had happened – not a man could I see – except Howlett and poor Besley lying groaning at my feet, on his face. Who'd won what was troubling me.

Arthur Charles Gordon Besley, a second lieutenant, was just out of his teens when he was shot. He came from a distinguished family, being the great-grandson of the ninth Marquess of Huntly, and his grandfather on his mother's side was the late Lord Cecil Gordon. He was educated at Wellington College and the Royal Military College, from which he graduated in August 1900, and was reportedly a first-rate rider and an accomplished shot. As the dust settled, du Maurier assessed the situation, addressing the immediate threat of a potential counterattack and the need to consolidate their position. From a vantage point he could see the Boers retreating at a gallop, and it dawned on him that he had successfully taken the kopje. The main column arrived, and the officer in charge, Major McMicking, met du Maurier and congratulated him on securing such a prized strategic position and preventing an attack on the main force. Characteristically, du Maurier played it down: '...although I didn't say so I knew it was all really a fluke 'cos when I assaulted the place I wasn't thinking of the column at all'.

The unfortunate Besley bled to death. The bullet had gone through his field glasses and severed the femoral artery. They returned to camp, and du Maurier presided over the burial by reciting some prayers. The grave was marked with a cross made of biscuit-box wood. The following day, du Maurier had the sad task of informing Besley's mother of his death:

> We moved off at 9 and cautiously moved on to the place about 10 miles further on, I was doing advance guard. We expected a fight but didn't get one – got here about 2. Camp in a very pretty wood on top of a small hill. Many outposts out, but I don't think we shall be attacked. I've just written a line to Besley's mother, giving her a few details she might care to have. He was a very nice boy though I used to get cross with him sometimes, and I am so awfully sorry about it. He was only 20.

Young Besley's death was proof, if it were needed, that the war was by no means over. With Kitchener's failed attempt to bring peace receding into the past, it was clear that the Boers still in the field – the *Bittereinders*, as they were known – would have to be reduced to a state whereby they couldn't function as a fighting force; they would have to be comprehensively and militarily nullified to bring an end to hostilities. This war had a long way to go.

Besley's life would be honoured by his brother officers, who installed a brass plaque in St. John the Baptist Church, Palmeira Square, Hove. Such ceremonies were repeated in churches and cathedrals across the country by many bereaved families during and immediately after the Boer War. Stone memorials were also erected in town centres and parks as whole communities needed to recognise the sacrifice of their kith and kin. It was nothing less than a national explosion of commemoration through public art and sculpture. This was the first conflict whereby a widespread remembrance of those who had fallen was carried out. It was a collective expression of grief that set a precedent for the Great War and would reach its full flowering with the establishment of the Imperial War Graves Commission (IWGC) in 1917.

Contained within the commemorations of the Boer War were the seeds of an egalitarian approach to the memorialising of those who had served during conflict. It elevated the ordinary soldier – the private and the non-commissioned officer to a state of remembrance that had previously been enjoyed only by the sons of the aristocracy and the landed gentry. Previously, working-class soldiers were nameless and often buried in mass graves. There was a historical disregard for the life of a soldier from a lower socioeconomic background; his contribution was not considered worthy of remembrance. Although he may have been much loved by family and friends, his life was considered less valuable than that of a person from a higher stratum of society. And although my grandfather hadn't died in action, that attitude chimes with the inadequate memorialisation of his life – that of being buried in a common grave purely on account of his economic status, with no acknowledgement of the distinguished service he gave his country – and it rankles still.

Alan Bennett addresses this phenomenon in his play, *The History Boys*. The relevant scene is set in a large urban grammar school in Yorkshire. Hector, a schoolmaster, enters his classroom after lessons have ended for the day to find one of his most talented students, Posner, still there. Hector asks him what he has learned this week. Posner tells him that he's been studying Hardy's *Drummer Hodge* and then recites the poem in its entirety:

*They throw in Drummer Hodge, to rest*
*Uncoffined – just as found*
*His landmark is the kopje crest*
*That breaks the veldt around;*
*And foreign constellations west*
*Each night above his mound.*

*Young Hodge the Drummer never knew –*
*Fresh from his Wessex home –*
*The meaning of the broad Karoo,*
*The bush, the dusty loam*
*And why uprose to nightly view*
*Strange stars amid the gloam.*

*Yet portion of that unknown plain*
*Will Hodge for ever be;*
*His homely Northern breast and brain*
*Grow to some Southern tree,*
*And strange-eyed constellations reign*
*His stars eternally.*

Hector explains the significance of the poem:

Mmm… The important thing is that he has a name. Say Hardy is
writing about the Zulu Wars, or later or the Boer War possibly,
and these were the first campaigns when soldiers … or common
soldiers … were commemorated, the names of the dead recorded
and inscribed on war memorials. Before this soldiers – private
soldiers anyway – were all unknown soldiers and, so far from being
revered, there was a firm in the nineteenth century, in Yorkshire
of course, which swept up their bones from the Battlefields of
Europe in order to grind them into fertiliser. So, thrown into a

common grave though he may be, he is still Hodge the drummer. Lost boy though he is on the other side of the world, he still has a name.

In her biography of Thomas Hardy, Claire Tomalin definitively identifies *Drummer Hodge* as referring to the Boer War and regards it as perhaps the finest of a series of poems that he wrote at the start of the conflict. Both Bennett, in his play, and Tomalin, in her biography, note the similarity between Hardy's:

> *Yet portion of that unknown plain*
> *Will Hodge for ever be;*
> *His homely Northern breast and brain*
> *Grow to some Southern tree*

And Rupert Brooke's:

> *If I should die, think only this of me:*
> *That there's some corner of a foreign field*
> *That is for ever England. There shall be*
> *In that rich earth a richer dust concealed*

Tomalin goes further, suggesting that Brooke may have been influenced by Hardy's poem, but there is a distinct difference in tone between the poets' approaches; Hardy does not glorify the death of Drummer Hodge as Brooke does that of his subject. Perhaps this is because Hardy's soldier is explicitly working class; his humble origins emphasised by the description of his remains as *homely* in contrast to the *richer dust* of Brooke's hero. Hodge's motive for joining up would have included pragmatic reasons such as regular income, meals, clothing, and shelter – or wanting a life less ordinary than that which awaited a youth of the labouring class in Victorian Britain – as opposed to the romantic ideology of Brooke's soldier. Emily Orr's cry for the working-class soldier: 'What has your country done for you?' – conflicts with the original concept of 'Dulce et decorum est pro patria mori.'

Our working-class soldier, William, was still a teenager, due to turn twenty later that year. Within a few months of his birthday, he would be involved in an ambitious military operation designed to capture Kitchener's nemesis, Christiaan De Wet. He would need to utilise all of his shooting and riding prowess over the coming months if he wasn't to share the same fate at exactly the same age as 2nd Lt Besley and, like Drummer Hodge, come to be thrown, discarded, to rest 'uncoffined' in a common grave on the other side of the world.

CHAPTER SIX

# LIFE IN THE SADDLE

*I wish my mother could see me now, with a fencepost under my arm,*
*And a knife and a spoon in my putties that I found on a Boer farm,*
*Atop of a sore-backed Argentine, with a thirst that you couldn't buy.*
*I used to be in the Yorkshires once*
*(Sussex, Lincolns and Rifles once),*
*Hampshires, Glosters, and Scottish once!*
*But now I am M.I.*

RUDYARD KIPLING, extract from *M.I.*
*(Mounted Infantry of the Line)*

The lot of a mounted infantryman entailed hardship and privation, and life in the saddle required a high degree of self-sufficiency. He was not just responsible for himself; the welfare of his horse was of almost equal importance, and he had to carry sufficient kit and provisions to meet both his and his steed's requirements. Captain St. Leger of the 1st MI listed the equipment each man carried: 120 rounds of ammunition, one shirt, one pair of socks, one pair of drawers, a holdall, spare bootlaces, a rubber curry comb and brush, sponge, towel, soap, emergency rations, a canteen and a day's supply of oats for the horse. A blanket, a waterproof sheet, a greatcoat and a jersey for each and every man supplemented this equipment, carried by supply wagons that formed part of an MI column. The men slept under the stars; a night on the veldt could be freezing cold with just one blanket for cover. However, the supply wagons couldn't always keep up with the column when they were in hot pursuit and any number of days and nights could be spent out in the open, sleeping on the bare ground without any cover whatsoever. Kipling goes on to versify the travails of the MI:

That is what we are known as – we are the push you require
For outposts all night under freezin', an' rearguard all day under fire.
Anything 'ot or unwholesome? Anything dusty or dry?
Borrow a bunch of Ikonas! Trot out the —— M.I.!

('Ikonas' was a nickname for the Mounted Infantry believed to have derived from the Xhosa language.)

William was engaged in the continuing series of 'drives' across the grasslands of the Transvaal and the Orange River Colony (formerly the Orange Free State). This was frontier country. The pursuit of the Boers across the veldt in these corralling actions involved long hours in the saddle, similar to the experience of the cowboys engaged on the great cattle drives from Texas to Kansas across the prairies of North America. My grandfather bore a tattoo of Buffalo Bill on his left forearm; the Wild West hero would have completely recognised the life that the young fusilier was leading.

On the 12 September 1901, William's battalion arrived in Nylstroom for a break from the action. Du Maurier wrote:

> We've got in at last for a rest and if I said I didn't want one I should be telling you a lie. I was just fagged out.…. In the last 5 weeks trek we've killed about 6, wounded a dozen, say, and brought in 20 prisoners, and we've lost 6 killed and 8 wounded. I'm going to have an absolutely placid time while I'm here, just sitting in my tent trying to get the Battalion into order from an administrative point of view.

But he was warming to the life of a soldier on campaign. The idea of returning to service life at home was beginning to pall, and he was already thinking of life after the military, writing to his mother again a few days later on the 17th:

… there is no chance of my coming home this year. There will probably be many months' work for MI even after the war is really over, hunting down small parties of briganding Dutchmen all over the country…. I like this country and this life better than home work, besides, here I'm commanding a regiment and a horse regiment into the bargain and at home I must return to only a company and a fool company at that, leaving out of the question that I'm drawing 25/- a day instead of 13/- but of course they will soon begin to reduce the number of MI regiments and then, naturally, I shan't stand much chance of commanding one as there are so many others who have had many opportunities and have done more to deserve command of one then I have. If I can get some work at home in the event of them raising regular MI regiments I shall stay – otherwise I'm off the moment I have put in 20 years for a pension, or sooner if I can get one. Never could I go back to the Dover life again…

In October 1901, Lieutenant Ralph Verney, aged twenty-two, of the Rifle Brigade was seconded to du Maurier's battalion as a subaltern. He wrote to his father on the 5th of the month from Spruyt's Hotel in Pretoria:

Don't think that I have somehow exchanged into another regiment, because I haven't, but I am now in the 20th Battalion, Mounted Infantry…. I came here on Friday last, and am off to a place called Neylstroom (or Neilstroom) on Wednesday next. This place is about half way between here and Petersburg on the Northern Line…. In my opinion it is a great thing to be in the Mounted Infantry, and if ever I want to get a job in it again later on, of course I shall have much more chance of being taken for it, if I have served in MI out here. It is a great change for me, and it probably means that I shall not be with my regiment again for two years or more.

Nearly three weeks later, on the 24 October, Verney writes of the activities of the 20$^{th}$ MI during what was a very busy time. After an unsuccessful attempt to capture a Boer commandant named Hans Botha, the battalion made a perilous journey through the narrow valley of Zand River Poort. Surrounded by high hills and vulnerable to an ambush by the enemy, they made it through unscathed en route to three Boer encampments over thirty miles distant. Upon arrival, one company dismounted and stalked one of these *laagers* (camps formed by circled wagons) under cover of darkness. Just as the sun rose, they rushed the camp shouting, 'Hands up!', thereby taking the sleeping Boers by surprise. They captured over forty fighting men, hauling them bleary-eyed out of their wagons. They followed this up by capturing more from a smaller laager, bringing the total to sixty-two prisoners, and taking possession of their wagons and cattle. After returning to the convoy of their own wagons, which was about twenty miles behind, they'd covered a hundred miles in two and a half days – tiring work for both horses and men.

There was to be no let-up for the battalion. Verney writes home, detailing that, on the 10 November, they had captured another twenty-five prisoners during twenty-seven hours of continuous duty with hardly anything to eat. On the 6 December, he recounts the fact that they had been on trek for fourteen days in pursuit of a Boer officer named Badenhorst. At one stage, having left the supply wagons behind, they trekked for four days and nights, living only on the provisions they could carry – basically tea and biscuits – riding at night and snatching a little sleep during the day. They finally caught up with their prey on the 13 December, capturing him and fifteen other prisoners, although Verney admits they had some good fortune in doing so. The top brass were very pleased; Kommandant Chrisoffel Petrus Stephanus Badenhorst was a high-ranking officer and, as such, was a prize catch. He was exiled to St. Helena along with 5,000 other prisoners of war.

As the year neared its close, the day before Christmas Eve 1901, du Maurier writes of the preparations for the holiday:

We are making great arrangements for dining together on Xmas day, all the officers, each bringing with them some contribution. I've got a turkey that has been trying to get fat for some weeks but constant trekking is against superfluous adipose tissue. Your pudding and your cake – Alas the crackers and cigars haven't come. There may be one more train up with parcels, but it's a near thing. Like the Xmas dinner of the 'Trois Angliches', in Trilby [du Maurier's father's best-selling novel].

The war was dragging on into 1902 with no end in sight. On New Year's Eve 1901, Verney writes enthusiastically of his appointment as du Maurier's quartermaster, a role that in the MI also included that of 'galloper'. In a standard regiment of foot, a quartermaster is responsible for the organising of supplies, whereas a galloper acts as an aide-de-camp or assistant to a more senior officer:

Major du Maurier, who is commanding the 20th MI, has taken me on his staff as Quartermaster. In ordinary infantry battalions, the Quartermaster has risen from the ranks, but in an MI Battalion, the Quartermaster is chosen from one of the officers of the Battalion, because when on trek he acts as galloper to the Commanding Officer. I am awfully glad to have got it, as I hear all that is to be heard in the way of news, and it is a very nice job, being galloper. Of course I have had a lot of work to do these last few days, as I am in charge of all the food and rations both of men and horses in the Battalion. Also I have to draw from the Ordnance Store everything we want in the way of saddlery, clothing, etc, etc.

The unrelenting campaigning was taking its toll on du Maurier. On the 9 January 1902, writing from Dyson's Farm in the Orange River Colony:

I'm tired of war and would prefer Sicily. But I'm not allowing any hopes of finishing it off in 2 or 3 months to buoy me up – I think another year may see us on the way home and we shall all be glad and then I know we shall look back upon the campaign as the best time we ever had in our lives. It's curious how very childish it sometimes seems to one to see a whole lot of really grown-up men shooting at each other for apparently no reason.

In a letter dated the 24 January 1902, he shows his dry sense of humour as he expresses his healthy disregard for rank and privilege, having received a distinctly underwhelming gift for his men:

I've just received 7 pipes from the Queen to distribute among the Battalion – rather funny. I'm afraid I don't gush much over Royal presents and it was suggested by the Head of the Army that they should be given to men who have distinguished themselves in the field. I thought the reward was hardly adequate though they are quite nice pipes, so I have given them to the non-commissioned officers in order of seniority...

The work of the 20th Mounted Infantry was about to intensify. Kitchener was feeling under immense pressure to bring the war to an end, and he saw the capture of Christiaan De Wet as key to achieving this. De Wet was one of the most successful Boer leaders during the guerilla phase of the war. A number of notable victories over the British, combined with a Houdini-like ability to escape and evade capture, had gained him folk-hero status with the Boers. His name was celebrated in song. Kitchener devised a strategy whereby a 'drive' carried out by four reinforced troop columns – nine thousand men acting in concert – would pursue De Wet and his men from east to west into the maw of a large fifty-mile-square enclosure formed by connected blockhouse lines. The British columns would set off from the 'open side', the men spaced at approximately every ten yards, forcing De Wet against the blockhouse-protected Kroonstaad-to-Wolvehoek railway line to the west, from where there should be no escape. That was the theory, anyway. My grandfather was under the command of Colonel Rawlinson, the officer in charge of an enhanced column – composed of veterans of a series of successful night raids – that was described by Thomas Pakenham, the author of what has become an essential history of the Boer War, as Kitchener's 'best MI columns' and 'the elite of the army'.

At first light on the 6 February, the four column commanders opened their sealed orders and directed their troops to begin the huge pressing movement westwards into the maw of the pen formed by the lines of blockhouses, like a giant ramrod down a barrel. The garrisons manning the blockhouses had been reinforced and were further supplemented by seven heavily armed trains ranging up and down the tracks with searchlights sweeping and guns raised. The juggernaut was now in motion, and all Kitchener could do was wait, as the chain of command was all but broken once the operation commenced. Unable to contain himself, he left Pretoria on the 7th to travel to the western end of the trap for the anticipated denouement. To the intense frustration of Kitchener, De Wet had managed to escape in the early hours of that day, using wire cutters to break the line in the southwest corner of the trap, eluding his adversary once again along with nearly seven hundred of his men.

However, the operation wasn't a complete failure. On the morning of the 8th, a reckoning was carried out that showed that 285 Boers had been captured (140 of which had been taken by Rawlinson's column, who were on the right flank of the advance, to the north), and herds of cattle, along with many horses that had been ridden to exhaustion and then abandoned, were rounded up. It was a partial success, and it demonstrated that the degree of harassment inflicted upon the Boers was having a significant effect.

A week later, clearly acting on intelligence received, Kitchener ordered the juggernaut, now augmented by even more troops, to roll back east from whence they came. Using the same tactics, the men lined up like beaters on a shoot, but this time they would drive their prey into the southeastern corner of the rectangle. Once again, the wily De Wet escaped, and it seemed that this drive was to be even less successful than the first. That is, until the last day, the 27 February, when, once again, Rawlinson's column covered themselves in glory by capturing 650 men of General Lucas Meyer's commando by encircling and taking his laager at Lang Riet. The fact that William played a part in these successes fires my imagination. My mind's eye pictures him riding into action, slouch hat protecting his head from the fierce South African sun, bandolier slung diagonally across his shoulder and chest, with rifle in hand.

This second great drive ran from the 13 to 27 February. Verney wrote to his mother on the 22nd from the Klip River, describing an encounter with a Boer commando group on the third day of the march. They had been forewarned that this unit was in the general vicinity but hadn't anticipated meeting them for a good few miles yet. Consequently, the officers were standing in a group, some way ahead of the men, rather than keeping in extended order to present less of a target. This was an irresistible target for the Boers, who had stationed themselves amongst the rocks some 300 yards ahead. They lost no time in opening fire on them, a colonel amongst them by the name of Dawkins being a particularly attractive quarry. Fortunately, none were hit. The column promptly mounted their horses and rode hard towards them, but the Boers managed to escape. The 20th MI bivouacked at Klip River Station that evening, settling down to a cold night without blankets as the supply wagons had taken a different route.

On the 4 March, they embarked on a third drive that would be the least successful of the three. Heading west again, they managed to capture only a meagre one hundred Boers, and De Wet eluded them once again by breaking undetected through no less than three blockhouse lines. He reached the relative safety of the Western Transvaal, where, due to the scarcity of water, no blockhouses had been constructed. The British policed that region using roving mobile columns instead.

Following the conclusion of the third drive on the 11 March, the 20th MI were not allowed to rest on their laurels. On the 19 March, du

Maurier writes that he is looking forward to a rare half-day off: 'No rest for us and we are off tomorrow morning, I don't know where. Thought I would have a bath and a quiet afternoon instead of going in to see the sights of Potchestroom.'

Five days later, William's battalion set off during the evening of the 24th as part of a huge force given the objective of capturing Generals Koos de la Rey and Jan Christoffel Greyling Kemp, two high-ranking Boer commanders. It's a curious thing that our particular hunter – my grandfather – and one of the hunted – Koos de la Rey – were both of Huguenot descent. Many Boers shared the same ancestry, having descended from an estimated 400 French Protestants who had fled to the Cape of Good Hope during the same seventeenth-century diaspora that had brought William's ancestors to England.

The 20th MI, led by Colonel Rawlinson as part of one of the enhanced columns, along with those led by Generals Walter Kitchener (the younger brother of the C-in-C) and Robert Kekewich, were on the move again – 16,000 mounted troops in all. They had intelligence of a Boer laager at Hartebeestefontein and marched all night, overshooting the encampment by some twenty miles as part of a deliberate ploy to convince the Boers that they remained undiscovered. At dawn, the British began the drive back towards Hartebeestefontein, with Kekewich's column on the left, Walter Kitchener's on the right, and Rawlinson's in the centre. Eventually, three hours into the drive, a convoy was spotted on the horizon, initially believed to be British. By noon, they'd ascertained that there were no infantry with the convoy, suggesting that they were Boers. Still not completely sure, Rawlinson's men accelerated and cantered into the hills on the flank of the unidentified convoy to overtake them. From the hills, they could see that the convoy was heading for a nek (a mountain pass) two miles ahead. Breaking into a gallop, the column managed to reach the nek shortly before the convoy. When they saw the vanguard trot into view about 1,500 yards away, they were finally able to confirm them as the enemy. They opened fire on the Boers, who promptly turned tail and looked for an escape route. Kekewich's column had one flank covered, but the Boers managed to slip the net to the south, where Walter Kitchener's column should have been, but who had lost touch for some reason. Nevertheless, the endeavour was a partial success; the Boers had fled in haste, leaving behind a number of artillery pieces, including four guns and two pom-poms.

The pursuit carried on until nightfall, and approximately 170 of 600 Boers were taken prisoner. The column had been in the saddle for twenty-six hours non-stop, and their mounts had been ridden to near exhaustion. Nearly a hundred miles had been covered during this period, and the horses had not been fed for all of that time. They were rewarded with some well-earned oats before the men lay down to rest and slept like logs.

The following day, du Maurier writes:

Today we are resting and tomorrow we have at them again. I'm afraid there is a lot more rain to come and it is very wretched work in the wet, not that it's perfect bliss in fine weather. I do not like fighting. I read in a book of Seton Merriman's the other day that a man who has once heard the Siren Song of the bullet cannot live without it. I think I can exist without it…

His pessimism is evident yet again in his next letter dated the 16 April 1902:

It's much too early to think yet of plans 'when the war is over', there is plenty more of it to come. But it must end some day and then there will be so many people to provide with nice fat billets that with my absence of push and interest I'm bound to be far behind. Perhaps also my lack of merit, but judging from what I can see that is a very common complaint. I certainly cannot see myself returning to the old groove. Of course I must go on till I complete 20 years for a pension, but no further unless the road to something really good lies before me. I should be happier far farming with you [his mother] than vegetating and fossilizing in a mess with a herd of uninteresting boy officers…

Whilst he was writing this, fresh peace negotiations were in progress, having begun in Pretoria on the 11 April. The basis for the talks were the conditions laid out in the previous discussions that had taken place in Middleburg over a year earlier, on the 28 February 1901. Verney writes home on the 21 April and is much more positive regarding news of a possible end to the war. He is excited that these negotiations might be decisive. The day after, du Maurier also writes, returning to the themes of farming as a future career and his disillusionment with the army and his commanding officers, but he is optimistic about the negotiations and seems to agree with Verney, signing off his letter from Schoon Spruit, near Klerksdorp, with his view that peace is on the horizon:

I'm very fit except for veldt sores which are a bore. I had rather a bad one on my ear but it's getting better. From what I've seen of generals out here I give you my word I'd sooner be a farmer. A more borne lot of self-important duffers I never want to come across. Besides, the only point in being a general is to be one in war – and I don't suppose if I ever were a general there would be a war, and I know I don't possess the qualities which make a great war general. England doesn't grow those men, and a general in peacetime I consider a contemptible occupation. Farming is more dignified and infinitely more useful. Besides, it looks as if there are better times coming for farmers in general now that they've put a tax on imported corn. I've got a good head for business and I know a good deal about men, and something about horses, and these qualities are wasted in the army and I'm sick of it. Of course I've thoroughly enjoyed it all out here and I wouldn't have missed it for anything. But I've seen the absolute rottenness of our system, or rather want of system – and the hopeless amateurishness of the whole profession and I'm convinced it's no place for a grown-up person, splendid for boys and old women and I'm not the former and I want to get out of it before I become the latter… I'm getting 40 remounts today, and I'm told I shan't get any more so it looks as if the peace conference was expected to come to something.

His perception of the army's senior command expressed here foreshadows a post–First World War view held by many veterans, historians, politicians, and commentators, including Basil Liddell Hart, Siegfried Sassoon, A.J.P. Taylor, David Lloyd George, and Alan Clark, who were equally critical of the generals, both as individuals and as a collective. Du Maurier develops his argument when referring to army reform in his next letter on the 27 April:

I've just been reading Mr. Broderick's great army reform scheme and I don't think it is epoch-making and he won't get the men he wants for another sixpence. I'm amused at the great talk about the education of the officer and how he is to be made to take a far greater interest in his profession and how much more work is to be got out of him and how vastly superior he is to be in a few years. If they want that sort of men they will have to pay for him. The market price of intelligence is much higher than the rate they pay at present. I don't know if I really want peace or not. Of course I'm not bloodthirsty and don't love fighting, and I also want to come back to you, but I do like the life out here more than any life I've lived yet, and I know when it's over I shall regret it. There is generally a purpose in everything you do, which is so different to the life of a soldier in peace time at home, and I do love being in the open air all day and all night and there is so much room in the country – no one to push against you. Ten minutes in one of the towns though makes one loathe South Africa. Now that the war is closing all the money makers are flocking back and nothing is talked of or thought of but gold, till one gets sick of the sound of the word and I hate gold mines and all connected with them.

Passed one some time ago just before we were going to camp for the night, and I felt quite pleased when the men demolished all the buildings and everything to get firewood.

Du Maurier is speaking purely from the viewpoint of a soldier here; his revulsion at the avarice and rapacity of the prospectors and speculators (the 'goldbugs', as they came to be known) is plain to see; he wants no part of it. However, so focused is he on the military imperative, he is blind to the contradiction in his stance; the army is executing the aims of the British government in prosecuting this war, and they stood to benefit from the mineral resources extracted from the ground in the event of victory.

Although the victory would come, the war wasn't quite over yet. Verney wrote on the 14 May of the capture of 352 Boers of Kemp's commando on the completion of their latest drive. On the 19 May, peace negotiations resumed in Pretoria with De la Rey and De Wet amongst the Boer delegation sitting around a table with Lord Kitchener and his staff. These renewed negotiations produced three additional questions to be resolved: whether and in what form amnesty for colonial rebels in the Cape and Natal would be granted; when (if at all) the franchise would be granted to black Africans; and the amount of financial help that the Boers could expect from the British to settle their debts and rebuild their economy. A draft agreement cabled to London for the Cabinet's consideration arrived on the 22 May.

On the same day the missive was sent, du Maurier writes another letter:

Got into the Blockhouse line and are resting. I got two mails from you and some parcels. The lifeguard coat is lovely and will keep me beautifully warm. I also got a welcome addition of 200 men and horses from the different regiments I'm composed of to bring me up to strength again. No news of peace and I don't know what my future movements are. Of course beloved if I get a good job out here I suppose I shall take it as the pay is good – but for your sake I will own that I don't expect to be honoured with the offer. I don't think I've impressed my immediate commanding officers very much. They certainly haven't impressed me, and I haven't taken much trouble to prevent them seeing it and we've had many arguments. I say, if I command a regiment I'll do so in my own way, and if they don't like it they can lump it or get me removed.

Again, du Maurier reveals his frustration at what he perceived as incompetence in his senior officers, and he states his refusal to progress his career by sycophancy. It's a damning indictment of the institutional mindset of the army at that time that they couldn't accommodate an officer of du Maurier's ability. After all, he came from the same gene pool that produced three generations of extraordinarily talented individuals: his father, George, who wrote the best-selling *Trilby*; his brother Gerald, the much-lauded actor and theatre manager; and his niece Daphne, one of the most successful authors of the twentieth century. Major du Maurier's irreverence and honesty were obviously qualities that didn't endear him to his superiors. His own talent was there for all to see when he went on to write the smash hit play *An Englishman's Home* in 1909, a prescient drama that foresaw the threat posed by Germany – a threat that became real and played out to its awful consequences in 1914.

On the 31 May 1902, peace terms were finally agreed, and the war ended with the signing of the Treaty of Vereeniging. To modern eyes, it is utterly predictable and deeply depressing that the postponement of black enfranchisement was one of the compromises that was made. So much for Secretary of State for the Colonies Joseph Chamberlain's statement that 'we cannot consent to purchase a shameful peace by leaving the coloured population in the position in which they stood before the war.' The issue was kicked into the long grass, to be decided at a future unspecified date when the British would be prepared to concede self-determination to Transvaal and the Orange Free State, who would be trusted to resolve the matter. Of course, the question of the black franchise was not to be properly addressed until universal suffrage was achieved with the end of apartheid in 1994. The war had cost Great Britain over 200 million pounds (equivalent to nearly 25 billion pounds today); 500,000 British troops had ultimately been deployed; and the conflict had cost the nation dearly – not just financially but also in terms of international relations and the reputation of the armed forces.

Verney wrote to his mother on the 3 June, providing news of how the peace was received at camp:

> You will have heard long before now the great and joyful news that Peace was signed at Pretoria last Saturday night. On Sunday morning we were sitting in our tent, having just finished breakfast, when, like a thunderclap, we heard a great burst of cheering from the direction of Church parade, which we did not attend on that morning. We rushed out to hear the news, which we had guessed already, and which Colonel Rawlinson had formally given out as soon as service was ended. He had received a telegram from Lord Kitchener, which he read out on parade. Each different camp took up the cheering, which lasted for nearly an hour. We could hear General Walter Kitchener's columns cheering nearly 3 miles away, and the Imperial Light Horse had taken it up from us in the next camp. Sports and impromptu smoking concerts have been the order of the day (and night) ever since. On Sunday night, du Maurier, Deedes and myself dined with Colonel Dawkins to celebrate the occasion.

On the 18 July, writing from Elandsfontein, du Maurier writes of an inspection by a senior officer and his chief staff officer:

> General Oliphant who commands here inspected us on Tuesday. I don't think he'd seen any MI before. He's an old Guardsman who commanded at Aldershot for the last year or two and was sent out here a few months ago to be ready on the declaration of peace to

take command of the garrison town. He didn't seem to me to quite grasp the situation and didn't know or care whether the men rode well or the horses looked fit, etc., but seemed chiefly concerned at the way the men were dressed. As a matter of fact, I haven't seen them so well dressed since they left England and I don't know how they managed it. But he seemed to think otherwise. He's a nice little old thing, though, but an ideal cup of tea. His chief staff officer though seems a most offensive person, a colonel with a very military face with all the signs of a military brain. While I was waiting for the general to ride down the ranks with me, the Colonel, looking very fierce, said to me: 'I don't know whether you know it, but your officers aren't sitting to attention'. Well, I didn't know it and I could have bet they weren't because I'm sure not one of them knew what sitting to attention was – I didn't. I'd told them not to talk and not to smoke, and to stay in their proper places. However, the Colonel had such an eagle eye, so I shouted out: 'Will those officers sit at attention please'. They looked most dismayed and at once sat in the most ridiculous attitude they could think of at the moment, and the Colonel looked fiercer than ever as I smiled sweetly at him and said I thought that was better...

Reimagine such a farcical situation during the Second World War, and you have a scene that wouldn't be out of place in Joseph Heller's satire *Catch-22*. In this letter, du Maurier perfectly articulates the absurdity of a certain type of military mind; the colonel concerned displays the reactionary, unimaginative, inflexible attitude of a career soldier whose high rank has been gained simply on the grounds of seniority rather than ability ('Buggins' turn'). As du Maurier had stated in his previous letter of the 22 May, his response to the Colonel's request with an air of amused detachment wouldn't have 'impressed my immediate commanding officers very much'; in fact, he would have been seen as subversive. The Colonel's insistence on parade-ground standards of dress and drill as if they were taking part in a passing-out ceremony at Aldershot was completely inappropriate and ill-judged when applied to combat veterans who had lived in the saddle for months on end. And asserting his authority through rigidly applying the rulebook no matter what the circumstances showed a remarkable lack of leadership. The sight of these officers trying to 'sit to attention' in a variety of contorted or unnatural postures was too much for du Maurier's highly developed sense of humour.

On the 1 August, du Maurier writes of the winding-up of the 20th Mounted Infantry:

> I got definite orders about my battalion last night and we start breaking up at once. Everyone, officers and men, are to be returned to their infantry battalions except myself, and I am appointed 2nd in command of the 5th MI at Modder River, Cap Colony. I can't say I think I have been well treated. The future Commanding Officer is a good deal junior to me, and had not been so long in the Mounted Infantry, so it's rather a blow to one's self esteem, and I must consider myself as a bit of a failure. It will take me about a fortnight to wind things up here and then I shall go to Modder River and see what chances there are of getting leave, and of course I shall come home as soon as possible. I might, of course, write and refuse to take the job and ask to be returned to my regiment, but I don't want to act like an aggrieved child, and as I've got to put in some years' service somehow or somewhere it don't very much matter how or where I do it. I'm bound to get four months' leave either at once or in four months' time, and I will content myself with looking forward to that…

The British Army had learned a great deal from the experience of the Boer War; the 'lesson' of Kipling's poem that had been taught was instrumental in the development of tactical reforms that, by the beginning of the Great War in 1914, produced the most highly trained, well-skilled, and professional army that had ever served crown and country. In particular, the marksmanship of the British soldier was second to none. Improved training exercises involving shooting from cover, lying prone and kneeling, at both moving and pop-up targets, and subject to time limits, simulating a combat situation far more effectively than the old system of firing at static targets. Intense musketry practice was encouraged by the award of extra pay for those who attained first-class marksman status; men would practice working the breach on their rifles in their own time in order to increase the rapidity of reloading, the most expert reaching an impressive twenty aimed shots a minute, the record an astounding thirty-eight rounds. Further inducements included shooting competitions, such as the Evelyn Wood Trophy – which William competed for with the 1st RF as pictured in the photograph so treasured by my Aunt Florrie – all of which resulted in a proficiency that astonished the Germans in the initial stages of the Great War. One German observed that 'section after section ran into the well-directed fire of experienced troops. Every effort had been put into our training, but it was completely inadequate preparation for such a serious assault on battle-hardened, long-service colonial soldiers.'

The British view of the Great War is so dominated by the tragedies of the Somme and Passchendaele that scant attention has been paid to the fact that the Germans went through a similar trauma during the initial, mobile phase of the conflict when thousands of their men, including many young, idealistic students, had marched towards the British lines singing songs of the Fatherland only to be mown down in rows by the lethal marksmanship of the regular Tommy. Such was the intensity of fire that the Germans believed that the British were equipped with a large number of machine guns. In fact, the opposite was true; at the beginning of the Great War, the Germans had a marked superiority in machine guns – the whole of the British Expeditionary Force (BEF) had only 150 compared to an estimated 12,000 issued to the Germans – and it was one of the biggest failings of the British high command that they had initially not recognised the importance of this highly effective weapon and, thus, the resulting tactical disadvantage under which the BEF laboured. Of course, the Germans were totally unaware of this;

their misconception was solely down to the superb marksmanship and rapidity of fire of the British infantryman.

But all this was yet to come. The 20th MI was disbanded in short order, the horses sold off, and the records show that my grandfather was transferred back into the regular infantry with the 2nd Battalion Royal Fusiliers on the 11 August 1902 – back to soldiering on two legs rather than four. William had loved working with horses in the Mounted Infantry, developing a deep affection for these much put-upon animals. He was to work with horses later in civilian life, too, and my father spoke often of grandfather's strong affinity with those noble creatures.

William arrived back in England on the 22 October 1902 to serve a 'home' posting with the 2nd Battalion, where he would resume the rounds of training, manoeuvres, drill, and soldierly routine that were part of barrack-room life. This came to an end on the 9 February 1904 when he was transferred to the 1st Battalion and his next overseas deployment beckoned. The exotic mysteries of the East awaited him... on the 11 February, he embarked for India, the jewel in the British Empire's crown.

# CHAPTER SEVEN

# INDIA

*When the 'arf-made recruity goes out to the East*
*'E acts like a babe an' 'e drinks like a beast,*
*An 'e wonders because 'e is frequent deceased*
*Ere 'e's fit for to serve as a soldier.*

RUDYARD KIPLING, from *The Young British Soldier*

My grandfather was no 'arf-made recruity' when he embarked for India. Although only twenty-two years old, he had already served for nearly four and a half years, five and a half if you count his year in the militia. And, critically, he'd seen active service. He was a combat veteran, a badge of honour that some of the 'old sweats' that he'd be joining on the subcontinent could not claim; many had never fired a gun in anger. In addition, his year and 112 days of home service following his return from South Africa had served him well; he was well-versed in barrack-room life and wise in the art of soldiering. Without the benefit of a first-person account to work with, there is one soldier's record that I can turn to in reconstructing this stage of my grandfather's life: that of Private Frank Richards of the Royal Welch Fusiliers, whose army career followed a remarkably similar path to William's and who was also stationed in India at the same time, albeit in a different part of the country. Of a similar age and also from a working-class background, it can be reasonably assumed that they would have viewed army life through the same cultural prism and held and exhibited similar attitudes and behaviour; Richards can be relied upon as a wholly authentic witness in recreating William's story.

William set sail on the 11 February 1904, towards the end of what was known as the Indian 'Trooping Season', which ran throughout the cooler months from October to March, thereby avoiding travelling in the heat of summer. The troopships carried about 2,000 men accommodated below decks in an unventilated environment that would have been unbearable – and a major health hazard – in the higher temperatures of April to September. During the autumn and winter months, reinforcement drafts were sent out to India, and, in accordance with the terms of the Short Service engagement, time-expired men returned home after completing their seven years with the colours. William was no stranger to a long sea voyage; it would be twenty-four days before he made landfall.

Frank Richards had sailed to India with a draft from his own regiment just over a year earlier, in October 1902, and had thoroughly enjoyed the voyage, documenting life onboard and how his time was spent. Each morning, an hour was given over to 'Swedish Drill' – a system of gymnastic floor exercises originally devised in the nineteenth century by a pioneer of physical education named Pehr Henrik Ling. The rank and file would parade on deck and follow the barked commands of the instructor, performing knee bends and stretching and balancing exercises. Apart from these sessions and the occasional boat drill involving parading with lifebelts on, much of the troops' time was spent gambling. Card-schools would form on the upper decks playing Brag, House, and Kitty-nap, and dice games such as Crown and Anchor and Under and Over. The ship's crew had a sideline in selling penny buns and 'Bombay fizzers' (a sherbet drink) to the soldiers, supplementing their own pay as well as the troops' diet. Richards described the food provided on board as 'excellent'. They slept on hammocks, which were issued of an evening and hung on hooks below decks, to be returned in the morning. To escape the suffocating heat, Richards chose to sleep on the upper decks, which they were allowed to do (weather permitting) once they'd passed Gibraltar.

William arrived in India on the 5 March 1904. His eventual destination was Darjeeling, a hill station 6,700 feet above sea level in the northeast of the country, lying in the shadows of the mighty Himalayas and close to the borders with Tibet, Nepal, and Bhutan. On a clear day, he could see the spectacular Mount Kangchendzonga, the third highest mountain in the world. Arriving as he did at the start of spring, he saw the rhododendrons and magnolias blossom as the mountains turned a lush green. As spring turned to summer, fog billowed upwards from the plains, climbing the *khuds* and *ghats* until the town was enveloped in mist, obscuring the majestic Kangchendzonga from view until the rains came. The rain fell incessantly during July, August, and into September, the sun a distant memory, hidden by the grey cloak of the monsoon season. The humid climate provided a fertile environment for the tea plantations surrounding the town. And then, as September grew old and the monsoon receded, women in their hordes appeared on the verdant slopes in the early morning to pick the autumn flush, their traditional blouses and saris providing splashes of colour amongst the thick green blanket that draped the foothills. They plucked the tea dextrously with both hands and filled the large baskets on their backs that were secured by straps around their foreheads, deftly casting the leaves over their shoulders in expert, fluid movements.

The 1st Royal Fusiliers were stationed in an army depot at Lebong, five miles from Darjeeling itself. Two and a half months after William's arrival, an extraordinary expedition known as the Younghusband Mission took place, an adventure that would prove to be one last hurrah of British imperialism. Charles Allen, in his book *Duel in the Snows*, details the involvement of the 1st RF in this curious exploit led by Francis Younghusband, soldier, adventurer and mystic, whose ambitions aligned with Lord Curzon, the Viceroy of India's obsession that Russia, with the collusion of China, had designs on Tibet, thereby threatening the British Empire's status and influence in India and the East. Curzon's fixation had its roots in 'the Great Game.' Played out in the mountainous regions of Central Asia earlier in the 1800s, the Great Game, or 'The Tournament of Shadows', as the Russians called it, was a clandestine contest between British and Tsarist agents vying for political control of these high-altitude lands sandwiched between the two empires. The protagonists included adventurers and army officers in disguise – posing as correspondents or hunting parties – criss-crossing these borderlands in intelligence-gathering and surveying operations. Younghusband was one of the most active of these freelancers, making a name for himself as a most daring explorer. The Tibetan 'mission' of 1904 was portrayed as a peaceful, purely political affair involving a delegation sent across the border to talk trade, but it was nothing less than a British invasion. Allen writes that, on the morning of the 14 May 1904:

> … the normal routine of the 1st Battalion of the Royal Fusiliers was disturbed by buglers sounding for colour-sergeants to report to the adjutant at the double. By the time the men were at their ablutions rumours of mobilisation were flying – soon confirmed by the return of the colour-sergeants with the news that four companies were being sent on active service to Tibet.

At that time, a British battalion consisted of eight companies of approximately one hundred men each (prior to Army reforms that changed the composition to four companies of 200 men). William was in one of the four companies that remained in India, and I can imagine his frustration at watching his fellows march off on the 22 May on their Tibetan adventure. The incongruity of cockney rhyming slang echoing throughout the Himalayan mountains is suggested by the observation of Richard Holmes, the military historian, that '…it was here that the Raj's imperium was carried up to the roof of the world by pipe-smoking norff-of-the-river boys from Stepney and Bow'. Predictably, armed only with ancient matchlock muskets and swords, the Tibetans were no match for the firepower of the British. To avoid further bloodshed, they were eventually forced to accept unfavourable terms in a peace treaty (there proved to be little or no evidence that the Russians had been interested in establishing a presence here.)

In India, generally, the routine of a soldier's life in these outposts of empire was largely determined by the weather. Drill would take place in the morning and early evening, and the troops would be left to their own devices during the heat of the afternoon. Without the raison d'être of a full-blown military campaign, and when not involved in organised sports or on a field day, policing the empire left the men with time on their hands, and, inevitably, much of that time was spent gambling and drinking. All of the old favourites were played, including Crown and Anchor, Under and Over, Brag, and Kitty-nap, but the most favoured was House because, as Richards puts it, 'it was the most sociable and one could not gain or lose much at it, and it was leisurely and long drawn-out'.

The men would look forward to 'Canteen-time' of an evening when beer, nicknamed 'purge' or 'neck-oil', was on tap. Consuming beer was the favourite pastime of the troops, and a fair proportion of their pay went on it. A common complaint was the suspicion that the canteen sergeant was watering down the beer for his own benefit. Richards records a conversation he'd had with an old ex-soldier who'd served originally with the East India Company. He had enlisted way back in 1837 and had settled in India upon completion of his service, marrying a woman of mixed-race heritage and thirty years younger, and thereafter living off his army pension of a shilling a day. The veteran, whilst talking to Richards in the canteen, complained of the quality of the 'neck-oil':

**Sonny, the soldiers of the old John Company [East India Company] drank rum and not shark's piss. This rotten stuff will wash a man's kidneys away before it will make him drunk. In my old days it was a common sight by stop-tap to see practically every man in the Canteen as drunk as rolling f—ts: yet if they had not been put in clink meanwhile they would all wake up in the morning as happy as larks.**

Three or four men would form a 'boozing school', each of them contributing to a kitty to cover this and all of their leisure pursuits, including tobacco or cigarettes, with one of them acting as treasurer. The members of such a 'school' would share a basin holding a quart of beer, passing it amongst each other until it was empty, whereupon it would be taken to the bar to be refilled. When the 'school' eventually ran out of money, they would raise funds by borrowing from all and sundry and selling kit. When the debt reached a limit of two hundred rupees, the 'school' would 'go on the tact' – abstaining from alcohol (but not tobacco or other pursuits) and living on their rations until they'd built up enough capital to replace the kit they'd sold and amass an excess credit of two hundred rupees as a fresh kitty to carry on the 'school'. The cycle could take about six months and would usually only be broken when the members of the 'school' were entering the last year of their service before they became time-expired. In that final year, they would dissolve the 'school' and pay up all their debts, and they would 'go on the skin'. Practically all expenditure would cease, often including on tobacco, so they could save money before returning to civvy street.

Another pursuit occupied the soldiers' time: sex. Depositing multitudes of young, hormonally charged males in a foreign country cut free from family and community ties presented the army with an age-old problem. Inevitably, many were unable to deny their natural urges. The soldiers followed a two-tiered rank-based approach to fulfilling their needs. Single officers – as well as some unaccompanied husbands – took Indian mistresses; the other ranks relied on prostitutes.

The army took a pragmatic stance. They recognised that sexual activity had to be regulated if sickness rates through sexually transmitted disease were to be kept low. Regimental brothels, known colloquially as 'Rags', were established for the exclusive use of white soldiers. The women were subjected to regular medical check-ups by the army's medical officers. Richards comments on the efforts made to prevent the transmission of disease:

> Each girl had a couple of towels, Vaseline, Condy's fluid and soap; they were examined two or three times a week by one of the hospital-doctors, who fined them a rupee if they were short of any of the above requisites.... There was always a number of

men in hospital with venereal, but it was very rarely that they contracted it in the Rag.

He describes it as 'a horrible form of suicide' if one were to pay for the services of a girl outside of the regulated brothels. The Rag's business hours were from noon till eleven at night. The girls solicited trade by standing on the thresholds of their shacks and loudly proclaiming their proficiency and skill at their craft, in the fashion of stallholders at a bazaar.

The Regimental Police patrolled the Rag to prevent any contact between the native population and the girls. These measures were highly successful; hospital admissions due to sexually transmitted diseases fell from a substantial 483 per thousand in 1890–93 to 67 per thousand in 1909. Richards was of the opinion that the Rag had some positive aspects, in that the girls were paid well and their well-being was attended to, which was more than could be said for those in the unregulated trade. And unlike the unfortunates practising outside the Rag, his view was that they were mistresses of their own destiny; there was no exploitative master controlling them and taking the bulk of their earnings.

He relates the tale of a 'magnificently-built' fifty-year-old prostitute who had chosen to retire during the Delhi Durbar of 1903 – a two-week-long festival organised by Lord Curzon, celebrating King Edward VII's and the Queen Consort's succession as the Emperor and Empress of India. She had serviced the British army for thirty-six years and had made her fortune, enough money to keep her comfortable in her retirement. To mark this auspicious occasion and to show her fondness for the men of the British Raj, for one night only, on her last working shift, she offered her services for free, giving preferential treatment to regular customers.

But soldiers also passed the time in more constructive pursuits such as playing chess and reading. Libraries and reading rooms were provided, and a surprisingly large number of the men took advantage of them. Frank Richards worked his way through Dickens, Dumas, and Kipling, although he also read popular novels of the day by Nat Gould and Paul de

Kock. He graduated to history, reading the works of Macaulay, Plutarch's *Lives*, and Bourienne's *Memoirs of Napoleon Bonaparte*, highbrow stuff for a former pit boy from Wales who'd left school at the age of twelve.

Needlework was also a popular pastime; soldiers would sit on their *charpoys*, skilfully embroidering elaborate regimental emblems. They also knitted for extra income. Richards mentions two soldiers who were '…expert knitters: they bought wool from the Bazaar with which they knitted jerseys with fancy designs, and blow-belts, for keeping money in, which a large number of men wore around their waists. They made a handsome profit out of their work…' This is undoubtedly where William developed his knitting skills, those that my Aunt Florrie recalled.

On the 1 April 1904, the conditions of Royal Warrant Army Order 66 of 1902, governing 'service pay' for the other ranks, came into effect. These extraneous payments were awarded to those with over two years' service who could display competence and skill in performing their duties and were instituted in an effort to improve retention rates and stem falling establishment and recruitment levels. William took immediate advantage of this by signing on for an extra year; his statement of service was stamped with 'Extended his Army Service to complete eight years with the colours, auth. Orderly Room, 1st Royal Fusiliers, and elected to come under the conditions of Special Army Order 66 of 1902,' and it was duly signed by him on the 1 April 1904.

In practice, a sliding scale of payments based on whether a soldier had achieved certain competencies was applied; accordingly, there were three rates of service pay. William was eligible for the middle rate and was thus awarded the payment on the day the order was enacted. It was the same for Frank Richards, who explains,

> To qualify for the top rate of pay a man had to have at least a third-class certificate of education and also be a first-class shot. Men of two to five years' service who possessed both these qualifications were entitled to sixpence a day extra pay; if they had only one of them they received fourpence, unless they were only third-class

shots, in which case three pence was all they got. The top rate, for a man with five years' service or over, was seven pence a day, which could be dropped to five pence and three pence, according to his qualifications.

William's statement of service shows that he was categorised as 'Class II @ 4d' on the 1 April 1904; he was awarded the second-class rate of pay on account of his being a first-class shot but lacking a third-class certificate of education. Richards was in exactly the same position. He goes on to state:

> I knew many first-class soldiers who never received the top rate of pay, merely because they did not have a third-class certificate of education. Some of them could read and write a little, but they hated the thought of going to school again and would rather be paid less than do so. I hated the idea of school myself, but I did not intend to have two pence a day less than another man, not if I could help it. I started to attend afternoon school a fortnight before an examination came off, and then sat for it. The teaching was something similar to what my cousin Evan and I had been given in Standard Three of our board-school when we did not happen to be playing truant. I managed to pass the examination and was awarded my third-class certificate.

And it is clear that William did likewise, going back to school and passing the self-same examination. On the fifth anniversary of his enlistment, the 4 October 1904, he was awarded the top rate of pay recorded as 'Class I @ 7d.' As much as I'd like to think his motive was self-improvement, as in Richards' case, the higher rate of pay was the likelier incentive.

William eventually completed his extended period of service in October 1907 – that he had signed up for on the 1 April 1904 – and was now deemed 'time-expired' and, therefore, able to set sail for home. In the years before William departed from India (the practice had ended by the time he embarked), a soldier who had not extended his seven-year term of service and who was time-expired after the critical date of 1 October would find himself in a state of limbo. Richards' explained:

> ...so that time-expired men sent to Deolali from their different units might have to wait for months before a troop-ship fetched them home. Moreover, if a man completed his seven years with the Colours on the 30th September he caught the last boat of that trooping season; but a man who completed his seven years on the 1st October would have to serve another year with his battalion and catch the first boat home the following trooping season.

These men would be transported to Deolali when their time was up. Around a hundred miles northeast of Mumbai, Deolali was a British Army depot, a transit camp for troops arriving at and departing from the subcontinent. Having handed in their arms and equipment before leaving their battalion, those due to return to England were left with nothing to do for months on end but kill time. The devil made work for these idle hands. Soldiers with unblemished disciplinary records got into trouble and were imprisoned; many that had previously been careful contracted sexually transmitted diseases and had to be hospitalised. The ennui and tedium experienced by these troops was the cause of some strange behaviour in the men, leading to the phrase 'Doo-lally tap' ('Doo-lally' derives from 'Deolali' and 'tap' is a root word from the Sanskrit meaning 'to be hot or feverish'), which became common parlance for mental illness or eccentricity of any sort.

William arrived back in England on the 8 November 1907. He had completed eight years and thirty-nine days with the colours, five years and 126 days of it overseas. On arrival at Southampton, he was sent to the discharge depot at Fort Brockhurst, Gosport, with other time-expired men, where his transfer to the Army Reserve was formalised.

Richards underwent the same experience in 1909. He exchanged his khaki for a cheap, Army-procured, off-the-peg 'civvy' suit at the same depot and, once the process of becoming a reservist had been completed, was sent on his way home.

Before catching his train, Richards enjoyed a few jars of neck oil in the depot canteen with his fellow returnees. Barely recognising each other out of uniform, the experience of seeing their former fellow soldiers as civilians was disconcerting. He refers to an army pal's analogy of two caterpillars meeting subsequently as butterflies. No doubt William also raised a glass or two with his cockney comrades, and although the freshly minted reservists would not express openly what must have been an emotional moment, theirs was a reluctant goodbye to what had been an extraordinary way of life. They would have savoured every drop in those mugs of beer before boarding their transports to their hometowns. For William, Bethnal Green beckoned.

Upon his return to Wales, Richards initially revelled in the greenery and birdsong of his homeland. He found the food, generally, and the meat, in particular, far more flavoursome than what he'd been used to for the past six and a half years. But after finding a job in a tinworks in Caerleon, the novelty wore off, and he began to feel nostalgic for the subcontinent. He pined after the sounds of the indigenous wildlife – the cheetahs and the jackals, the bullfrogs, and the constant buzzing of the insects. He tried to re-enlist but was unable to as he was bound by the conditions imposed on him as a reservist. He even considered re-enlisting under an assumed name but could not bear the thought of serving with any other regiment and was well aware of the consequences should he be discovered: he would be arrested and imprisoned for fraud and desertion in contravention of his terms of engagement.

Richards couldn't bear civilian life. He eventually cracked, leaving his job and tramping the countryside to live rough for a couple of weeks. Feeling reinvigorated by his escapade, he found work in the colliery at Blaina when his money ran low. There he contented himself with regaling his workmates with tales from the East – an everyman version of Kipling.

When his first period of engagement finished in 1912, he extended it for a further four years, regularly attending reunions with other reservists in convenient hostelries on 'pension day' and chewing the fat over pints of neck-oil before finishing the evening in general agreement that they should never have left the army: 'By stop-tap most of us had said what utter fools we had been to leave the service, and that if we had our time over again we would not leave the army until we were damned well kicked out of it.'

I wonder if William felt the same way when he returned to the soot-stained surroundings of the East End. For him, the stark contrast between the lush green foothills of Darjeeling and the drab monochrome streets of Bethnal Green must have been even more disorienting than that experienced by Richards. He secured a job at a vinegar factory in neighbouring Hoxton. The 1911 census shows his 'personal occupation' as 'Labourer, Vinegar Brewery' and records him as living with his widowed mother, Frances – listed as 'head of the household' – at 59 Russia Lane, along with his younger sister Florence, aged twenty-three, who was employed as a 'Hose Suspender (Corset Grade)'.

During this mundane interlude between their return from India and 1914, it is doubtful that either William or Frank Richards were overly concerned or possibly even fully aware of what was happening on the continent. The geopolitical elements of militarism, international alliances, imperialism, and nationalism coalescing there would culminate in the assassination of Archduke Franz Ferdinand in Sarajevo on the 28 June 1914, an event that became the catalyst for Britain's eventual declaration of war on Germany on the 4 August. Oblivious to the catastrophe that was about to engulf the world, they were too busy earning a living.

Saturday, the 5 September 1914. William had finished his morning shift at the vinegar works just off City Road. He hung up his work apron, put on his jacket and cap, and strode purposefully out of the complex of warehouses, offices, and stables. He headed out on to the main thoroughfare, passing the site of the old turnpike before crossing the main junction with Old Street. He walked southwards alongside the bustling traffic – motorised omnibuses and taxis, horse-drawn delivery vans and carriages – on one of the main north–south arterial routes into the City of London, towards Finsbury Barracks, the home of the Honourable Artillery Company, pressed into service as the local recruiting office.

As he approached the gates to the barracks, he joined the – in Larkin's words – 'long uneven line' of men from all backgrounds, a stream of flat caps interspersed with straw boaters, bowler hats, and the odd top hat. The queue shuffled past the ancient burial ground of Bunhill Fields (the resting place of William Blake, John Bunyan, and Daniel Defoe) on their right, just to the north of the barracks. As the prospective recruits glanced through the railings at the rows of headstones within, would they have grasped the symbolism of the scene before them? That the presence and proximity of this graveyard on their route that day was a forewarning, a portent of the wide ribbon of cemeteries that would track the old front line of Belgium and northern France, marking the fortunes and the toing and froing of the British Army along the Western Front. William's walk of just under half a mile from the vinegar works to the barracks took somewhere between five and ten minutes. Was it to be a path to glory or the road to hell?

The 5 September 1914 was a notable day for a number of other reasons apart from William's re-enlistment. On this day began the First Battle of the Marne that, crucially, would prevent the Germans from taking Paris; the iconic image of Lord Kitchener declaring 'Your Country Needs You' first appeared in the *London Opinion* magazine; Thomas Hardy completed his pro-war poem *Men Who March Away*; and HMS *Pathfinder* was sunk off the coast of Scotland by a German submarine, with the loss of 260 lives. This last event, the first successful U-boat attack of the war, would, though William did not know it at the time, have a profound effect on his life.

It would also determine my very existence.

# CHAPTER EIGHT

# TO FRANCE

*Quiet night-time over Rouen, and the station full of soldiers,*
*All the youth and pride of England from the ends of all the earth,*
*And the rifles piled together, and the creaking of the sword-belts,*
*And the faces bent above them, and the gay, heart-breaking mirth.*

MAY CANNAN, extract from Rouen: 26 April–25 May 1915

William sailed into Rouen on the 2 April 1915. Having left Southampton the previous night, his draft arrived in the morning on a transport ship escorted by destroyers, completing a voyage made in blackout conditions – no lights onboard and smoking on deck prohibited. Sailing past the Channel port of Le Havre at the mouth of the Seine, the soldiers travelled another fifty or so miles east along the river to reach their destination. They passed cheering French peasant workers in characteristic *bleu de travail* workwear on the banks of the river, taking a break from toiling in the fields to wave at them. The cheering continued from the residents of Rouen as they disembarked and marched through the city to the base camps that surrounded it. By this time, eight months since hostilities had begun, a whole complex had been developed as a British Army supply depot and logistics centre, and military hospitals had been established on the southern edge of the city and on the racetrack. Earlier in the conflict, shortly after the outbreak of war on the 10 August 1914 when Frank Richards had arrived in Rouen with the 2nd Royal Welch Fusiliers – they were the first infantry battalion to disembark there – the British Army had had to find quarters wherever they could, and the 2nd RWF were billeted in a convent. They had also received a rapturous welcome on the march from the docks to their billets. But once they'd fallen out and dumped their kit, the old sweats of the battalion had their own priorities:

'On arrival at a new station we pre-war soldiers always made enquiries as to what sort of a place it was for booze and fillies. If both were in abundance it was a glorious place from our point of view. We soon found out that we had nothing to grumble about as regards Rouen.'

William reported with his draft to the 6th Divisional Base overlooking the port. The men fell into the usual camp routine of drills, training, inspections and parades whilst awaiting orders for the Front. William would have no doubt been delighted when he was told he would be posted to his old battalion, the 1st Royal Fusiliers, who, at that time, were deployed in the trenches at Chapelle d'Armentières near the Belgian border. The 1st RF formed part of the 17th Brigade of the 6th Division, who were an 'old army' division composed of seasoned troops. These were regular soldiers who had already been serving or had served prior to the war breaking out, as opposed to the territorials and the freshly minted civilian volunteers from all over Britain who had rushed to join up at the declaration of war.

A little over a week later, William had received his orders to join his battalion and found himself on a train, consisting of compartmentalised carriages for the officers and bare, unfurnished trucks marked '40 Hommes 8 Chevaux' for the other ranks, on a seemingly interminable rail journey to the Front. Captain F.C. Hitchcock of the 2nd Battalion, the Leinster Regiment, a sister battalion to the 1st RF (along with two other battalions that completed the 17th Brigade), made the same journey over five weeks later, taking eighteen hours to reach the railhead at Bailleul, travelling approximately 190 miles via a circuitous route through Abbeville, Boulogne, Calais, Saint-Omer, and Hazebrouck. His service with the 6th Division coincided with William's, including at Ypres and the Somme. Although serving in a different battalion, it was part of the same brigade, and therefore Hitchcock's memoir – *Stand To: A Diary of the Trenches 1915-1918* – features some of the events that would have also been experienced by my grandfather.

Charles McMoran Wilson, the medical officer of William's battalion, is an even more valuable witness. This was the man who would treat

William when he was wounded in July 1916 at Guillemont and who would later become Churchill's personal physician from the Second World War onwards. His diary of his time with the 1st RF formed the basis for his book *The Anatomy of Courage*, a study of the effects of war on soldiers. Wilson had landed in France towards the end of October 1914, initially serving at No. 8 General Hospital, Rouen, before being posted to the 1st RF. The customs and behaviour of the men of the London-based regiment were a culture shock to him. He found the cockney character to be utterly alien: 'Whenever I imagined I was beginning to understand them something happened and I was utterly non-plussed. They are extraordinary people, I kept saying, just like children.' Along with his fellow officers, he learned to view the activities of the men with 'affectionate amusement'.

And it wasn't only their own officers who viewed the Londoners with amusement. Hitchcock of the 2nd Leinsters, which often occupied the trenches alongside them, observed the following incident on the 9th of September 1915:

> The Germans yelled across to the 1st Royal Fusiliers, 'London is on fire' and 'What about the Dardanelles now?' The RFs, being Cockneys, strongly objected to the first remark, which happened to be the first news they had heard of the Zeppelin raid on their capital. The Fusiliers got on their fire steps, and never did I hear more amazing language than this Cockney regiment shouted across to the Huns!

The 1st RF, as an 'old army' battalion, still contained a strong core of regulars that had been part of the pre-war, highly trained professional army, and it is clear that the battalion had a policy of reinforcing with reservists and re-enlisted men. The official 1st RF war diary for the 16 March 1915 states that 'Reinforcement (No.15) of 89 other ranks joined battalion, 87 of these had been with the battalion previously,' and on the 11 April 1915, William's arrival with his draft is mentioned: '25 other ranks joined battalion – the 16$^{th}$ reinforcement. All re-enlisted men.' Some of these reinforcements were veterans of the Boer War, like William, and all were experienced men, thereby maintaining the professionalism, integrity, and regimental ethos of the battalion. On the 27 April, another draft of eighty-five men joined, 'of whom 59 were returning sick and wounded'. Sergeant W.J. Collins of the Royal Army Medical Corps asserts that the 'old army' soldiers 'were a wonderful generation … let's face it, there were we, at the beginning of the war, the regular soldier, tough hardened from India and South Africa'. He could have been describing William personally.

Wilson believed that the character of these old sweats – Britain's 'contemptible little army', as the Kaiser reportedly dismissed them – equipped them with the resilience and ability to perform courageously under fire and manage fear to a far greater extent than the 'new army' of civilian volunteers who, but for the war, would have never considered a career in the military; and, even more so, from the spring of 1916, those who had no choice in the matter – the conscripts. During the Somme offensive, Wilson observes that '…it tells something of the battalion that during the battle there were no sick, for none would ask for an easy ticket to the rear', and 'it was the unwritten law among the men that they should not go sick.' Wilson quotes a veteran from the battalion who notes that 'during a gas attack a hundred and fifty men drifted away from the battalion on our right while only ten left the fusiliers, though the conditions were the same'. In his book, Wilson goes further:

Likewise in the English professional army of 1914, which the Germans themselves called 'a perfect thing apart', there were battalions which were more than usually resistant to the corroding effects of strain and battle. It is from such a battalion [the 1$^{st}$ RF] that I have taken my illustrations of the birth of fear. These men had resolved to do nothing to besmirch the name of the Regiment, however fearful they might be in their hearts. They would rather have gone out than own defeat. I do not doubt that in less seasoned troops, where the idea greater than fear had taken no very definite shape, and the preparation of the individual mind for sacrifice had in consequence hardly begun, the birth of fear may have taken on ruder shapes.

This was illustrated to great effect when, in October 1915, the 1st RF along with the rest of the 'old army' 17th Brigade were removed from the 6th Division and exchanged with a brigade from the 'new army' 24th Division. The 24th had suffered badly at the Battle of Loos, not entirely due to their inexperience. Following an exhausting forced march, they were thrown, not fully prepared, into the heat of battle, with predictable results. The morale of this 'new army' division having been shattered, the seasoned troops of the 17th Brigade were brought in to provide a professional spine to the 24th. By their example, the 1st RF and the rest of the 17th Brigade were to teach them how to soldier. This caused some resentment on one occasion, when the men of the 1st were left in the line for an extraordinarily long spell to allow time for their relief, a 'new army' battalion, to come up to scratch. The old sweats of the 1st saw these newcomers as amateurs, no more than civvies in uniform.

Wilson noted the contrast when walking with his batman through the trenches held by one of these 'Kitchener' battalions:

> The sentries when they saw an officer approaching bobbed their heads up over the parapet and down again at once. 'I spy,' grinned my servant who was with me. It was a curious sight to eyes accustomed to see our fellows resting on the parapet at night as old sailors lean over the wall looking out to sea…. When we got back, I overheard my servant unfolding the tale of the sentry to the other servants. 'Gawd's truth,' he added, 'where 'ave these blokes come out of? They're scared pink.'

Wilson comes to the conclusion that the men of the 'old army' are a breed apart whose choice of career is a result of Darwinist natural selection, and he does not entirely agree with the commonly held notion that these are the unemployed and the unemployable. He sees something different in these men, that they 'do not seem to fit into the structure of society' and are 'vaguely discontented' with the humdrum existence of scraping a living; for them, the army is an escape from the suffocating and mundane labouring life.

Routine manual work was anathema to the professional soldier. Wilson quotes Francis Bacon to illustrate this: 'All warlike people are a little idle, and love danger better than travail.' But in addition to his employment of this generalisation to characterise an old army regiment, Wilson identifies the Royal Fusiliers as having their own distinct qualities. 'The cockney soldier has become a legend', which is explained 'by more careful folk' as being due to the 'quickness and shrewdness of the non-commissioned officers'. This, in essence, is the inherent ability of the resourceful cockney to live on his wits, a streetwise approach that enabled him to effectively adapt to the battlefield in an agile way. The survival skills that served him so well in peacetime were easily transferable to the art of soldiering.

But Wilson believes there is more to it than that. He suggests that, amongst a city of eight million people, a few thousand drifters, nonconformists, mavericks and misfits will be drawn to the army, seeking a life less ordinary – their sense of adventure overriding any tendency to domesticity, if any such tendency ever existed in the first place – giving the Royal Fusiliers its own particular character. Wilson also refers to the ability of the Londoner to use humour as a coping mechanism – mocking himself as much as he ridiculed the situation in which he found himself – contrasting him with his colonial colleagues: 'this gift of humour which encased our cockneys like chain-armour was not to be found among the Australians and Canadians. Perhaps nations in their infancy cannot afford to laugh at themselves.' Second Lieutenant Donald Hankey of the 1st Royal Warwickshire Regiment described the 'Cockney warrior' as 'infinitely brave without vindictiveness, terrible without hate, all-enduring and yet remaining his simple, kindly, jaunty self'.

The soldiers of the 1st RF, both officers and other ranks, were the subjects of Wilson's recorded observations on the psychology of men at war that formed the basis for his book. Wilson had a long-standing professional interest in psychology. For a period, he had held a post at the London County Lunatic Asylum at Hanwell. In the acknowledgements section of his book, he thanks 'the officers and men of the First Battalion The Royal Fusiliers, who taught me what men can do in war'.

Wilson served in the trenches with the 1st RF as their medical officer from late 1914 to early 1917. In his diary, he records numerous instances of behaviour by officers and men that he was able to analyse and draw conclusions from, thus formulating his theories relating to the quality of courage and how it is manifested. Wilson concluded that there were four categories of men whereby courage could be measured: those who were fearless; those who experienced fear but concealed it; those who experienced fear and displayed their anxiety but functioned nevertheless; and those who experienced fear and displayed their anxiety and acted upon it by deserting or refusing to soldier.

One of his most insightful observations is that a soldier could move between these four states; that is, occupying a particular category was not necessarily a permanent condition. 'At Ypres I was beginning to understand that few men spent their trench lives with their feet firmly planted on one rung of this ladder. They might have days without showing fear followed by days when their plight was plain to all the company.'

He accepted that his classification system could be perceived as crude and open to challenge, but he developed a coherent argument based upon his informal method of naturalistic observation. He identified the first category (fearlessness) as the rarest, citing a colonel who 'became a legend, as if men could scarcely believe what they had seen with their own eyes'. However, he deduces that this apparently awe-inspiring individual's 'courage' was the result of insensitivity to danger – a complete lack of imagination that had made him totally unaware of the potential consequences of his recklessness. This view suggests that he sees the two following categories as more admirable: that the ability to overcome one's fears, whether such fears are apparent or not, requires true courage.

Perhaps the most significant conclusion that he reaches is that the capacity for courage is finite; each man has limited reserves of this quality that can be exhausted, which often happens. He uses analogous financial terminology to illustrate this: 'A man's courage is his capital and he is always spending. The call on the bank may be only the daily drain of the front line or it may be a sudden draft which threatens to close the account.' In other words, courage is a well from which a man can drink for only so long. Eventually, it will run dry.

Wilson had also endured the tortuous rail journey from Rouen to the Front back in November 1914. He described the progress of the train as similar to that of a trotting horse but with numerous unscheduled stops. Likewise, William arrived at Bailleul in 1915 after a long and uncomfortable journey. Alighting from the train and shaking off the stiffness induced by sitting cramped on bare wooden floorboards in the overcrowded truck, he assembled with his draft in preparation for the march to the Front at Armentières, about eight miles away.

Sunday, the 11 April 1915, the day William joined his old battalion, was a beautiful day. Chapelle d'Armentières was a small commune a short distance southeast of the larger town of Armentières. At that stage of the war, it was a quiet sector of the line, and a post there was considered 'cushy'. So relatively few were the casualties that the official war diary frequently mentioned 'Other Ranks' killed and wounded by name, an undertaking that would have been totally impractical at the busier sectors of the line where the casualty lists were greater – and wholly impossible during the major offensives of the war. An example of this is shown in an entry on the 2 April, just over a week before William arrived, recorded thus:

Private W. Thurston of 'A' company volunteered to accompany Lt. James (attached Shropshire Light Infantry) on a dangerous reconnaissance. Their movements were observed by the Germans who put up 2 or 3 flares and then opened with machine guns. Private Thurston though mortally wounded insisted on Lt James continuing the reconnaissance. Lt James spoke in the highest terms of Private Thurston's conduct. Unfortunately Private Thurston died just before being brought back to the trenches.

Private 15452 Wallace Alfred Thurston is buried at La Chapelle d'Armentières Communal Cemetery.

William's and Frank Richards' paths converged at Armentières. Also forming part of the 6th Division was the 19th Brigade, one of whose component battalions was Richards' 2nd Royal Welch Fusiliers. This battalion was extraordinary for the remarkable amount of Great War literature and poetry produced by officers and men serving in its ranks, including *Memoirs of an Infantry Officer* by Siegfried Sassoon; *Goodbye to All That* by Robert Graves; *The War The Infantry Knew* by Captain J.C. Dunn; and Richards' own *Old Soldiers Never Die*. William's and Frank Richards' battalions served alongside each other in this sector for seven weeks until the end of May, when the latter's 19th Brigade was transferred to the 27th Division and the 6th Division received orders to move to Ypres.

William's first spell in the trenches began on the 15th of April, when the 1st RF relieved the 3rd Rifle Brigade. Routine tasks included maintaining and improving the trenches, repairing revetments, and laying fresh barbed wire in no-man's-land. Frequent sniping and short bombardments from both sides punctuated the execution of these tasks. The Germans used high explosive (HE) shells on specific targets, often causing surprisingly few casualties or little or no substantive damage. The war diary records a number of such instances, including on the 15th: 'About 20 shells landed rear "B" company between 3pm and 4pm,' resulting in one man wounded. The following day: 'Enemy fired about 50 shells along our line during day without effect'; and on the 20th: 'Enemy put 5 shells rear "D" company's HQ, during afternoon 50 shells landed rear Chards Farm (16th Infantry Brigade),' with one wounded man the only reported casualty from William's battalion.

On the sixth day, the 1st RF was relieved by the 3rd RB. The casualties for the preceding six-day period were two men killed and eight wounded, with one of the deaths and four of the wounded caused by sniper fire on the 17th. This pattern of six days in the trenches and six days out continued until they left the sector at the end of May. The casualty figures at the end of the month were seven killed or died of wounds and twenty-seven wounded. The war diary lists a running total for the battalion since the commencement of the war. At the end of April 1915, the diary shows 129 killed or died of wounds and 283 wounded.

When the soldiers were out of the line and in billets, the days were taken up with drill, inspections, route marches, and practising on the rifle range. The men took turns bathing by company, and they meticulously carried out ablutions; personal cleanliness was of paramount importance to the professional soldiers of the old army.

Any leisure time was invariably spent playing football – although matches were prone to stoppages due to shrapnel exploding overhead now and again – and both officers and men could enjoy the delights of Armentières itself. For officers, these included a subterranean teashop; a 'first-class confectioners'; and the Café Comte d'Egmont for alcohol. The 2nd RWF rented premises at No. 37 rue Nationale for junior officers to rest and recuperate from sickness and fatigue, and there were many other eateries and *estaminets* for every rank and to suit all purses. The men would tuck into egg and chips, and the novelty of omelettes was much enjoyed.

The theatre in the town had been requisitioned by the 4th Division. They had formed a troupe named 'The Follies' that was helped by two ingénues from Paris whom the men had promptly nicknamed 'Lanoline' and 'Vaseline' – and who would soon be replaced by female impersonators. Establishments boasting pianos were the most popular amongst those who favoured more spontaneous entertainment. From such places would issue bawdy, drink-induced ditties, including the aptly titled *Mademoiselle from Armenteers*, of which there were numerous variations:

*Mademoiselle from Armenteers–Parley vous!*
*Mademoiselle from Armenteers–Parley vous!*
*Mademoiselle from Armenteers–*
*She hasn't been kissed* [an expletive was more commonly used]
   *for forty years–*
*Inky-pinky parley-vous*

After a night on the town, the overstayers, if they weren't too much the worse for wear and incapable of doing so, had to avoid the Military Police post on their return to billets. They would have had to previously arrange for pals to answer for them at roll-call from the shadows of whichever quarters served as accommodation; otherwise, the ordeal of Field Punishment No. 1 awaited them. FP No.1, as it was known, consisted of the offender being tied up or fettered to a gun carriage wheel or other fixed object for two hours a day and could also involve carrying out menial or unpleasant tasks.

The 22 April 1915 proved to be another warm spring day. Apart from a rain shower on the night of the 16th, the good weather that had greeted William upon his arrival had continued. He had completed his first spell in the trenches a couple of days before, and the 1st RF were now out of the line. Two companies were practising on the rifle range, and the other two were the subjects of an inspection by the battalion's commanding officer. Although routine, life was not altogether unpleasant for the men of the 1st RF during this period.

Fourteen miles to the north at Ypres, it was an entirely different matter. At 5pm on the 22nd, the German heavy artillery commenced a furious bombardment of the salient using 17-inch and 8-inch howitzers. It was the opening salvo of what has become known as the Second Battle of Ypres. The barrage was accompanied by two greenish-yellow clouds – bisected by the town of Langemarck – that emerged from the direction of the German trenches, watched keenly by the men of the French 87th Territorial and Algerian 45th Divisions, who were manning the trenches to the northeast of Ypres. As the two clouds spread and merged into a single body of mist that was carried by a light wind towards the French lines, the *poilus* and *tirailleurs* observed it with curiosity more than anything else. They noticed an odd smell when it reached their trenches, then their eyes began to sting, and they felt a burning sensation in their respiratory tracts.

The cloud was chlorine gas, prolonged exposure to which could result in significant damage to the corneas and lungs, and in a high enough concentration, would prove fatal. This was the first use of poison gas in the war. The line broke as the French and Algerians fled – running, stumbling, crawling, half-blinded and choking, back westwards to the rear echelons – leaving a huge gap in the line and exposing Ypres to attack. Although the German forces were able to penetrate the Allies' front to a depth of around two miles, they failed to capitalise on the breakthrough they'd made, partly due to hesitancy on their part but also as a result of a determined defence by the Belgians and Canadians on either flank of the 8,000-yard breach who managed to stem the tide. The Canadian forces were prominent in subsequently reinforcing and holding the line.

Although the use of gas was a shock to the men in the trenches, it is even more shocking to note that the French and British high commands had been forewarned; they had received intelligence that gas was going to be deployed. Over a week before the attack took place, a German soldier named August Jaeger of the 234th Infantry Regiment deserted and gave himself up to the French. He provided details of how the gas was to be used and, as evidence, produced a protective pad that he'd been issued with, which covered the nose and mouth.

Although the officers of the French 11th Division who interrogated him had no doubt as to the veracity of his story, when the intelligence was sent up the chain of command, senior officers suspected that Jaeger was a 'plant' sent to propagate fear and ensure that the French kept large numbers of troops and reinforcements at that part of the line, thereby preventing resources from being deployed for planned allied offensives elsewhere. Despite their scepticism, they passed the intelligence to the British, who also doubted its credibility. However, the British did carry out aerial reconnaissance, the results of which were inconclusive, and they carried out a token bombardment of the German lines in an effort to destroy any gas cylinders that might have been stored there.

The French had also received intelligence from sources in Ghent, Belgium, relating to the manufacture of 20,000 respiratory masks by the Germans in preparation for a gas attack. The date of the planned attack was given as the 16 April, so when that date came and went without incident, it seemed to confirm the suspicions of both high commands that this was either a devious ploy by the enemy or the intelligence simply lacked credibility. But neither seemed to have looked into the possibility that the wind direction might have been a decisive factor in its not taking place on that day. The French 11th Division, which had originally received the intelligence and, to its credit, given it credence, had prepared for a gas attack by fashioning nose and mouth pads with a damp straw filter, but they had been relieved in the line by the 45th Algerian Division prior to the attack. The commanding officers of the 45th, for whatever reason, had seen fit to disregard both the intelligence reports and the undertaking of any countermeasures to cope with a potential gas attack.

Both the Hague Declaration of 1899 and the Hague Convention of 1907 had prohibited the use of poison gas in conflict. The Allies were appalled at its deployment. Sir John French called it 'a very dirty "low-down" game to play shooting out that damnable "gas"' and Edward Grey, the British Foreign Secretary, wrote that its use was 'an offence not only against the rules of war, but "against all humane considerations"'.

Immediate steps were taken to manufacture protective masks for the troops, and officers were sent urgently to Paris to procure large quantities of material and elastic. French and Belgian women living in towns and villages near the front were tasked with making the respirators on their sewing machines, and the *Daily Mail* 'called on the women of England to make a million'. These masks were issued to the soldiers at the front fairly swiftly; William and the 1st RF received their protective equipment two and a half weeks after the first gas attack. The war diary entry for the 8 May details 'all ranks fitted with respirators and about half with goggles in case of use of asphyxiating gas by enemy', and, the following day, '550 goggles issued which completed battalion.'

The action taken by the Germans on the 22 April had effectively normalised the use of poison gas as a tactic, and both sides took it up. On a personal level, its use affected my great-uncle James – William's younger brother – later in the war. Eventually contracting bowel cancer as a result of mustard gas poisoning, he was successfully operated on at St Mark's Hospital, London, in 1936 and lived to the ripe old age of eighty-nine.

The outrage expressed by the brass hats and the politicians at the use of chemical warfare didn't seem to affect how the 1st RF viewed their German counterparts. The cockneys' legendary sense of humour shaped their attitude towards the enemy. They ridiculed the Germans' standard greeting of 'Gott Strafe England' with their own parodied versions and joined in enthusiastically with the patriotic Teutonic war songs drifting over no-man's-land. One can only imagine how puzzled – and frustrated – the Germans must have been at the Londoners' response to their 'hymns of hate' that were meant to curdle the blood and intimidate. The cockneys simply didn't take them seriously. They did not bear any ill will towards the men opposite them. Second Lieutenant Donald Hankey of the 1st Warwicks observes that 'the Cockney warrior does not hate the hun. Often and often you will hear him tell his mate that "the Bosches is just like us, they wants to get 'ome as much as we do; but they can't 'elp theirselves".' Captain Charles Wilson confirms this: that they 'are not good haters. During the thirty months I was with the 1st Royal Fusiliers, I cannot recall a single man who lost his temper with the enemy.'

The only instance of anything approaching hostility towards the Germans that he could recall involved the following chain of events. About half an hour before midnight on the 11 May, a skirmish took place in the darkness when a patrol from the 1st RF came across an enemy patrol in no-man's-land. The resulting firefight ended with the Germans fleeing, but one large fellow stood his ground and put up a fight before he was hit by a British bullet. The war diary contains a mention of this incident: 'a German sergeant belonging to 139 Regiment, 19 Saxon Corps was shot about 11:30pm while on patrol near "C" company's listening post (Pigots Farm) by Private Mustart of MG section and his body brought in'.

Early the following morning, before the sun rose, the British sent a working party to retrieve the German's body and bury it behind the line. However, they found he was still breathing, barely. He was taken to the dressing-station but was pronounced dead upon arrival. Wilson was struck by the appearance of the soldier. His remarks on the German's physical characteristics confirmed the stereotype of the brutish 'Hun'; he noted his shaven 'flattened' skull, his 'great bull neck' and the 'nailed soles of his enormous boots'.

The body was left in a farm outbuilding awaiting interment, and for the rest of the day, curiosity got the better of the troops in reserve, who came to gawp at the body of the unfortunate German. Eventually, some of the men started stripping pieces of uniform from the corpse as souvenirs until an adjutant noticed what was going on and had a guard placed on the door.

Shortly afterwards, the body of a fusilier who had recently died from a sniper's bullet was carried from the trenches for burial at a section in the French cemetery set aside for British soldiers. This was likely the body of the only soldier who was mentioned in the war diary as having been killed that day, a Private Higginbotham of "C" company. (Private 9116 William Higginbotham is buried at the La Chappelle d'Armentières Communal Cemetery, where his grave is maintained by the CWGC.) Wilson attended the ceremony along with the adjutant. The padre conducted the service. Afterwards, the men of the deceased's company silently drifted away in small groups, leaving Wilson with the adjutant and the drum major. The three of them then went to an adjacent field where the body of the German had been placed in a freshly dug grave. The drum major haltingly read some appropriate passages from a prayer book before the adjutant told him to fetch a working party led by a corporal to fill in the grave. Wilson overheard one of the men say, 'Anyway, mate, that's one bloody Hun less.' When he reflected on this event, Wilson regretted the German's burial in unconsecrated ground – 'outside the pale', as he puts it.

Wilson finds this incident remarkable, as it is the only exception he can find to the lack of animosity shown by the men towards their adversaries. As far as the Tommies were concerned, the Germans were only following orders – as they themselves were. It was nothing personal; they were soldiers, and this is what they did. If anything, they spoke of their counterparts with an almost affectionate respect.

And certainly, for the Saxon regiments, the respect was often mutual, possibly due to the common Germanic roots they shared with the English. There were instances when a Saxon regiment would shout words of encouragement across no-man's-land, urging the Tommies on to greater efforts when they were directing their fire at a Prussian or Bavarian regiment (the young Hitler served in a Bavarian regiment). Dunn of the 2nd RWF wrote of a short bombardment followed by two volleys of small-arms fire in which they had participated on the 27 January 1915: 'While our guns were giving the Prussians opposite us hell, the Saxons opposite the Middlesex applauded the hits. Later, they shouted across, "We are being relieved by Bavarians tonight. Give us time to get out and then shoot the [expletive deleted]."'

Vera Brittain relates a tale told her by a patient of hers when she was serving as a nurse. A Scottish sergeant said that:

…when [we] were opposite the Saxons near Ypres, [we] and the enemy made a mutual agreement not to shoot one another. In order to appear active [we] continued to use [our] rifles, but fired in the air. Occasionally [we] met and talked in the space between the trenches, and when, finally, the Saxons had to change places with the Prussian Guards, they promised to fire a volley as warning. This promise they faithfully observed.

Instances of good humour such as these humanised the adversaries in each other's eyes. Wilson believed that, as a result of this attitude of 'amusement and tolerance' towards the enemy, and certainly after the initial stages of the war, the use of propaganda to instil a martial spirit would be useless; any attempt to demonise the Germans would fail. The Tommy's motive to kill was not inspired by hot-blooded hate but, rather, a dispassionate professionalism in getting the job done.

On the 1 June, the 6th Division received orders that they would be relieved by the 27th Division and were to begin preparations to move. The following day at 5pm, the 1st RF set off on a gruelling three-and-a-half-hour march in the hot sun – carrying all of their equipment in their backpacks and on their webbing, weighing anything between fifty and eighty pounds – to billets at Bailleul eight miles away. It was a tribute to the stamina and fortitude of the men that no one had fallen out along the way.

Two days later, on the 4 June at 5am, they were on the move again. The whole 17th Brigade paraded. The order of march was the 1st North Staffords, 1st Royal Fusiliers, 2nd Leinsters, and the 3rd Rifle Brigade. They marched eleven miles, crossing the border into Belgium and arriving at 1:30pm into the woods northeast of Poperinghe, where they bivouacked. The transport arrived shortly afterwards with the cookers to feed the footsore soldiers.

When darkness fell that night, the men had already settled into camp, laying out their groundsheets and lighting fires to gather around and brew their tea. The officers from the 1st RF, along with their counterparts from the other three battalions in the 17th Brigade, left the other ranks to their rations in order to reconnoitre the trenches that were to be taken over from the 10th and 11th Brigades. For William, his 'cushy' sojourn in Armentières was over. He was about to enter the much-fought-over amphitheatre that was the Ypres Salient.

# CHAPTER NINE

# YPRES

*Day dawns in a mist. A veil hides the inner reality of Ypres, and as a visitor says – 'It looks more picturesque in the mist'. Ypres however is an altar to which the nation must return.*

STEPHEN GRAHAM, from *The Challenge of the Dead*

On the 5 June 1915, a day after their arrival at the salient, William's battalion went into the trenches two and a half miles north of Ypres. It would be twenty days before they were relieved – a lengthy spell without respite for their initiation in the Belgian front line. Captain Hitchcock, whose 2nd Leinsters were in support of the 1st RF, described the trenches there as 'well-made and revetted, but the parapets were much lower than those at Armentières', and he went on: 'everywhere there was the sickly smell of the gas which had been used on the Canadians in the Second Battle of Ypres'. The 17th Brigade was deployed at that sector of the line where the Germans had made their furthest advance on the 22 April – the date of the gas attack. The enemy artillery was far more active here compared to their compatriots at Armentières; on the 8 June, Hitchcock observed, 'we were all greatly astonished at first by the colossal shell-fire and the continual bombardment of Ypres'. Captain Charles Wilson also commented on the heavy shelling at Ypres that took its toll on some of the troops, eroding their martial spirit.

The combination of a prolonged stay in the front line along with the incessant shelling caused an increase in the number of casualties sustained by the 1st RF. The totals for their first month at Ypres were seventeen killed and forty wounded, compared to eleven killed and fifteen wounded the previous month at Armentières.

Over the coming months, the 1st RF would man the trenches at practically every sector along the front line of the salient that fringed

Ypres and its surrounding villages. Protecting the bulging line of a salient that projects into enemy territory obviously requires more manpower and matériel than are needed to hold a straight defensive line, as the length of the front is extended and the holders of the salient are vulnerable to fire from three sides.

The topography did not favour the Allies; the salient can best be described as a large shallow bowl or saucer with Ypres at the centre. The Germans occupied the high ground along an arc to the east of Ypres – the curving eastern edge of the bowl's 'rim' – with a view down into Ypres and beyond, including the supply lines to the west. Their artillery was able to target the roads from Ypres that headed east towards the British front line like the spokes of a wheel, and that caused difficulties for the movement of men and guns to and from the trenches and artillery emplacements. The sound military tactic would have been to withdraw from the salient and straighten the line, and there would have to have been a compelling reason not to do so. There are two main explanations as to why the salient was not given up, one of which is that the Ypres region was being held as a buffer zone to protect the supply lines between the Channel coast and the British sectors on the Western Front to the south of Flanders. But there were also powerful political and symbolic reasons for holding Ypres; having entered the war to defend Belgium's neutrality, it would have been unthinkable to abandon this last corner of Flemish Flanders still occupied by the Allies.

However, following the gas attack on the 22 April and the failure of the French 87th and Algerian 45th Divisions to hold the line, the British high command was of the view that, unless the French improved their position, they would do precisely that and vacate the salient, thereby flattening the line. Field Marshall Douglas Haig made the following entry in his diary on the 30 April 1915:

... at 11:30 Sir John French came to see me to tell me of the situation generally, and to ask my opinion regarding the withdrawal from the Ypres salient. Lee MP [Arthur Lee, MP for Fareham and personal commissioner to Lord Kitchener serving with the rank of temporary colonel] arrived while we were talking, with a letter from C.G.S. [Sir William Robertson, Chief of the General Staff] and enclosing one for Sir J's signature to Foch [General Ferdinand Foch, Commander of the northern group of French armies]. Sir J. read me the latter. It was of the nature of an ultimatum, and stated that the withdrawal of the British troops from the salient would commence tonight, unless the French had succeeded in advancing their line.... As to the policy of retiring, I said that I had no doubts in my mind as to the wisdom of such a step if the French did not regain the old front but continued in their present position. Our troops are now in a very sharp salient. This will be untenable under hostile artillery alone, while they will find it most difficult to withdraw, when forced to do so. They will also suffer most terribly from hostile artillery, which almost envelops them at the present moment. I considered that it was the C in C's duty to remove his men from what was really a 'death trap'.

And as Hitchcock and Wilson attested, this is the position in which the 17th Brigade, including the 1st RF, found themselves – besieged by hostile artillery.

Ypres itself was a small Flemish city that had prospered during the Middle Ages as a centre for the manufacture and trade of linen and textiles. The magnificent Cloth Hall, one of the largest commercial buildings in medieval Europe, was built in the thirteenth century, confirming Ypres' pre-eminence as a hub for the industry. By the end of the Great War, along with the rest of the city, the building lay in ruins. Hitchcock described the scene before him when he visited Ypres on the evening of the 17 June 1915:

The city was deserted and desolate. The atmosphere was heavy with the smell of decaying bodies, for the first shells had surprised the inhabitants, and had caught many in their beds. A number of the houses had been knocked down by direct hits, and others had one of the walls blown down, showing the furniture of the stories above, like scenery in a theatre. Few houses had been left unscathed. The square in front of the Cloth Hall was in a dreadful state, strewn all over with parts of British G.S. wagons, bones of dead horses, broken rifles, and web equipment. The streets throughout Ypres were pitted with shell craters, beside the Cloth Hall there was a crater of a 16-inch shell. I measured it, and found it was fifty-two paces around, 30 feet deep and 48 feet across from lip to lip.

In October 2005, nearly six months after I'd first stood by my grandfather's grave, I travelled to Ypres. It was the first visit of what would become an annual pilgrimage to the battlefields of Belgium and France, chasing the ghost of Corporal William Charles Blumsom. I travelled with six workmates, each of whom had varying degrees of interest in the Great War. This three-day trip had to cater for everyone, so, armed with *Major and Mrs Holt's Battlefield Guide to Ypres*, I devised a bespoke itinerary that would give an overview of the salient and take in as many of the major memorials, museums, CWGC cemeteries, and other places of interest as could be crammed in. Within this customised tour, we would visit sectors where William had served in 1915–16.

Travelling in two cars, we set off early on a Friday, crossing the Channel on the Eurotunnel service, then driving from Calais to arrive in Ypres mid-morning. After parking in the main square – the Grote Markt – I unwound myself from the car and slowly took in a 360-degree view of the city centre. I had, of course, previously seen photographs of Ypres, both as it is now and as it was during 1914–18. But by being there in person, the postwar reconstruction that had been carried out could be fully appreciated, particularly the Cloth Hall, the rebuilding of which was an astonishing achievement. It had been practically razed to the ground by the end of the war. Work started in 1928, and it was finally completed in 1967, having been painstakingly rebuilt to its original medieval specifications. Even when measured against today's colossal structures, it is massively impressive; in the Middle Ages, it must have been awe-inspiring.

I felt immediately at home here, and that wasn't due to any Anglicisation of the city. The place is obviously and distinctly mainland Europe. Physically, most of the handsome buildings in the square had the crow-stepped gables typical of the Flemish vernacular style, and to my eyes there was no sense that the local shopkeepers and tradesmen were looking to exploit the large number of British visitors that come here in an overly tacky or cynical fashion. Certainly, there were souvenirs bearing iconic imagery of the Great War, some more tasteful than others, but nothing to excess and not more than I would expect for an event that had become so inextricably linked with the city's history. No, it felt familiar for a different reason, and I can only put it down to something intangible, something residual that came from almost four years of a solely British Army presence. Hundreds of thousands of troops had eaten, drunk, slept, exercised, rested, fought, and died here and in the surrounding countryside. The whole salient was steeped in the blood of the British and its empire. These men had left an indelible imprint that I connected with; it was as if they were speaking to me from ninety years past – as if they were welcoming one of their own.

We checked into a two-star hotel on the Grote Markt within a hundred yards of the Cloth Hall. The accommodation was basic by any standards, but it served us well enough. Having agreed to rendezvous later for our first excursion, I took the opportunity to venture out on my own for an exploratory visit to take in the famous Menin Gate memorial. As I walked from the Grote Markt into Menenstraat leading towards the Menin Gate, my first impression of the monument as I left the square did not do it justice. The narrow, converging building lines on either side of Menenstraat 'cropped' the view of the Gate, literally clipping its wings; only the central arch is visible. As you approach from the west towards the crossroads immediately in front of the monument – the junction of Menenstraat with Bollingstraat and Kauwekijnstraat – step by step, the whole of the imposing structure slowly reveals itself as your perspective widens, and as you break free from the congested street, the crow-stepped gables of Flanders give way to the Doric columns of Imperial Britain, and the full panoramic view of this masterpiece is revealed in all its grandeur. Designed by Reginald Blomfield, who was a firm adherent of the formal, classical style of architecture, the Gate references the triumphal arches of ancient Rome, although there is no sense of triumphalism conveyed by its form, majestic as it is. As you breach the massive archway, you step through a portal into the familiar. The Portland stone–faced panelled walls of the memorial are engraved with the names of 55,000 soldiers of the British Empire who have no known grave, arranged under the names of the units they served with, county and regional regiments steeped in history, including the Argyll and Sutherland Highlanders, the Loyal North Lancashire's, the Duke of Wellington's Regiment, Royal Welch Fusiliers, the Duke of Cornwall's Light Infantry, and the Royal Irish Fusiliers. The list of famous old regiments is a roll call of the British army.

Blomfield's lengthy archway cuts through the town's 133-foot-deep ramparts, creating the Hall of Memory, the roof of which is punctuated by three circular open skylights that illuminate what Sassoon called the 'intolerably nameless names'. He famously described the memorial as a 'sepulchre of crime', but, understandable as Sassoon's bitterness and cynicism might be, anger is not the emotion one feels when standing under its vaulted ceiling and struggling to process the vast multitude of humanity memorialised here. Rather, one feels a mixture of sadness, reverence, awe, and admiration; this place is sacred.

I walked through the length of the arch, and as I emerged onto the bridge crossing the city's moat, I stopped and looked back, taking in what is the best view of the memorial. From here, the magnificence of the building can be truly appreciated. Atop the monument, facing east towards the old front line, is a stone lion recumbent, its head erect and watchful. It symbolises Britain and its empire, in Blomfield's words, 'patient and enduring, looking outward as a symbol of the latent strength and heroism of our race', but simultaneously chiming with the pair of original stone lions that, prior to the war and the devastation wreaked upon the city, had stood flanking the old Menin Gate, having been installed there in 1862. The German author and pacifist Stefan Zweig, writing in 1928, made perhaps the definitive judgement on the memorial: 'Ypres has gained a new monument, and – let me say at once – one that is, both spiritually and artistically, profoundly impressive: The Menin Gate, erected by the English nation to its dead, a monument more moving than any other on European soil.'

Our group mustered at the appointed time. The first port of call was the In Flanders Fields Museum, an essential experience for the first-time visitor. Housed within the Cloth Hall, the museum is very well curated and an ideal introduction to touring the battlefields, albeit a victim of its own success. It was a bit too crowded for my liking, although I was anxious to get out to the old front line, and my impatience might have added to my irritation.

After completing the tour of the museum, we set off to explore the salient, leaving the city by the Meenseweg. We drove to Hooge, a village three miles east of Ypres, passing Hellfire Corner, so named because this crossroads (now a roundabout) had been perpetually shelled by the Germans – it had been a through route to Potijze and Zillebeke and a busy junction for the movement of troops and artillery – before stopping at the Hill 62 Museum, a privately run affair situated in Sanctuary Wood just south of Hooge and boasting a large section of preserved trenches revetted with replica sandbags and corrugated iron. The museum building itself is a converted private house, including a café with extensions housing displays of Great War artefacts to the side and rear of the property. It was a peculiar and fascinating experience, but one not to be missed.

The café doubles as the ticket office, and from there the first room entered is lined with glass display cabinets containing helmets, uniforms, medals, weapons, and all sorts of Great War detritus, exhibited fairly haphazardly and seemingly without any sort of thematic progression or coherence. My first impression was that it really needed a professional curator to make sense of it all, but then maybe the randomness is part of its charm.

The main attraction is the stereoscopic viewers fixed to the benches that run down the middle of the room; they draw you in. They contain graphic images of the conflict that, once seen, cannot be forgotten. The gruesome sights brought home the catastrophic impact inflicted by industrial warfare upon humanity, but the images that affected me most were those of horses blown to kingdom come, including complete carcasses hanging in the branches of trees. It was the animals' lack of agency that I found so ineffably sad. They had trusted their handlers, drivers, and riders implicitly – of whom, no doubt, most had the horses' best interests at heart – and I know that my grandfather would have grieved at the suffering of these innocents. And Robert Graves was of the same view: 'I was shocked by the dead horses and mules; human corpses were all very well, but it seemed wrong for animals to be dragged into the war like this.'

We finished the tour and exited the museum to the rear to explore the preserved trench system within the grounds. It sits within a small wood, new growth having long replaced the blasted, blackened, splintered stumps described in Great War literature and poetry and depicted in Paul Nash's art. As I negotiated my way through the maze of earthworks, I naturally wondered if my grandfather had inhabited these woods ninety years before.

A stone's throw from the museum is the Sanctuary Wood Cemetery, a beautiful CWGC graveyard designed by Sir Edwin Lutyens and laid out in the shape of a fan. It was a brilliantly sunny day, and as I inspected the headstones, I reflected on my reaction to what I'd assumed would be a purely sombre and sobering experience. As expected, it was just this – of course it was – but it was also simultaneously a surprisingly positive and even uplifting one. This is a tribute to the architects and gardeners of the Commonwealth War Graves Commission, who have managed to sensitively create these sites of contemplation and mourning, where healing and closure can take place. It is difficult to imagine a greater contrast to the carnage that had raged all around them all those years ago. Those who were able to visit these places in the years following the war – the wives, mothers, fathers, sisters, and brothers of these men, and succeeding generations of their descendants – were and are able to draw consolation from the beauty of these surroundings.

This was where William had served in the trenches, including a particularly eventful period from the 9 to 24 August 1915.

At that time, the front line ran through the village of Hooge at the easternmost extent of the salient following the successful German gas attack in April. The sector incorporated, from north to south, Bellewaerde Ridge, Hooge village itself, Zouave Wood, and Sanctuary Wood. The Menin Road bisecting the front line between Hooge and Zouave Wood on an east–west axis was a focal point for much savage fighting that continued almost unabated throughout the war. Hitchcock noted that 'Hooge had been continually under shellfire since the First Battle of Ypres in October, and the ridge … had been captured and recaptured five times since April.'

Ever since the end of the Second Battle of Ypres and the resulting gains made by the Germans, including the Bellewaerde Ridge and Hooge Chateau, the British had been at a distinct disadvantage in this sector. With the Tommies having been driven out of the redoubt that they'd been constructing in Hooge, the enemy enjoyed a commanding view over the British line, and it was considered vital to retake this position.

A surprise attack was planned that would involve driving a mineshaft under the German fortification and terminating in a chamber packed with ammonal. After the explosives were detonated, the 4th Middlesex Regiment was tasked with taking and holding the position. There would be no preparatory barrage, so that the Germans would be caught unawares.

On the 19 July 1915, the 175th Tunnelling Company of the Royal Engineers detonated the mine, just north of the Menin Road, producing a crater 120 feet across and 20 feet deep. It worked perfectly. The 4th Middlesex rushed the crater and drove the enemy out, including from the trenches immediately on either side. They held the position by reinforcing the north- and east-facing lip of the crater with sandbags.

The Germans responded furiously, shelling the crater intensely whilst the British held on doggedly. It was only a matter of time before a counterattack would come.

When it did, on the 30 July, it was as if the fires of hell had been unleashed. The Germans chose to deploy the *flammenwerfer*, it was the first time that flamethrowers were used against British troops. Great jets of liquid fire shot towards the crater, momentarily turning their world red. These were real 'shock-and-awe' tactics that had the Tommies reeling. There followed a hellish bombardment of all types of shell and ordnance, including high explosive, shrapnel, and machine-gun fire, creating a terrific noise, and the British were forced to relinquish the crater. The line had to give, but it did not break; the 8th Rifle Brigade and the 7th King's Royal Rifle Corps withdrew and established a new line 200 yards further west across the Menin Road.

The Hooge Crater was too crucial a position to be allowed to remain in German hands. Whilst they held such a commanding position, their artillery and machine guns would be used to maximum effect, causing excessive British casualties. To retake Hooge would require an extremely well-planned operation executed with precision and great military force. The 6th Division was chosen to carry out the attack. The Order of Battle was decided on the toss of a coin, and the 17th Brigade, including the 1st RF and the 2nd Leinsters – in Hitchcock's words - 'lost out'. For the initial phase of the attack, the 17th would be in reserve, with the 16th Brigade leading the assault and the 18th in support. On the 9 August, the day of the attack, the 1st RF war diary details the day's events: 'Attack on enemy's position near Hooge. Guns bombarded from 2:45am to 3:15am, 16 Bde on left and 18 Bde on right took trenches without difficulty. 17 Bde in reserve. Stood by all day. At 7pm received orders to be at Lille Gate at 8:15pm en route to Maple Copse; owing to enemy shelling did not arrive there till 11:30pm.'

As the 1st RF were in reserve, their war diary naturally contained just the briefest details of the assault, not reflecting how well the attack was executed. The battle has been described as a 'model of how an operation could be conducted'. In the days leading up to the attack, the plan involved the divisions to the north and south of the attack fooling the Germans by apparently carrying out preparations for an offensive, including the digging of 'jumping off' trenches, suggesting that operations were to take place in those sectors rather than Hooge itself.

To disguise the conventional immediate bombardment preparatory to the attack – a surefire warning that one is about to take place – the artillery began shelling in the early hours on a daily basis some days previously, thus establishing a pattern of behaviour that would not suggest that anything out of the ordinary was about to take place on the actual day of the assault. Air support was used to identify enemy artillery positions for counter-battery purposes. It was an all-arms approach of infantry, artillery, and air force working in unison.

During the initial bombardment and just before zero hour, between 2:45 and 3:15am, the men crawled out undetected into no-man's-land just yards from the German front line in readiness for the attack – some actually entered the enemy's trenches, causing mayhem even before the barrage had ended. Subsequent waves of infantry reinforced the leading units. The Germans were taken completely by surprise. Fierce hand-to-hand fighting took place, and the enemy was soon driven out of their front line. One unidentified Tommy gave the following account:

We lay there waiting for the order to charge. It came and we lost all control of our senses and went like mad, fighting hand-to-hand bayoneting the hounds. I did not like to kill, but it was sport-like so I did it, and wanted more. We got in to the first line and went straight on to the fourth, and past it, and then dug ourselves in under hell's flames.

The German artillery responded with a very heavy bombardment commencing at 9:30am and rising in intensity and continuing until nightfall, but no counterattack was mounted.

The following day, whilst still in reserve, the 1st RF were employed in building dugouts for the wounded in Maple Copse, a small wood to the south of Hooge. Their war diary records that the front line at Hooge was now divided into two sub-sectors, the Menin Road forming the boundary between the two. At dusk on the 10th, William entered the trenches, the 1st RF having relieved the Queen's Westminster Rifles in the sub-sector south of the Crater and the Menin Road. Approximately twenty-four hours later, the 2nd Leinsters, their sister battalion, relieved the 1st East Kent Regiment in the northern sub-sector above the Menin Road, incorporating the crater and the area towards Bellewaerde Lake. Hitchcock recorded that D Company of the 2nd Leinsters, who held the line immediately north of the Menin Road, 'connected with the 1st Royal Fusiliers, who held the line running through the Zouave Wood'. The 1st RF, in their first full day in the Hooge trenches, was employed in improving the earthworks. B and C Companies on the left were 'urgently' working on 'Bond Street' trench to make it tenable; the state of it was so bad that contact between the crater and Zouave Wood had been lost. A and D Companies were busy reinforcing a stronghold known as 'the appendix' in Sanctuary Wood. Such are the vagaries of fortune that the two battalions, although occupying the line adjacent to each other, were to undergo two very contrasting experiences over the following days.

On the 12 August, the 1st RF war diary's Summary of Events records: 'Fine day. Enemy shelled Zouave Wood. B and C continued work on Bond and Fleet Street trenches. Nothing unusual occurred. *Crater was bombed by enemy*. 6 men wounded.' To the immediate north, the 2nd Leinsters were going through a much more torrid time. The brief mention of the activity at the crater on the cockneys' left flank was elaborated upon in great detail by Captain Hitchcock's version of events.

Having taken over the crater the night before at 11pm, Hitchcock describes the devastation around him when the sun came up at 4am on the 12th: 'Everywhere lay the dead. The ridge in our rear was covered with dead men who had been wiped out in the final assault of the German position.' Hundreds of decomposing, dismembered, bloated, and blackened corpses surrounded them. An official report estimated that the bodies of 200

Germans littered the crater and 300 more lay in the vicinity of the Hooge stables, most of them having been bayoneted. The sheer number of dead Germans packed into the captured enemy dugouts rendered them unusable by the Leinsters, and on parapet and parados, in no-man's-land and in the trenches lay the bodies of men from the 2nd Durham Light Infantry and the 2nd Yorks and Lancs, the reek of decay permeating everything. 'A few solitary stakes and strands of barbed wire were all that was left of the dense mass of German entanglements by our artillery. Several khaki figures were hanging on these few strands in hideous attitudes.' There were sections of the trench where German arms and legs protruded from between the disrupted sandbags, and fragments of their field-grey uniforms steeped in dark-red blood were scattered all around.

Hitchcock concluded that 'Serving in the Ypres salient one was not unaccustomed to seeing men blown to pieces and, therefore, I expected to see bad sights on a battlefield, but I had never anticipated such a dreadful and desolate sight as the Hooge presented, and I never saw anything like it again during my service at the front.'

At 5am, a small number of enemy shells fell on the Leinsters portion of the line, tracking across in a methodical fashion. In the ensuing silence following this very brief flurry of shelling, it became obvious that the German artillery had been registering their range in preparation for a sustained bombardment, and as expected, it duly started a quarter of an hour later. The deadly accuracy of the German guns eventually took its toll. The 2nd Leinsters suffered significant casualties. This carried on until 12:30pm when the shelling slowed, and in the lull they began to suspect a counterattack and made preparations accordingly.

It never came. Instead, a second bombardment began at 3pm. The sky turned black from the sheer number of high explosive shells coming over and the resulting eruptions of soil and debris rocketing up towards the heavens. Hitchcock observed that 'we could not have been in a worse position, and it seemed that every enemy gun around the salient was turned on to our 400 yards of trench on the left of the Menin Road'. Their trench defence works, the parapet and parados, were effectively destroyed, replaced by gaping holes and craters red-hot and smouldering, leaving them with little protection from the deadly shrapnel fragmenting around them, accompanied by its banshee wail. Hitchcock feared that they would not be able to hold the crater if this continued: 'If this went on much longer, the Boches would walk into our position without any opposition, as we would all be casualties.'

Just as he began to despair at the lack of a counter-barrage from the artillery, the British guns opened up with an almighty roar, the trajectory of the shells so low it seemed as if they were skimming the heads of the 2nd Leinsters. Although the tremendous noise and the percussive effect might not have been to their liking, it improved the morale of Hitchcock and his men no end. SOS rockets were launched all along the German line, which cheered them even more. At 5:30pm, the enemy's artillery fire suddenly ceased, allowing Hitchcock to take stock of the casualties. Of the three platoons in the front line, they had sustained a casualty rate of more than fifty per cent, losing 65 of 120 men over a period of seven hours. The war diary for the 2nd Leinsters records a total of seventy-five casualties for the day – ten killed and sixty-five wounded 'almost all from shell fire'. Compare this with only six wounded suffered by the 1st RF immediately on their right on the same day, and the concentration and accuracy of the German bombardment of the crater can be appreciated.

Hitchcock listed the total casualties for the fighting at Hooge throughout August 1915 as two officers killed, six officers wounded, forty-nine other ranks killed, and an estimated 250 wounded. In contrast, the 1st RF sustained about a sixth of their sister battalion's total for the whole of the month of August, detailing fourteen killed and forty-two wounded. These statistics brought home to me how narrow were the margins that determined whether one lived or died, and I reflected on the happenstance that increased the chances of my grandfather's survival; the two battalions' deployments could have easily been the other way around.

Walking slowly along the rows of headstones in the Sanctuary Wood Cemetery, I was looking to connect with my grandfather through the names of his 1st Battalion Royal Fusiliers comrades who had fought alongside him but never went home, to honour them – some of whom might have been his friends – and pay my respects. There in the cemetery lie six of his colleagues who lost their lives at Hooge:

**Private 4660 Charles John Wicks of King's Cross, London, who died on the 11 August 1915, aged 40.**
**Private 9583 Ernest James Arnold, who died on the 14 August 1915.**
**Private L/15297 Thomas David Edgar Cooper of Camberwell, London, who died on the 14 August 1915, aged 18.**
**Private 9984 George Francis of Fulham, London, who died on the 18 August 1915, aged 33.**
**Lance Corporal 9611 Alfred Knight, who died on the 20 August 1915.**
**Private L/11854 William John Beer of Leytonstone, Essex, who died on the 24 August, aged 19.**

Also buried here is Lieutenant Richard Kellock Stirling, who died on the 21 August 1915, aged 22. Originally serving with the 5th Battalion Royal Fusiliers, he was attached to the 1st RF at Armentières, having arrived in France almost directly from Exeter College, Oxford. Captain Wilson, the medical officer, refers to Stirling in a section of his book wherein he considers the qualities and virtues of leadership and what makes an inspirational and authoritative officer. Apparently Stirling, although reserved and lacking experience, had an indefinable quality, a way about him that clearly convinced the other ranks that here was a man they could follow. There was no shortage of volunteers to accompany him when he went out on patrol in no-man's-land; they had complete confidence in him. He died, shot through the head by an enemy sniper, whilst surveying the German front line through binoculars.

Led by the company commander Barty Price, the men of C Company assembled at the edge of Zouave Wood to bury him at nightfall. No padre was available, so Price read the service. The odd shell was coming over, so he ordered the men to keep their heads down. They did so, albeit resentfully, as they took umbrage at the enemy's intrusion on their need to pay their respects. Presently, it fell quiet, and Wilson describes the touching ceremony:

The moon had risen above the blackness of Zouave Wood in which it was no longer possible to make out the broken shapes of individual trees. The men were half-kneeling, their eyes on the ground; Barty, who was standing a little apart appeared extraordinarily tall and thin against the sky. He looked up. 'You have lost a good officer, men,' and then after a moment's silence, 'Put him with his head to the enemy.' He read the short service, stumbling as he failed to make out the words by the uncertain light of a torch. Then we got up and went away and no one spoke. Today before we were relieved I walked over to the grave and found that the men of Stirling's company had been working on it overnight. They had marked it out with stones and had planted moss and a few wild flowers that drooped before they took on fresh life.

While I was researching the 1st RF's war diary for the month of August 1915 in relation to these men, I came across an entry listing other comrades of William that deserve mention. In an unusual report dated Tuesday, the 31 August, was the following:

Information received that the following NCOs and men had been awarded Russian Decorations:

13719 Sgt. W A Burdett – Medal of St George (2nd Class)
11366 A/Sgt B Nice – Cross of the Order of St George (4th Class)
9176 L/Cpl A Greenfield – Medal of St George (4th Class)
15457 Pte. W J Agland (since deceased) – Medal of St George (3rd Class)

The awarding of Russian medals to British soldiers was a gesture that allowed the Tsarist government to show their appreciation for the support of their allies. This was a common practice amongst the armies of the Entente. Britain reciprocated, awarding medals and decorations to foreign troops, as did Belgium and France, whose awards of the Croix de Guerre to allied soldiers are more well known.

I delved into the records to find out more, in particular regarding the last-named: William Joseph Agland. He is mentioned in the *London Gazette* dated the 24 August 1915 in relation to his decoration. The entry reads that he 'was awarded the Russian St. George Medal [aka Bravery Medal] 3rd Class, by His Imperial Majesty the Emperor of Russia [Tsar Nicholas II], for gallantry and distinguished service in the field'. He had died three months earlier, on the 20 May, and the Medal Roll for his 1914 Star lists his cause of death as 'Mastoid'. This clearly refers to an infection of the mastoid bone behind the ear known as mastoid disease or mastoiditis. He was buried at Boulogne Eastern Cemetery, one of the town's civil cemeteries, in a CWGC plot set aside for soldiers who had been hospitalised and had died there. I was intrigued to discover that he had been a neighbour of William's back in Bethnal Green; the Agland family lived in Russia Lane, at 115 Quinn's Buildings. Within the close-knit community of an East End backstreet, the two families likely knew of each other. And the residents, upon hearing of William Agland's medal and of my grandfather receiving the Military Medal, too, would have celebrated that two of their boys had been decorated for bravery.

We gradually drifted back to the cars in twos and threes to set off for the next stop on our itinerary. I had to say goodbye to William and the 1st RF for the time being and put aside my personal pilgrimage for the interests of the collective.

As much as I wanted to walk my own Via Sacra and follow my grandfather's every footstep on the salient from the north of Ypres at the old front line near La Brique down to Ploegsteert in the south, there is one place that looms large in British Great War history that cannot be passed over. Leaving the ghost of my grandfather there in Sanctuary Wood, we set off to visit Tyne Cot Cemetery, the largest British war cemetery in the world, forever linked with Passchendaele.

William Charles Blumsom marching on a country lane near Runfold, Surrey, c.1904 - *Photo: Author's Collection.*

William Charles Blumsom in Darjeeling, India, c.1905-07.
*Photo: Author's Collection.*

A British soldier catches up with the latest war stories from 'Balkans News', the official organ of the British Salonika Force. It was published from November 1915 until May 1919. *Photo: National Army Museum NAM. 1978-11-157-29-6*

Lieutenant Colonel Guy du Maurier 3rd Bn Royal Fusiliers (City of London) Regiment. Uncle of the famous writer Daphne du Maurier. He was awarded the DSO in October 1902 for bravery during the Second Boer War where he commanded a mounted infantry company. Killed in action 9th March 1915, Kemmel, Belgium. P*hoto: Wikipedia*

Part of the old Sarson's Vinegar factory in Southwark, London, on the southern approach to Tower Bridge. *Photo: Charles Watson / Historic England.*

The stables were situated in the railway arches on the right in the above photo. *Author's collection.*

Above: The author as a tour guide, speaking at Hooge Crater, Flanders, Belgium. *Photo: Stephen Mulford.*
Below: The mighty Thiepval Memorial to the Missing, Somme, France. *Photo: Stephen Mulford.*

The author paying his respects at Guy du Maurier's grave, CWGC Kemmel Chateau Military Cemetery, Belgium - *Photo: Stephen Mulford.*

Menin Gate from the Grote Markt, Ypres - *Photo: Stephen Mulford.*

Corporal WC Blumsom MM.

Remembrance Sunday 2005 at the Royal Fusiliers War Memorial, Holborn, London.
*Photo: Carole Maybank.*

Aunt Florrie at her father's inscription at the Royal Fusiliers Regimental Chapel, Holy
Sepulchre Church, Holborn, London - *Photo: Carole Maybank.*

William Charles Blumsom's headstone at Nunhead Cemetery, South London - *Photo: Carole Maybank*

# CHAPTER TEN

# WAR PILGRIM

*The war pilgrim, paying his due of honour to those who came
that day, cannot follow very far on their road unless he die also.
If he chooses to follow any one soldier, will he not very likely
come soon to the road's end and a grey wooden cross where his
soldier's destiny dipped into eternity?*

STEPHEN GRAHAM, from *The Challenge of the Dead*

Graham wrote these words in 1920, two years after the war had ended. He
was revisiting the battlefields to reflect on the experience of 'the common
soldier', having served himself as a private in the latter stages of the conflict.
He used the term 'war pilgrim' to describe those travellers, mainly relatives,
who had lost a loved one and who craved the comfort and consolation
that a visit to their grave provided – the widows and mothers, fathers,
sisters and brothers, fiancées and friends, who visited in the immediate
aftermath of the war. In the ensuing years, their sons and daughters would
visit, and as the twentieth century wore on, so would my generation –
the grandchildren. And so it goes on. Today, the great-grandchildren and
great-great-grandchildren flock to Flanders and Picardy, war pilgrims all,
walking in the footsteps of those that came before them.

The initial postwar boom in battlefield tourism spanned the years
1919 to 1923, with the Church Army, Salvation Army, and the YMCA
conducting tours and escorting tens of thousands of bereaved relatives.
Two years after the war, in 1920, the travel agents Thomas Cook
observed 'that there had never been such a demand for tickets to the
Continent at Easter'. The second boom of the late 1920s to early 1930s
was influenced by the spate of 'war books' published during this period,
including memoirs and novels by Siegfried Sassoon, Edmund Blunden,

Robert Graves, Ernest Hemingway, Henry Williamson, and Erich Maria Remarque's classic *All Quiet on the Western Front*, along with R.C. Sheriff's 1928 play *Journey's End*, and the third boom occurred during the years 1936 to 1939.

David W. Lloyd, author of *Battlefield Tourism*, identifies the two main groups that make these battlefield pilgrimages – ex-servicemen and bereaved relatives – and goes on to distinguish between these pilgrims and those he labels tourists. He links the tourists to (what the pilgrims would view as) a commercialism and a trivialisation of the war. It was feared that charabancs of tourists on organised whistle-stop tours would career around Belgium and France without any understanding of or reverence for the hallowed ground they would tramp across, ghoulishly searching for souvenirs such as spent bullets or twisted military insignia. Lloyd also points out that many ex-servicemen viewed the difference between the pilgrim and the tourist as an extension of the divide between those serving at the front and those safe at home during the war. However, it could also be seen as a coming together: those 'tourists' that might not have suffered a direct bereavement (although the reality was that few could have escaped some kind of loss) were coming to pay their respects alongside the relatives and the old soldiers. It might not be morbid curiosity but, rather, a need to honour the sacrifice of the fallen.

But there was, and is, a sub-category of war pilgrim whose road's end does not, in Graham's words, lead to a grey wooden cross. Those like me, whose relatives survived and lived a life after the war, and who are haunted by the part played by their flesh and blood in the conflict and the after-effects they might have suffered. A hundred years after the event, war pilgrims still visit the battlefields in their droves. Graham, writing in 1920, believed that time would see a tailing-off of these pilgrimages: 'most of the cemeteries in the more obscure places will be half-forgotten and gone desolate'. He equates this to the dwindling numbers of visitors to the cemeteries in the Crimea.

But he failed to take into account the dedication and determination of those working for the Imperial War Graves Commission (now the

CWGC), whose sacred task is to maintain these burial grounds in perpetuity. His assertion that 'so it will be with us; we shall join the authentic dead, and the young ones will have forgotten whilst chattering of some other war' is powerfully contradicted by the coachloads of British schoolchildren who visit Belgium and northern France every year. The Great War features regularly in the national curriculum.

And the cataclysm of the Second World War has failed to eclipse the earlier conflict, even for one who served in the latter:

> *And I remember,*
> *Not the war I fought in*
> *But the one called Great*
> *Which ended in a sepia November*
> *Four years before my birth.*
>
> From *The Great War,* by Vernon Scannell

The experience of the Great War is embedded in the national consciousness in a unique way, and even though we have lost the last of those who had a living memory of the conflict, the work of the CWGC and the annual ritual of Remembrance Day perpetuate and refresh those memories for succeeding generations; the baton is passed on.

And so, today, we, the descendants of these men, come back again and again, crisscrossing the 'fatal avenue' of the Western Front, each of us on our own personal odyssey. Oftentimes, our touring party would pull into a lay-by adjacent to one of the CWGC cemeteries and note the presence of a car bearing a GB plate already parked there, or one that arrived subsequently. We would exchange nods of recognition with the occupants of those cars as our paths crossed amongst the headstones – kindred spirits chasing ghosts.

But is this need to walk in our ancestors' footsteps also about something else? Is my generation – and succeeding generations – attempting to retrospectively experience the Great War vicariously through our forefathers? Does this tendency chime with Dr Johnson's view that 'every man thought meanly of himself for not having been a soldier'? Unlike the two cohorts preceding it, my generation has not had the horror of a world war to fight – my grandfather and father, professional soldiers both, served for practically the entire duration of their respective world wars. There has been no need for us to raise a great citizen army as there was in 1914–18 and 1939–45. We have not had to prove ourselves on the battlefield. Private Harry Wells of the 23rd Battalion Royal Fusiliers expressed this perfectly: 'In a way, although it's not something they would have wanted to be involved in, the young people today seem to have missed something in their lifetime. Every generation had a war.' And, surely, he is right. We, the descendants of those soldiers, would not want to go through what they went through. It is more a question of hypothesis. Awestruck, we look at what they endured and wonder how we would have fared, both individually and collectively, as a society.

For the war pilgrim, no visit to the salient is complete without visiting Tyne Cot CWGC Cemetery. The largest of the British 'Cities of the Dead', it contains nearly 12,000 souls, of whom over two-thirds are unidentified. Another 35,000 names of soldiers who have no known grave are engraved on the curved Memorial Wall at the rear of the cemetery.

Tyne Cot must be the most-visited British cemetery on the Western Front. It will be forever associated with nearby Passchendaele, the town whose name has become shorthand for the Third Battle of Ypres, the main assault of which took place between the 31 July and the 10 November 1917. I have visited Tyne Cot several times since, but on this, my first visit, I was struck by the enormity of the place. I would learn that it is best appreciated on a late afternoon during an Indian summer: when the sun is low and the shadows are lengthening, the visual effect on the seemingly endless rows of Portland headstones is spellbinding.

No other place brings home to you as this place does the sheer scale of the loss suffered during the Great War. Each grave represents a family shattered, a wife widowed, a child made fatherless, a mother bereft, and for those young men whose potential would never be fulfilled, all those lives unlived, all those sweethearts unwed, all those children unborn, their lineage dying with them in the mud of Flanders.

Here in this place, to a far greater degree than anywhere else, are Thomas Hardy's and Rupert Brooke's words made solid, the 'homely northern breast and brain' and the 'richer dust', all that remains of the thousands of British soldiers that lie here, each occupying their own portion or corner of a foreign field.

The layout of the cemetery has been likened to that of a cathedral. The high, curved panelled wall on the eastern boundary connects with a low, flint wall that defines the rectangular northern, western, and southern boundaries of the cemetery. The walls enclose countless ranks of headstones lined up like row upon row of pews. A main, central aisle leads up the slope towards the altar-like Stone of Remembrance and the Cross of Sacrifice.

These two symbols were the subject of much controversy in the formative years of the Imperial War Graves Commission. The driving force behind the Commission was a remarkable man named Fabian Ware, a former editor of the *Morning Post* who, on account of his age, was rejected for military service and who subsequently secured the post of commander of the Red Cross Mobile Ambulance Unit in October 1914. His appointment to this position would eventually lead to the founding of the Commission.

Ware was a contradiction in many ways. He was simultaneously an individualist and a collectivist; he was interested in social reform, and he held some very progressive views, but he was also a committed imperialist.

Early in the war, Ware's unit was initially tasked with searching for wounded and missing British soldiers in the wake of the Allies' retreat from Mons and Le Cateau to the River Marne and conveying them back to British field hospitals and bases behind the lines. This work necessitated liaising with Lord Robert Cecil, also appointed by the Red Cross and in charge of the Wounded and Missing Department, which was likewise involved in similar searches. Initially undertaking his searches on an ad hoc basis following inquiries to Cecil's department, Ware was often able to verify wounded or missing soldiers as being killed.

When he located the burial sites of those who had died, Ware concerned himself with the conditions of those graves, taking ownership of the upkeep of the wooden crosses and ensuring that the details of the deceased were accurate, clearly marked, and recorded. By May 1915, he had registered 4,300 graves. Ware described this as a 'most useful piece of work' and saw this endeavour as a natural extension of his activities with the Mobile Ambulance Unit.

This was to become a colossal undertaking, but Ware was the right man for the job. The energy he would bring to this role was extraordinary. He saw his opportunity and presented himself to Nevil Macready, Adjutant-General to the British Expeditionary Force, at the end of February 1915 to formalise his work and obtain official standing with the Army.

It was a match made in heaven.

Macready was not a conventional military type; as a young man he had had ambitions to be an actor, but he had conformed to his father's wishes and joined the army instead. Ware's dynamic approach and life experience appealed to him. As a result of that meeting, Macready founded the Graves Registration Commission, the first incarnation of the organisation that would eventually become the CWGC. Ware was put in sole charge and had the rank of major conferred upon him.

Ware, for all his contradictions, was a visionary. He assembled an eclectic group of architects, horticulturalists, politicians, soldiers, and writers to undertake the creation of what can only be described as a modern wonder of the world, a global architectural expression of remembrance and of a nation's grief. Kipling described it as 'The biggest single bit of work since any of the Pharaohs'.

Ware was, as much as anything, an egalitarian, and he developed very definite ideas as to the form that this memorialisation should take. Officers and men would be treated exactly the same; the privileges of rank would not be reflected in the design or nature of the memorials. The cross was rejected as a grave marker in favour of a uniform-sized headstone bearing the name, rank, and regiment of the deceased, along with the date of death.

The policy of treating all of the fallen equally in the form of a headstone was to cause outrage and offence amongst some, including one of the most powerful and influential families in the land, the Cecil clan – notably Lady Florence Cecil and the aforementioned Lord Robert Cecil. They were the most vociferous of those ranged against Ware's egalitarian approach. Lady Cecil presented a petition containing thousands of signatures to the Prince of Wales, appealing for an alternative memorial in the form of a cross.

Ware and the Commission would not be moved; there would be no exceptions. It was a fundamental principle born of the fear that ostentation and bad taste might prevail in individual gravestone designs. This approach would avoid the prospect of a kind of hierarchy of the dead developing in the cemeteries, whereby those of high social status would install the most elaborate and extravagant memorials, and the markers would gradually diminish in size and decoration down to the most basic for the ordinary Tommy – something akin to the 12 x 12 inch tablet that marked my grandfather's common grave in Nunhead – the British class system writ large.

Ware had a powerful ally in Edwin Lutyens, one of the Commission's three distinguished chief architects, who shared his egalitarian ethos. A parliamentary debate resolved the matter, with impassioned and emotive contributions from both sides. The Commission had Kipling and Asquith, who had both lost sons to the war, and Churchill arguing their case. Eventually it was accepted that it was inappropriate to put such a sensitive matter to the vote, and the way was clear for the Commission to proceed.

The question of a central memorial still had to be settled. Lutyens's response was his design of the iconic Stone of Remembrance, an altar-like monolithic block measuring twelve feet long with Kipling's choice, the phrase from Ecclesiasticus, 'Their Name Liveth For Evermore', inscribed on the main aspect of the monument. Stones of Remembrance are installed in hundreds of CWGC cemeteries and sites containing more than 1,000 graves or commemorating more than 1,000 dead. Although altar-like, it was intended as a secular symbol. In accordance with Ware's principles, the overarching egalitarian philosophy of the Commission not only included rank and social status but also religion, too. This was not meant to be a Christian device but, rather, one for all faiths and none. Lutyens insisted that:

> All that is done of structure should be for endurance for all time and for equality of honour, for besides Christians of all denominations, there will be Jews, Mussulmens, Hindus and men of other creeds, their glorious names and their mortal bodies all equally deserving enduring record and seemly sepulture.

But once again, the Commission met with fierce opposition. The Anglican Church demanded the presence of a monumental cross in each cemetery, and, unfortunately for Ware and Lutyens, Herbert Baker, one of the other principal architects for the Commission, agreed with the clergy. The controversy raged with no resolution in sight, and the Commission was forced to appoint a referee in the shape of Sir Frederic Kenyon, the Director of the British Museum. Kenyon was tasked with carrying out a wide-ranging consultation with religious groups, taking into account their views, and forming a committee from interested parties to consider the proposals for the design and architecture of the cemeteries before reporting his recommendations to the Commission. Kenyon's report would, with the possible exception of this contentious issue – prove to be a masterpiece of precision, reason, and sensitivity; he laid out clear and detailed recommendations for the form the cemeteries should take. And in the main, most of Ware's philosophy prevailed: 'the principle of equality of treatment' with regard to the headstones; all inscriptions to include name, rank, regiment, date of death, and regimental insignia; and the presence of a central monument in the form of a memorial stone – the non-aligned Stone of Remembrance – were formalised.

The only battle that Ware lost related to the symbolic cross. Kenyon felt that as the British Empire was a Christian empire, the cemeteries would suffer for the lack of a cross and that its omission would cause much distress. The obvious flaw in Kenyon's conclusion was that the British Empire was not wholly Christian – particularly millions of subjects on the Indian subcontinent. It was a circle that could not be squared, for the Hindus, Muslims, and Sikhs who had fought so hard for the 'mother country'; those of the Jewish faith; and the Taoists, Buddhists, and Confucianists of the Chinese Labour Corps who worked alongside the troops would also lie in these cemeteries. As would those of no faith – the atheists and agnostics, the humanists and Darwinists – and those that had become godless, proselytised by the trauma of war.

It is doubtful whether the presence of a monumental cross ever exercised the minds or passions of those working-class Tommies that survived the war. Historian David Stevenson, when examining the reasons behind the men's willingness to fight and endure the hardships of war, concludes that the established churches played very little part in influencing their thoughts, attitudes, or behaviour; that 'organised religion seems to have been conspicuously absent'; and that 'the surviving first-hand evidence – naturally with many individual exceptions – makes little reference to the official faiths'. This view is supported by Private Frank Richards, who states, 'if we happened to be out of the line on a Sunday we were compelled to attend Church parade which ninety-five per cent of the Battalion thoroughly detested'. The men's irreverence included parodying some of the hymns, for example…

> *John Wesley had a little dog,*
> *He was so very thin,*
> *He took him to the Gates of Hell*
> *And threw the bastard in.*
>
> [Sung to *O God, our Help in Ages Past*]

…with each succeeding verse becoming ever more blasphemous.

And who can blame them? Many had felt God-forsaken in their civilian lives, low-paid in often dirty and dangerous jobs, or mind-numbingly repetitive manual work, reduced to factory fodder. Only to be transformed into cannon fodder. And if they were lucky enough to have survived in one piece, they reverted to factory fodder when the war was over. Or, worse, unemployed and homeless. The institution of the Church, in all its guises, had no relevance to their deprived lives. Both the Church of England and nonconformist denominations had failed to engage with the working class since the Industrial Revolution. It was a state of affairs on which Charles Booth reflects in his study of the people of London, wherein he quotes a London City Missionary who 'says that the great difficulty is the general indifference; adding, "it nearly crushes me". To quote figures, we hear that of 70 families in one street only 2 attended a place of worship, while of 1199 persons in 3 streets only 29 were accounted "professed Christians".'

And when the army chaplains sent the Tommies on their way – supposedly with God's blessing, if not actual divine encouragement – to slaughter the enemy, mirrored by their German counterparts exhorting their own troops likewise, the ordinary soldier might legitimately ask whose side God was on. This question was tackled by the poet J.C. Squire:

> God heard the embattled nations sing and shout:
> 'Gott strafe England' and 'God save the King' –
> 'God this', 'God that' and 'God the other thing.'
> 'My God', said God, I've got my work cut out.'

For the Commission, taking on the Church establishment was a step too far, and Ware and Lutyens had no choice but to cave in. The result was the installation of the Cross of Sacrifice, a tall stone cross inlaid with a bronze sword and standing on an octagonal base. This monument was designed by Reginald Blomfield, the third of the triumvirate of great architects engaged by the Commission (the other two being Lutyens and Baker).

The writer Vera Brittain was a notable early war pilgrim, visiting the battlefields of Italy and France in 1921. She was able to identify with both classes of pilgrim – the relatives and the veterans. She had lost four of those dearest to her: her brother Edward Brittain; her fiancé Roland Leighton; and two close friends, Victor Richardson and Geoffrey Thurlow. And she had served as a Voluntary Aid Detachment nurse in Malta and France, treating wounded and dying soldiers straight from the battlefields.

She documented these shattering bereavements in her best-selling book *Testament of Youth*, which was published in 1933. Her brother was killed in action whilst serving on the Italian Front on the 15 June 1918; his grave is situated within the British military cemetery on the Asiago Plateau near Granezza. Earlier in the war, her fiancé Roland had been shot through the stomach by a German sniper as he repaired the defensive wire in no-man's-land that protected the trenches. He died of his wounds on the 23 December 1915; he was twenty years old. He is buried at Louvencourt CWGC Cemetery within the Somme sector.

Brittain made her pilgrimage in September 1921 with her close friend Winifred Holtby, first visiting her brother Edward's grave in northern Italy. She described it as 'this grave on the top of a mountain, in the lofty silence, the singing, unearthly stillness, of these remote forests!' Eventually making their way to France by train after having spent some time in Florence, they hired a car in Amiens to visit Louvencourt. Edward had himself visited Roland's grave here during the run-up to the Battle of the Somme. Whilst billeted in Albert behind the lines in April 1916, he had cycled to Louvencourt.

Brittain felt that the cemetery in Italy suffered by comparison with this idyllic spot in France:

We found the cemetery, as Edward had described it, on the top of a hill where two roads joined; the afternoon was bright and sunny, and just beyond the encircling wall a thin row of elms made a delicate pattern against the tranquil sky. The graves, each with its little garden in front, resembled a number of flower beds planted at intervals in the smooth, wide lawn, which lay so placidly beneath the long shadow of the slender memorial cross. As I walked up the paved path where Edward had stood in April 1916, and looked at the trim, ordered burial-ground and the open, urbane country, I thought how different it all was from the grey twilight of the Asiago plateau, with its deep, sinister silence. The strange irony which had determined the fates of Roland and Edward seemed to persist even after death: the impetuous warrior slept calmly in this peaceful, complacent earth with its suave covering of velvet lawn; the serene musician lay on the dark summit of a grim, far-off mountain.

In fact, she eventually came to view the aesthetic appeal of the IWGC cemeteries as a 'cheating and a camouflage'; to her, the tasteful and dignified appearance of these places was man's attempt to sanitise and even glorify the war. And a number of writers agreed with her that the elegantly inscribed Portland stone grave markers and the carefully chosen plants and flowers, along with the meticulously kept lawns, made fair what was once a nightmarish landscape of death and mutilation. But these critics were outnumbered. Many, including ex-servicemen, felt that the sheer number and scale of these graveyards scattered across Belgium and France were a searing indictment of war and that they provided the greatest advocacy for a lasting peace. In truth, the latter view prevails today. For visitors to these cemeteries and memorials, there is no sense of triumphalism or of glorifying war. There are no grand statues of victorious generals on horseback à la Napoleon or Wellington. Ware's egalitarian vision has been realised to an exceptional degree.

And, anyway, what would have been the alternative? Should the designs of these places have physically reflected the horrors of war? How would the relatives of those fallen have felt visiting their loved ones in their eternal resting places if they had been manifested in such a way?

A markedly different architectural expression of grief and memorialisation can be seen at Langemark in Belgium, where a German military cemetery is located. There are 44,000 burials there, with flat stone tablets marking the graves of individual soldiers, in contrast to the upright headstones seen in the CWGC cemeteries. There is also a mass grave containing 25,000 souls, half of whom remain unidentified. The plot is planted with great oak trees – towering sentinels watching over the dead. The oak, symbolising strength and endurance, is the national tree of Germany, and those trees, along with the dark grey-coloured stones used for the grave markers and the stout basalt crosses, create a powerful, brooding atmosphere in complete contrast to the CWGC cemeteries. There, the brilliance of the Portland stone and the vibrancy of the flowers provide an altogether sunnier outlook.

The difference between the two architectural and landscaping styles is very clear. To my mind it echoes the difference between German and British Romanticism, and I see the parallels in art and music: between the dramatic, wild landscapes of Caspar David Friedrich and the rural, idyllic country scenes of Constable; of an epic opera by Wagner and the orchestral reworking of an English folk song by Vaughan Williams; differences in the artistic interpretations of each people's cultural identity and in how they see themselves. I came away from my visit to Langemark in a sombre mood, filled with a deep sadness, in contrast to what I felt at Tyne Cot and other CWGC cemeteries, where such emotions were leavened by an instinctive response to the peaceful *green and pleasant* pastoral beauty of the surroundings.

Leaving Tyne Cot towards the end of our first day in Belgium, we headed back to Ypres and the hotel for a shower, rest, and refreshment before attending the Last Post ceremony at the Menin Gate, the mightily impressive monument to the missing of the salient. This was due to be performed at 8pm by a team of buglers drawn from the local fire brigade, playing it as has been done every night – with the exception of a period of four years during the Second World War – since the 2 July 1928. At about half past seven, we headed towards the Menin Gate, mingling with the general drift of others doing likewise.

As I strolled leisurely along, I reflected on the fact that I was actually walking in my grandfather's footsteps. This street, Menenstraat, was but a portion of the well-worn path for thousands of Tommies making their way towards the front line. William was often billeted in the woods near Poperinghe to the west of Ypres, and his journeys to the trenches would have involved marches from there via Ypres and through the Menin Gate to all points east.

I envisage him marching alongside me, accompanied by the phantom figures of the rest of his battalion. My imaginary reconstruction echoes the imagery of ghostly soldiers that appear in art and literature, from Sorley's poetic *Pale Battalions* to Longstaff's painting titled *Menin Gate at Midnight*. These imagined ethereal figures represent the dead and the missing in the most powerful way. Will Longstaff, an Australian artist who served in the war, returned to Ypres in 1927 to attend the inauguration of the monument. He experienced a vision on a midnight walk – a host of steel-helmeted phantom soldiers emerging Lazarus-like ahead of the Menin Gate, as if they were in the process of forming up to march eastwards, back towards the old front line.

We arrive at the monument to join the throng that has already gathered there. The main thoroughfare is roped off in preparation for the ceremony. Police officers on point duty are stopping all vehicular traffic. As eight o' clock approaches, the sense of anticipation is palpable. As the general hubbub reduces to a murmur and then complete silence, four buglers march to their post under the eastern archway, stand to attention facing the town, and prepare to play.

The *Last Post* is a bugle call that was originally played to signal to the troops that the day's soldiering was over, the sentries had been posted, and the garrison was secure. It has become the custom to play the *Last Post* at military funerals, memorial services, and remembrance ceremonies to symbolise that the soldier or soldiers commemorated had performed their duty for the last time and could now rest in peace. It is a poignant and haunting refrain, and the acoustic effect of it being played under the vaulted ceiling of the Menin Gate made it even more so.

The playing of the *Last Post* at the Menin Gate is a deeply moving event. Having attended on a score of occasions, I can testify that it retains its power to affect you; there is no immunity, as each night is unique. For example, a significant anniversary for a particular regiment might be marked by a band followed by a detachment of present-day soldiers from that regiment marching to the memorial from the square to honour their predecessors. On one occasion, a Scottish regiment was represented by a lone piper playing within the Hall of Memory, and the sound of the pipes echoing throughout this sacred place was profoundly stirring.

At other times, descendants of the missing will lay wreaths in their memory. They come from far and wide; I have seen families honouring their ancestors who have travelled from Australia to do so. For the Menin Gate is also a shrine for these kinsfolk; they have no grave to visit. When the memorial was unveiled on the 24 July 1927, Field Marshal Lord Plumer addressed the assembled crowd, and in his famous reference to the soldiers being memorialised, he reassured the bereaved that *'He is not missing; he is here.'*

The following morning, I woke early, for our hotel faced directly onto the main square, and Saturday is market day in Ypres. From the early hours, I was aware of much activity outside my window as the market traders set up their stalls, unloaded their produce, and displayed their wares. Before long, the shouts of the stallholders started, and one particular Flemish word is seared into my memory. 'Koop!' ('Buy!'). Every time I return, I welcome the familiar cry like an old friend.

The early wake-up call did not faze me, for I was eager to return to the salient – I was back on the trail of William. After their stint in the Hooge sector, the 1st Royal Fusiliers returned to the trenches near La Brique, two and a half miles to the north of Ypres – where they had been in June 1915 – for the month of September. The following month, from the 2 to 11 October, they manned the trenches at St. Jean, to the northeast, before being relieved and returning to billets near Poperinghe.

On the 13th, the whole Brigade paraded on the polo ground in an open square formation with the three sides formed by the 1st Royal Fusiliers, the 1st North Staffords, the 2nd Leinsters, and the 3rd Rifle Brigade, in that order, for an inspection by the General Officer Commanding the 6th Division, Major General William Congreve VC. The General Officer Commanding (GOC) was making a farewell speech on the occasion of the 17th Brigade leaving the 6th Division to 'stiffen' the inexperienced 'new army' 24th Division that had suffered so badly at Loos. He referred to how well the Brigade had acquitted itself in various actions and expressed his regrets that they were leaving – understandably so, for he was losing a body of battle-hardened troops that largely belonged to the pre-war professional army.

The following day, the 14 October, the whole of the 17th Brigade marched to Reninghelst, about five miles southwest of Ypres, where they made camp behind the lines. There, the Brigade was broken up and reorganised to spread their experience amongst the brigades of the 24th. Each was reformed as a mixture of 'old army' and 'new army' battalions, the former providing an experienced 'spine' for the latter – professionals teaching volunteers how to soldier.

The rest of that month and into November, the 1st RF manned the trenches east of Voormezeele on the bank of the Ypres-Comines Canal in the southern sector of the salient. The whole of the month of December was spent out of the line in billets at Bayenham.

The last quarter of 1915 was a relatively quiet time for the battalion. The casualty figures were:

| October | 7 Killed | 22 Wounded |
|---|---|---|
| November | 9 Killed | 22 Wounded |
| December | 0 Killed | 0 Wounded |

Before they saw the year out, on the 27 December, none other than the newly appointed Commander in Chief of the British Army himself, Sir Douglas Haig, arrived to inspect the battalion at work.

When I had originally obtained the 1st RF's war diaries from Kew during my research, I found that the sheets for the first six months of 1916 were missing. The originals had been lost. To track William's movements for this period, I had to go back to other records. I consulted the war diary of the parent brigade of the 1st RF, the 17th, but it was not sufficiently detailed to track an individual battalion.

Therefore, I had to reconstruct the 1st RF's movements from the war diaries of its sister battalions within the 17th Brigade and the 24th Division. This I did by viewing the records of the 2nd Leinster regiment, the 3rd Rifle Brigade, and the 12th Royal Fusiliers, whose diaries contained the exact dates and trench deployments when they relieved the 1st RF – or were relieved by them. Thus, I was able to determine that William's battalion was in support at the Ypres ramparts from the 7 to 13 January 1916 before returning to the Hooge/Sanctuary Wood sector for just over a month.

After that, the whole of the 17th Brigade went into rest at a camp in Ouderdom near Reninghelst. After a month in billets, they were back at Sanctuary Wood on the 18 March, relieving the 12th Royal Fusiliers (Service) Battalion. For most of the second quarter of 1916, they were deployed in the trenches at Hill 63 near Ploegsteert, at the extreme south of the salient, again alternating with the 12th RF.

We tracked the battalion's movements, working from north to south and stopping at points of interest on the way. Northeast of St. Jean, we stopped at Vancouver Corner, where the Canadians distinguished themselves during the Germans' first gas attack in April 1915. Here stands a monument marking the spot, a 35-foot-tall column of granite topped by a sculpture of a steel-helmeted Canadian soldier with his head bowed and his hands resting on arms reversed, his torso emerging from the solid block of stone. *The Brooding Soldier* is a profoundly impressive piece of work. The column bears a plaque commemorating this extraordinary feat of arms:

**This column marks the battlefield where 18,000 Canadians on the British left withstood the first German gas attacks the 22-24 April 1915. 2,000 fell and lie buried nearby.**

The writer Henry Williamson, who served in the war, was similarly impressed. Returning to the Western Front in 1964, he wrote an article for the *London Evening Standard*, describing it as 'Surely the memorial for all the soldiers of all wars?' He observes that the memorial 'has the gravity and strength of grief coming from the full knowledge of old wrongs done to men by men. It mourns, but it mourns for all mankind.... The genius of Man rises out of the stone, and once again our tears fell upon the battlefield.'

We returned to the Hooge sector for our second visit, just as William had returned there in early 1916. We parked by the Hooge Crater CWGC Cemetery, another masterpiece of remembrance whose construction had been overseen by Sir Edwin Lutyens. Entering through the gates from the Menin Road, you are greeted by the Stone of Remembrance, which is placed within a large stone-faced circle mirroring the crater created on the 15 July 1915 by the British mine that had exploded under the German front line – on the other side of the road. It is the fourth-largest CWGC cemetery in Belgium, after Tyne Cot, Lijssenthoek, and Poelcappelle, and, in accordance with Herbert Baker's vision, it bears the imprint of 'a cathedral precinct like Canterbury or Winchester, its trees and gardens surrounded by stone walls with an arched gateway and chapel, perhaps, and covered cloister walks' as opposed to the smaller cemeteries, which he envisaged as 'an English churchyard' resembling 'a humble Stoke Poges'. We crossed the Menin Road to visit the Hooge Crater Museum opposite, an excellent, well-curated collection of Great War armour and equipment, and enjoyed a coffee at the attached café.

Back on the road, we headed west back towards Ypres before veering left and skirting the town to the southeast, then making another left turn south of the Lille Gate and heading towards the border with France. We crossed the Ypres–Comines Canal just a mile to the west of where William occupied the trenches on the canal bank in November 1915. Eight miles south of Ypres, we reached our destination at the Ploegsteert Memorial to the Missing, adjacent to Ploegsteert Wood (the name 'anglicised' by the Tommies to 'Plugstreet').

The memorial, designed by Harold Chalton Bradshaw, is a stunning piece of public art that takes the form of a circular stone structure supported by doric columns. Three-quarters of the circumference of the outer ring of columns is infilled with walls bearing the names of 11,370 of the fallen that have no known grave. The soldiers commemorated here fell in several larger battles, including Loos and Aubers Ridge, as well as at other times during the course of the war. The entrance to the plot is guarded by two stone lions recumbent, designed by Sir Gilbert Ledward. The memorial itself sits within the boundaries of the Berkshire Cemetery Extension, which contains the graves of 876 men.

William spent a long time in this sector, practically the whole of April and May 1916, as well as most of June. He was in exalted company; his time here overlapped with that of Winston Churchill, who served here during his tenure with the 6th Royal Scots Fusiliers as a lieutenant colonel from the 5 January to the 6 May 1916. It could be said that he spent that time as penance after his ambitious plan to defeat the Turks through the Dardanelles had ended with the tragic failure at Gallipoli. Moved from his post as First Lord of the Admiralty to the peripheral one of Chancellor of the Duchy of Lancaster, he eventually resigned in November 1915 to rejoin the army. A stone bas relief plaque installed at the main Ploegsteert crossroads commemorates his time here.

But Churchill wasn't the only future prime minister to serve almost cheek by jowl with William in this sector during the spring of 1916. Just to the south of the trenches adjacent to Hill 63, where the 1st RF was deployed, the 21st Battalion of the Kings Royal Rifle Corps occupied the eastern edge of Ploegsteert Wood itself. Within their ranks was Second Lieutenant Anthony Eden, whose future offices included Foreign Secretary during the Second World War and Prime Minister (1955–7).

The young Eden, known as 'the Boy' to those in the officers' mess, thought highly of the men under his command, many of whom were of the same callow age. Writing of his experiences at Ploegsteert Wood in his autobiography, published in 1976, all those years later, he was able to name those ordinary soldiers that he held in such high esteem, including

Riflemen Arthur 'Tiger' Pratt and Tom Liddell (infantrymen in a Rifles regiment are known by the rank of Rifleman rather than Private), and Sergeants Reg Park and Bert Harrop – men like William, from the same class and background. His relationships with these men had a profound effect on Eden's personal philosophy: 'Many of the ideas which I hold to this day stemmed from them, particularly a sense of the irrelevance and unreality of class distinction.'

Having parked the vehicles in a layby near the cemetery, we set off to walk the ground. Just to the north of the memorial, we turn left at a CWGC sign pointing towards Underhill Farm Cemetery. To our right is a wooded area on a steep slope. We enter the woods through a gate and then ascend the hillside along a rough paved track. Blowing hard, we reach the top of the wood and exit it through another gate to continue to the heights of the ridge.

This is Hill 63, a strategically important position that was occupied by the British for most of the war. The hill provides an excellent vantage point to view what was once the battleground of the southern sector of the Ypres front. The gentle undulation of the landscape here is easier on the eye than the flat, monotonous farmland to the north of the salient. Scanning the horizon from left to right, I can see significant landmarks that will be forever associated with the Great War: Kemmel Hill, the spire of Wijtschate church ('Whitesheet' to the Tommies), the Messines Ridge.

Underneath us is a sealed massive underground complex that was dug into the hillside by the 1st Australian Tunnelling Company in the autumn of 1917. Consisting of a subterranean network of nineteen 'streets' with a labyrinth of connected chambers and dugouts, it contained ranks of chicken wire–sprung bunk beds for the use of the troops in reserve and could accommodate 1,200 men. It also contained a General Office, a Signals Office, a small hospital, a canteen, and generators that provided electricity for lighting and power for the signals equipment. Outside the underground complex, there was accommodation for a further 250 men in steel-framed 'huts' rendered in clay spoil from the excavation. The complex was known by several names: 'the Catacombs', 'the Hill 63

Dugouts', 'Wallangarra', although it became most commonly referred to as 'The Hole in the Hill'.

We tramped off eastwards on a gradual descent from Hill 63 towards the old front line; the slope from west to east is much gentler than the south face of the hill that we had climbed. The line of the trenches had followed the eastern edge of Ploegsteert Wood. Skirting the northern edge of the wood, we briefly visit Prowse Point Military CWGC Cemetery before reaching our next destination: St. Yvon, a place forever associated with the famous Christmas Truce of December 1914.

Here, on Christmas Day 1914, British and German troops had initially sung songs and carols to each other from the trenches before meeting in no-man's-land, the khaki and field-grey uniforms mingling together. They swapped food, smokes, and souvenirs and shared rum and schnapps. Numerous anecdotes of football being played on no-man's-land have been recorded, either between the British and the Germans or games played between British units with the Germans looking on. 'The Christmas Day 1914 football match' has now entered Great War lore.

Marking the spot is a plain wooden cross, inscribed '1914–1999 – The Khaki Chums – Christmas Truce – 85 years – Lest We Forget'. Amongst the poppy wreaths at the base of the cross were footballs and football scarves that had recently been placed there by other battlefield tourists. The cross was erected by the Khaki Chums (The Association of Military Remembrance), a group of present-day enthusiasts who wear authentic Great War uniforms and tour the battlefields in an effort to educate and inform.

We leave the old front line to enter Ploegsteert Wood itself and visit three separate burial places within: Toronto Avenue, Ploegsteert Wood Military, and Rifle House CWGC Cemeteries. These sites provide a complete contrast to most of the other CWGC cemeteries that we had seen so far, many of which had been situated in open countryside and surrounded by farmland, each Cross of Sacrifice visible from far away. Coming across these three cemeteries, each hidden away from view in a wooded glade, provides a wholly different atmosphere.

Many of the men buried in these places were not killed in large-scale set-piece battles. Ploegsteert differs in that respect from Arras, Passchendaele, and the villages of the Somme region. These soldiers were casualties of the day-to-day routine of trench warfare, falling victim to sporadic shellfire, shrapnel, mortar bombs, and sniping.

We backtrack and leave the wood via the route we entered it. We then turn left onto a track that was known to the Tommies as Mud Lane and make our way westwards back to our cars.

William saw out June 1916 in billets at Locre to the southwest of Ypres. Seventy miles to the south, in France, the long-planned Allied offensive for the summer of 1916 was due to commence on the 29th of that month at the Somme, a province bisected by the river of the same name. However, bad weather postponed the beginning of the offensive by forty-eight hours to the 1 July. Although the 1ˢᵗ Royal Fusiliers had not originally been detailed to take part in the offensive, subsequent events would dictate otherwise.

On the 2 July, William's battalion occupied the trenches at Kemmel – where his old CO from the Boer War, Colonel Guy du Maurier, had been killed on the 9 March 1915 – staying there until they were relieved eleven days later by the 12ᵗʰ RF. They enjoyed a rest period in camp at Wakefield Huts for a week before crossing the border into France, where they were billeted at Saint Jans-Cappel on the evening of the 19th. On the 21st, they received orders to stand by, ready to move. They finally marched off at 11:45am, arriving two hours and fifteen minutes later at Le Steent'je, four miles south. Here they remained until the 24th, when they entrained at Bailleul to move south to the Somme. After a seemingly interminable stop-start sixty-mile journey due to the heavily congested rail network – trains carrying ever-increasing numbers of men and volumes of matériel, including vast quantities of shells and ammunition, clogged up the tracks heading south from the Channel ports to the battle sectors, with commensurate numbers of wounded men heading in the opposite direction – they eventually reached Longueau, four miles southeast of Amiens, at 6am on the 25th. They then embarked on a march of twenty miles west to Riencourt, arriving at 5:30pm, and spent five days training in preparation for joining the battle. The first week of August saw the 1st RF undertake further training, learning from the experience gained during the first month of the offensive. The training included practicing uphill attacks in camp at Sandpits, three miles southeast of Albert.

Going into the Battle of the Somme, the battalion was at full strength, with 41 officers and 1037 other ranks. They were as well prepared as they could be for what they were about to face.

# CHAPTER ELEVEN

# THE SOMME

*We were rushing along in Gillymong*
*We could hear the Boche a singing*
*They seemed to say,*
*"You have stolen our trench,*
*But don't go away,*
*And we'll pepper you with tear shells*
*All the day*

GILLYMONG
Soldiers' song, sung to the tune *Moonlight Bay*

The Battle of the Somme had been raging for over five weeks when the 1st Royal Fusiliers joined the fray on the 8th of August. The first day of the battle, the 1 July 1916, proved to be the most catastrophic day in the history of the British Army, when over 20,000 men were slaughtered, many within the first hour of the attack. In total, including killed, wounded, and missing, the British suffered 57,000 casualties.

The Somme would also cost the 1st RF dearly, and William would not escape unscathed. The preceding two weeks of training had been in preparation for an attack on the village of Guillemont – 'Gillymong', as the men nicknamed it – towards the southern end of the British sector on the Somme front. It was an important strategic point, the southernmost village on a ridge held by the Germans that ran from Thiepval, lying roughly to the northwest just over seven miles away, down through *Pozières* before reaching Guillemont, approximately four miles north of the Somme River. The capture of Guillemont was crucial as it would enable the whole of the right flank of the Fourth Army to advance, taking out a salient at Delville Wood in the process.

The village, or what little remained of it, commanded the surrounding countryside. Sitting at one of the highest points on the ridge at an elevation of over 500 feet, Guillemont was key to the whole advance. From their observation posts, the Germans could monitor the movements of the British – men and matériel – coming from Amiens into Albert eight miles to the west. They were determined to hold it at all costs, and they had the advantage of a network of concrete fortifications and underground tunnels from which to defend their position. It was considered an almost impenetrable stronghold.

Throughout July and into August, numerous attempts to take Guillemont had been attempted and failed. In Lyn Macdonald's words:

For six weeks, division after division battered up the slope against the defences of Guillemont village. Time after time they were thrown back again. Time after time the ragged remnants of battalions were withdrawn, decimated and demoralised. Like High Wood, Delville Wood, Mametz Wood, Thiepval and Beaumont Hamel, the name of Guillemont was already imbued with overtones of horror, which the passage of a whole generation would not erase.

These attacks ranged from the piecemeal to larger-scale operations and were unsuccessful for a variety of reasons, including poor planning and unimaginative tactics, seemingly contradictory or ambiguous instructions issued by the high command, and the perennial problem of inadequate artillery fire. The latter, in particular, contributed greatly to the lack of success. A shortage of guns and shells had meant that much of the German wire remained intact, and there was insufficient protection for the infantry, but equally damning was the failure to understand that the Germans had adapted their tactics and improved their defences. Previously, the British gunners, taking advantage of excellent observation posts, had been able to fix their sights with pinpoint accuracy on their opponents' trenches. And, accordingly, they wrought havoc on the German front line.

However, the Germans responded by relocating their machine gun nests out of the trenches and into outposts, shell holes, and the cellars of houses adjacent to and traversing their lines. In consequence, these 'pockets' of lethal firepower survived any preliminary bombardment and were able to inflict heavy losses on the attackers. On the occasions when the Tommies had managed to reach and enter the village, they were mown down by machine gun fire from the rear and the flanks.

The solution would have been to broaden the width of the target area to straddle the front line whilst intensifying the volume of shells, taking out the machine gun posts as well as the trenches, but the British lacked the necessary firepower; both guns and ammunition were in short supply at this stage of the war.

The 1st RF was deployed under these circumstances.

They entered the trenches on the 8 August, taking over 1,500 yards of the front line between Delville Wood and Trones Wood the following day, with the 'trench strength' (as opposed to the 'establishment strength') of the battalion standing at 21 officers and 866 other ranks.

Captain Charles Wilson, the battalion's medical officer, wrote a detailed account of the 1st RF's time in the front line. On the 10th of August, about mid-morning, a heavy barrage began, and Wilson made his way to the trenches to assess the situation. To his horror, he discovered that they were being bombarded not by German shells but by British, the result of a deadly miscalculation by the artillery. He met the officer commanding B Company, who went by the name of Burdett, who angrily exclaimed, 'It's *our* goddamned guns! I can't make out what the hell they're up to!'

The 'friendly fire' destroyed the trenches. The methodically dug earthworks were obliterated, pounded by their own shells into a crater-pocked mess. Men vanished from sight in an instant, and the trench furniture – the sandbag-revetted parapet and parados, the wooden duckboards, and the timber supports and corrugated iron – was smashed into fragments and littered amongst the great heaps of soil thrown up by the explosions. It was complete chaos.

As the bombardment continued, the men worked feverishly amidst the black smoke and deafening noise to rescue their buried comrades. They redoubled their efforts on hearing the muffled cries of their pals, discarding their spades through fear of harming them and frantically clawing at the soil with their hands. In their frenzy and fearful that they were running out of time, each man was oblivious to the fact that the 'spoil' his digging was creating was hampering his neighbour alongside him, working on his own rescue efforts.

Wilson worked steadfastly alongside the men, until eventually a shell landed close by – too close. He experienced 'a terrific noise; everything vanished for a moment'. When the dust cleared, he realised the officer and two men who had been toiling next to him had disappeared, buried under the debris of the explosion.

This particular blast proved to be the climax of the barrage. Whether this was because word had got back to the artillery that they were shelling their own lines or the fusillade had simply reached its intended conclusion is not recorded.

Wilson observed that 'The men were angry; they had been let down; if this thing happened once it might happen again.' This anger drove the men to even greater efforts; they picked up their spades again and dug them 'viciously' into the earth. Caution was thrown to the wind; it was a race against time.

Incredibly, only one fatality was recorded that day – and that was from an accidental drowning. Of the twenty-nine casualties listed, the majority were rescued from being buried alive by the efforts of their comrades, including Wilson. The official war diary detailed the events of the day as follows:

B Company were shelled by our own 9.2s losing 23 casualties mostly however were buried and bruised but all suffered severely from shock. Lt W van Greeson showed great gallantry in rescuing buried men, also Cpl J Scott who was himself buried, when dug out he rendered great assistance in getting others out. Capt. CM Wilson, our MO also distinguished himself at this time.

And the following day, he excelled once more:

> Bosch shelled us this afternoon from 3 to 5. Casualties were small. Captain CM Wilson again distinguished himself by rendering aid and evacuating Major Musgrove who was wounded by shell fire in a CT [communication trench] near Trones Wood when on his way to the front line.

On the night of the 11th, the battalion was relieved in the front line and retired to Breslau trenches, a support position. As a parting gesture, the Germans subjected them to a heavy barrage as they passed through Trones Wood – a wood now in name only, as all that remained were blackened stumps – causing several casualties. For the next few nights, until the 17 August, the battalion was engaged in digging 'jumping-off' trenches ahead of the front line, a hundred yards into no-man's-land, in preparation for the planned attack on Guillemont. The work was frequently interrupted by enemy attention, and the men had to take cover where they could, in shell holes and partly dug abandoned trenches.

Wilson looked on in dismay as he watched this body of highly trained fighting men reduced to labouring duties: 'This perfect unit of the old army has been turned into a labour battalion; they have been shot down with their eyes on the ground and spades in their hands like prisoners who are made to dig their own grave.'

On the 18 August, the battalion took up their position in Trones Wood in readiness for the attack. The Guillemont sector was only one element of a much larger assault across a broad front of 12,000 yards. The objectives included taking High Wood, Delville Wood, and Ginchy as well. The 1st RF was in close support to the 3rd RB and the 8th Buffs (East Kent Regiment), with the 12th RF in reserve.

The hot sun beat down out of a clear blue sky on Wilson and his orderlies as they moved their stretchers and other medical equipment into a dugout that had previously been used by the Germans to store ammunition. Live shells, simply abandoned, were piled up on three sides of the chamber, and a direct hit would have put paid to Wilson and his men in spectacular fashion. At 3:30pm, the preparatory bombardment began, announced by the apocalyptic roar of the guns. Wilson watched as 'the men grinned with glee and one big fellow, spitting on his hands, rubbed them on his hips … all at once the men ran out, in spite of the stuff that was falling all around'. The men went over the top, following a creeping barrage – a system of precisely calibrated 'lifts' whereby a coordinated bombardment would closely precede the advance of the troops at pre-set timings that would correlate with their progress, a 'curtain of fire' shielding the men and moving at a rate of fifty yards a minute.

Captain Hitchcock of the 2$^{nd}$ Leinsters, now with the 73$^{rd}$ Brigade, whose company was also in reserve to the main attack, watched from a vantage point on a ridge around a thousand yards from the jumping-off trenches, separated by a broad depression known as 'The Valley of Death'. He describes what happened:

> Simultaneously out got a line of forms from the British trenches, the first wave, and disappeared into the smoke. This cloud of smoke grew denser with the debris of brick and mortar from the ruins of Guillemont. The enemy was now retaliating with a vengeance on the slopes of the ridges to wipe out our supports, and the rattle of musketry or machine-guns could now be heard above the roar of the guns.

The artillery supporting the 17$^{th}$ Brigade carried out their task with great expertise and precision. The creeping barrage worked perfectly; when it was 'lifted' from the German front line, the infantry had only to cover fifty yards in a rush before entering the trenches, methodically bombing the dugouts, and engaging in savage hand-to-hand fighting. Hundreds of Germans surrendered and, with their hands raised above their heads, made their own way across no-man's-land to the British lines.

Wilson records that, within fifteen minutes of zero hour, a stream of

German prisoners were being escorted into captivity, testament to the initial success enjoyed by the 1st RF and the rest of the 17th Brigade. He busied himself with the few casualties, interrogating them as to the progress of the offensive, but they knew little. The gunfire eventually diminished, suggesting the fighting had stopped, and Wilson was desperate for news. He climbed to a high point in the trench system and scanned the horizon, finding the landscape practically 'deserted'. At dusk, he went to Battalion HQ to find out that the day 'had gone well' and they 'had succeeded in taking Guillemont station.'

It was at a cost, however. Wilson observed that 'the best of the men seemed to have gone out. Somewhere up there out of reach, the battalion was slipping away and I could do nothing.' However, this success, the greatest advance of the day, was not matched on the rest of the front. Although the 17th Brigade had achieved their objectives, taking Guillemont Station and 'ZZ' trench (so named due to the zigzag pattern of the earthworks), the 3rd Division on their right flank had failed to secure theirs, leaving the brigade vulnerable to an enfilading fire from that side.

Hitchcock had watched this failure unfold:

**Something had happened on the right. The Highlanders of the 3rd Division were coming back, and so were the attacking regiments of our Brigade [the 73rd]. They were not 'walking wounded' coming out of the smoke – wounded do not come back in lines. 'A failure!' It had been a fine sight seeing the leading battalions advancing into action, but it was a most depressing one seeing them retiring.**

Due to this failure on the extreme right of the division, a planned attack that was to take place the next morning at 5:30am was cancelled. Haig withdrew the shattered 3rd Division and gave the 24th – clearly due to the success of the 17th Brigade – the responsibility of resuming the attack on the 21 August.

Over the following days, the 1st RF consolidated their position before resuming the offensive, as planned, on the 21st, with the 3rd Rifle Brigade on their left and the 8th Queens on their right. At 3:30pm, they attacked 'Hill Street' and 'Brompton Road' in Guillemont. The war diary details that 'after a strenuous fight all opposition was overcome and enemy driven from his trench in front of Hill Street.' Although their strength had been reduced to about seventy men, 'A' Company played their full part in the attack. Their contribution was recorded as follows:

Capt. M.C. Bell took out his two officers and four other ranks as markers, also a Lewis Gun team, some distance in front in no-man's-land, for his Company to form up on, to enable the Company to start parallel to the objective. The whole Company moved out on to the alignment made by the markers, five minutes before 'Zero Time', under cover of our artillery barrage. Very few casualties were sustained in this movement. As soon as attack was launched a party of bombers including HQ bombers made an unsuccessful attack on a strong point between left of 'A' [Company] and right of RBs [Rifle Brigade]. Bombers were about 20 strong, and had heavy casualties amongst them, only three getting back to Company. Remainder of Company reached their objective as previously mentioned. Capt. M.C. Bell and Lt. F.E.B. de Uphaugh were both wounded early in the attack. Capt. Bell remained with his Company until consolidation had commenced, when 2nd Lt. J.H. Jacobs took command. 2nd Lt. L.O. Massey was killed when bringing up party with fresh supply of bombs. Capt. Bell and 2nd Lt. Jacobs displayed great coolness and courage. The bombers made a great and gallant fight against overwhelming odds. The strong point which they attacked having been overlooked by the Heavy Artillery. Sergeant Rye although wounded voluntarily took a message to his Company Commander and returned with the reply, being again wounded, in so doing. All ranks without exception upheld the traditions of the Regiment on this day.

Overall, one officer and fifteen other ranks were killed, and three officers and fifty-five other ranks were wounded during the attack, with four other ranks missing. In total, throughout their time at the Somme, the 1st RF was to suffer 403 casualties made up of 52 confirmed dead, 345 wounded, and 6 missing. As for William, his luck had finally run out; he was one of those wounded (conversely, some might say his luck was in; some would have welcomed a 'Blighty' wound, one that temporarily disabled but was not life-threatening); during the attack on the 21 August, he sustained a gunshot wound that was deemed serious enough for a return to England. The following day, the battalion was relieved for a well-earned rest at a camp in 'Happy Valley'.

Whilst marching towards Carnoy, they came across a 'new army' battalion that was sitting by the roadside en route to the front line. The reputation of the 1st RF went before them. As they passed the volunteers, one of the 'Kitchener' men looked on at the Londoners admiringly and said to his mates, 'Them's the First'. The cockneys, hearing this tribute, straightened their shoulders in pride, growing an inch taller, and covered off in parade-ground order as they marched on.

From this point the trail of William's movements goes cold, until he is passed as fully fit again in January 1917. His Army Form B103 ('Casualty Form – Active Service'), which forms part of his pension records, does not go into detail regarding his evacuation; it simply records that he was wounded in action on the 21 August and sails for England on the 27th. I go back to the records, researching the war diaries of the Assistant Director of Medical Services and the three Field Ambulance units attached to the 24th Division, in an attempt to reconstruct his movements. These papers show exactly how well organised and efficient the Royal Army Medical Corps (RAMC) was in establishing its medical chain of evacuation. The most useful document within these records is a map dated August 1916 showing the lines of evacuation from the front line where William was wounded to the various dressing stations and treatment points en route to the Channel ports. With this, I am able to plot William's progress with certainty up to a Casualty Clearing Station, and beyond that using informed guesswork.

William's evacuation journey started, naturally, with his being removed from the battlefield and taken by stretcher-bearers to the Regimental Aid Post (RAP), which was manned by the 1st RF's Medical Officer, Captain Charles Wilson, and his staff. The MO's responsibilities included checking field dressings, applying splints to fractures, and, most importantly, preventing the patient from going into shock by applying tourniquets and administering morphine. Those patients' foreheads would be marked with a corresponding 'T' or 'M', respectively, for the information of medics further down the line.

RAPs were generally located in as sheltered a spot as could be found within a few yards of the front line, usually in a dugout or a ruined building. Three RAPs, manned by the MOs of the three battalions involved in the assault, are shown on the map: the one occupied by Wilson at Waterlot Farm, adjacent to Guillemont Station and ZZ trench, and two farther south, adjacent to a communication line known as Scottish Lane. The lines of evacuation lead from these RAPs back through Trones Wood to two Advanced Dressing Stations (ADS) manned by the Field Ambulance units that serviced the 24th Division – one on the northern edge of Bernafay Wood, which William would have passed through, and one farther south at Briqueterie.

The ADSs, the next link in the chain, were ideally established around 400 yards behind the RAPs, although in this particular area, for operational reasons, they were around a mile away. The ADS was an intermediate stop allowing a more detailed assessment of the casualty – those casualties marked with an 'M' or a 'T' were given priority, and if the injuries were considered immediately life-threatening, surgery could take place here. The map shows a 'Loading Point – Motor Ambulance' on the western edge of Bernafay Wood (on the present-day route D197 named Grande Rue), which was roughly equidistant between the two ADSs. This was where patients were transferred from horse-drawn ambulances to their motorised counterparts.

Other urgent cases would be sent to the next stage of the chain, the Main Dressing Station (MDS). Non-urgent cases would bypass the MDS and go straight to the Casualty Clearing Station. The MDS also served as the headquarters for the relevant Field Ambulance Unit, in this case the 72nd, ideally sited a mile behind the ADS, although this was not always the case as topography and the size of the plot required dictated its whereabouts, and the MDS would often be a greater distance away. For the 24th Division, it was at Dive Copse, near the town of Sailly-le-Sec, located further westward on the route to the Channel. Again, surgery for serious cases could be carried out here. Bitter experience had shown that abdominal wounds had to be operated on within six hours of the event to ensure survival; thus, such injuries could not wait until arrival at a base hospital.

The next stop on the journey of the wounded soldier was the Casualty Clearing Station (CCS), where evacuated casualties were triaged into: non-serious cases – those who would recover to full fitness with basic treatment and rest; serious cases who were able to travel – continued evacuation to base hospitals; and serious cases in urgent need of immediate surgical intervention, including amputations.

Although originally intended as a sorting centre between the dressing stations and the base hospitals, they had to also develop an urgent care capability, essentially the same as a civilian hospital's Accident and Emergency department, for those in the third category. A CCS was invariably situated near a railhead to enable transportation by ambulance trains to stationary or base hospitals near the Channel ports, such as Rouen, Le Havre, Etaples, and Boulogne.

Thus, William would have returned to England, possibly in a straight reversal of the route he had taken when he had arrived in April 1915, eventually disembarking at Southampton. These train journeys, like all others during the war, were torturously long and could be agonising for casualties with serious wounds as a result of the jolting stops and starts and the bumpy crossing of points exacerbating their pain and discomfort. This was, unfortunately, unavoidable, what with the vast numbers of trains shuttling to and fro between the Channel and the front line and congesting the network.

The whole evacuation system was a model of meticulous planning and organisation with a built-in resilience and flexibility that allowed the chain to expand and contract, to ebb and flow, in line with the fortunes of the front-line troops whom it supported. As advances progressed and new front lines were established, the RAPs would keep pace and follow closely, with the ADSs moving into the vacated RAP sites, the MDSs taking over the ADS sites, and the CCSs occupying the old MDS sites, each moving up a link in the chain as ground was gained. If the infantry had to retreat, the process simply went into reverse, with the previous sites being reoccupied. The key to the whole operation was mobility, and the RAMC had mastered the logistical challenges to an impressive degree.

The system served William well. He was transported back to one of the ports before returning to England on a hospital ship, and then was sent on to a military hospital for further treatment. It was the last time he would serve with his beloved Royal Fusiliers.

For obvious reasons, I was particularly keen to visit Guillemont. In the autumn of 2006, on the second of what had now become our annual visits to the Western Front, we travelled to France and based ourselves in Arras. This gave us the opportunity to explore Vimy Ridge, about seven miles to the north, as well as Guillemont and the Somme battlefields, roughly twenty-two miles to the south.

As with our first trip, I'd been overambitious with the itinerary in the hope of visiting as many of the historic sites as possible. But it was immediately apparent that the areas we aimed to cover deserved much greater attention than could be paid over one long weekend – perhaps reading of Haig's repeatedly over-optimistic plans to stage a breakthrough by which the cavalry would pour through to rout the Germans had infected my thinking. The ground of the Somme region, in particular, requires numerous trips to gain a full understanding of each element of the battle. We would return many times, finding Amiens to be the most convenient base for exploring the battlefield in detail. On a personal level, I was thinking only of walking the ground where William had served in August 1916.

The day came, and we drove there, parking our cars in front of Guillemont Road CWGC Cemetery just outside and to the west of Guillemont village itself. The entrance to the cemetery is a very handsome portico-like structure built of Portland stone. Passing between the impressive stone columns, I make a beeline for the grave of Lieutenant Raymond Asquith of the 3rd Grenadier Guards – son of the then Prime Minister Herbert Henry Asquith – who, aged thirty-seven, took a bullet in his chest on the 15 September 1916 whilst leading his men in an attack and died shortly thereafter.

Having paid my respects, I carry on walking towards the rear wall. The ground gently falls away from the entrance in a northerly direction. As I descend the slope, I scan the surrounding countryside to take in the landmarks mentioned in the war diaries during the fighting that took place here. To the west is Trones Wood, which conceals Bernafay Wood beyond. Aerial photographs show that both woods occupy the same space as they had in 1916. Trones Wood resembles an elongated teardrop, and its neighbour Bernafay Wood is almost rectangular. The deep, rich green of the trees seems to belie the wartime descriptions of stunted, blackened stumps – a powerful reminder of the regenerative power of nature. It takes a leap of imagination to visualise the wasteland that was, not the thriving woodland surrounded by verdant, rolling chalk grassland that is.

Reaching the wall at the northern extent of the graveyard, I surveyed the ground's continued descent into a shallow depression which was known as Caterpillar Valley. Beyond, the ground rises again towards Delville Wood.

From here, looking north, I can orientate myself and pinpoint the exact locations of Waterlot Farm, site of the 1st RF's headquarters, almost directly north, and Guillemont Station and ZZ trench – taken by the 17th Brigade on the 18 August 1916 – a few degrees to the right at around one o'clock, both within a few hundred yards. It takes but a few minutes' walk for me to reach these landmarks over ground that was won at awful cost in a titanic struggle. It brings to mind one of the finest passages of Great War prose ever written, by F. Scott Fitzgerald, one of whose protagonists in his novel *Tender is the Night* visits the battlefields in 1925 and observes:

> See that little stream – we could walk to it in two minutes. It took the British a month to walk to it – a whole empire walking very slowly, dying in front and pushing forward behind. And another empire walked very slowly backward a few inches a day, leaving the dead like a million bloody rugs. No European will ever do that again in this generation...
>
> This western-front business couldn't be done again, not for a long time. The young men think they could do it but they couldn't. They could fight the first Marne again but not this. This took religion and years of plenty and tremendous sureties and the exact relation between the classes.

Here was where William fell wounded, and I lose myself in my thoughts as I try to reconstruct that day, the 21 August 1916, in my mind. The instant the whistles blew and he went over the top, cresting the parapet into a hail of gunfire and launching himself onwards across no-man's-land. It is moments like these – moments of contemplation and wonder; of barely comprehending how the human spirit could have withstood such an onslaught of the senses; of marvelling how these men were able to function and fight and succeed; of imagining what they went through – that bring the war pilgrim and all those who have developed a fascination with the Great War to these battlefields again and again. David Olusoga, the historian and television presenter, once spoke of this fascination in a radio broadcast:

> [T]here are places on the Western Front where if you can't feel the presence of a generation of doomed youth then I think there's

something wrong with you; there's fields where you can see fragments of metal and if you think for a second what that metal did or might have done and you can't connect with the horror of what happened in Flanders a century ago, then maybe history's not for you.

Reluctantly leaving Guillemont – at least on my part – we return to the cars and continue our tour. Later that afternoon, we arrive at our last stop, the colossal Thiepval Memorial, designed by Sir Edwin Lutyens and known as the Memorial to the Missing of the Somme. At 150 feet high, it is the largest British war memorial in the world, and it absolutely dominates the surrounding landscape. Although also based on the form of a triumphal arch, it is a radical departure from the classically influenced design of the Menin Gate. The memorial consists of an ascending set of arches twisting again and again on an alternate east-west and north-south axis. The structure is 'stepped' as it rises, pyramid-like, but takes on a complex and irregular form. All four sides of the building are pierced by three barrel arches of varying sizes that intersect, creating sixteen great piers. These piers bear forty-eight panels inscribed with the names of over 72,000 soldiers with no known grave.

It is a masterpiece, an abstract interpretation of the classical Roman arch with an entirely different character to the Menin Gate. Where the latter embraces you within its vaulted hall, creating a feeling of intimacy, Lutyens's memorial leaves you open to the elements, the huge maw of the main arch funnelling the wind, bringing with it a sense of desolation. Simultaneously sublime and terrible to behold, it is simply awe-inspiring. There is nothing else quite like it in the CWGC's body of work.

I am searching for one particular name. Although my branch of the family had been fortunate in that my grandfather and his brother, my great-uncle James, had survived the war, there were members of the extended Blumsom clan that had not been so lucky. My second cousin, three times removed, Private 26494 Allen Benson Blumsom of the 2nd Battalion Suffolk Regiment, was killed in action at Serre, north of Thiepval, on the 13<sup>th</sup> of November 1916. He was thirty-six. His body was never found; thus, his name appears here. His father, who we have met before in these pages, was my grandfather's first cousin and namesake, William Blumsom, the landlord of the Commercial Tavern in Spitalfields during Jack the Ripper's reign of terror. Prior to the outbreak of the Great War, Cousin Willam had taken over the Napier Arms public house in South Woodford, Essex, where Allen worked for his father. Cousin William died in March 1914, aged seventy-three.

Allen's battalion took part in the final battle of the Somme Front that brought to a close the great British offensive of 1916 that had started so disastrously on the 1 July. Serre lies just north of the Ancre River. In the autumn of 1916, the whole area in and around the Ancre valley was, due to the exceptionally wet weather and the effect of continual shelling, a muddy morass. Bad weather blighted the plans for the attack, alternating between rain and frost in the run-up, and the battle, already having been postponed from the 25 October, came close to being cancelled entirely. Would that it were; my cousin Allen would have lived to fight another day.

The 2<sup>nd</sup> Suffolks spent the frosty night prior to the attack on the 13 November squatting in the trenches trying to grab some sleep in whatever uncomfortable position they found themselves in. Mud would prove to be a contributory factor to the complete failure of the operation. The men were covered in it, and they were cold, wet and miserable. Some had had their rifles rendered unusable by the cloying mess, yet they still dutifully left their trenches at zero hour, only to stall in no-man's-land, stymied by the uncut concertina wire, leaving the troops at the mercy of German shelling and machine guns. Most of their officers had fallen in the first forty-five minutes. The 2<sup>nd</sup> Suffolks suffered an appalling casualty rate of eleven officers and 522 other ranks from a trench strength of 650.

And one of these casualties was Allen. Somewhere out on that battlefield, he lies there still.

The following day's itinerary included a side trip to honour another family member, Rifleman P/793 Robert Charles Blumsom of the 16<sup>th</sup> Battalion Rifle Brigade, who died on the 18 June 1916 whilst serving in the trenches at Festubert, near Neuve Chapelle. We are second cousins twice removed, and I felt a particular connection to him as he is the exact namesake of my younger brother, middle name and all. In his case, we know of his whereabouts. There is a grave where I can pay my respects at Le Touret Military Cemetery on the road from Bethune to Armentières. The cemetery boasts another distinctive piece of architecture. The memorial within was designed by the architect John Reginald Truelove, who also served in the war. It consists of an open courtyard surrounded by a colonnaded loggia, the panels of which bear the names of those with no known graves who fell on this front. Over 900 men lie here in these elegant surroundings.

I had researched the war diary for the 16th RB in an effort to establish the circumstances under which Robert had died. It seems he had been incredibly unlucky, for the month of June had been a quiet one for the battalion, with minimal casualties, as no set-piece offensive was being undertaken – there was only the daily routine of attritional trench warfare, with frequent sniping and shelling, including rifle-grenade attacks. There is no mention of Robert's death in the entry for the 18th, but there is one 'other rank killed' recorded in the entry for the 19th, indicating that he had died late the evening before, after that day's war diary entry had been completed.

Robert was just eighteen years old. I picture the telegram arriving at the home of his parents, Ann and George, in Stoke Newington, and their grief-stricken response to the news of his death.

The three cousins – my grandfather, Allen, and Robert – were direct descendants of Benjamin Blumsom, the Bethnal Green silk weaver whose fortunes had plummeted after the end of the Napoleonic Wars, and his wife Mary Ann Dubock. These reflections on my kinsmen bring me back to William's story and where we left him, convalescing in a war hospital in England. The army hadn't finished with him yet. This wasn't to be the end of his war; he had signed up for the duration, and once his recovery was complete, he was available to be redeployed within the ruthlessly remorseless war machine.

But he would not be returning to his fellow cockneys with the 1st RF. The powers that be had different plans. It is highly likely that he had never heard of his next posting, or had he heard of it, that he didn't know exactly where it was.

He was bound for Salonika.

# CHAPTER TWELVE
## SALONIKA

*I have watched a thousand days*
*Push out and crawl into night*
*Slowly as tortoises*
*Now I, too, follow these.*
*It is fever, and not the fight –*
*Time, not battle – that slays.*

RUDYARD KIPLING, Salonikan Grave, *Epitaphs of the War*

Leaning on the portside handrail, William was transfixed by the snow-capped peak of Mount Olympus, the seat of the gods, as the troopship steamed purposefully from the Aegean Sea into the Gulf of Thérmai. As they neared their destination, he moved further along the deck towards the bow of the vessel, catching his first sight of Salonika. From this viewpoint, it looked magical: the blinding whiteness of the tall, slender minarets from where the faithful were called to prayer; the sun glinting on the domes of the Byzantine churches; the sprawl of red-roofed, whitewashed, and wooden-shuttered houses rising into the surrounding hills; and the medieval White Tower with its ancient stone battlements. The architectural whole reflected the mix of Muslim, Jewish, and Orthodox Christian cultures that make up this city. This place, ruled in succession by Rome, Byzantium, and the Ottoman Empire, was, just as much as Constantinople, where east and west collided.

Reaching the safety of the harbour, the ship's crew and the soldiers alike could relax. The Mediterranean and Aegean seas were constantly being patrolled by German submarines. The troopships had been escorted by destroyers as they ran the gauntlet of these underwater predators; nevertheless, William still had to take his turn at guard duty on deck, scanning the horizon for an enemy periscope. If one were spotted, his instructions were to shoot out the angled mirror contained within, thereby incapacitating it. However, even he, a first-class marksman, would have found this a very tall order.

They arrived in Salonika on the 7 February 1917, after having set sail from Devonport on the 24 January. As they disembarked and set off through the streets, the aesthetic appeal of the city as viewed from the sea soon evaporated as they marched along the dirty and foul-smelling, straw-covered, cobbled roads. The reception from the local inhabitants was a complete contrast to that which William had experienced in Rouen nearly two years earlier. There was no cheering or flag-waving here; instead, there was a sullen resentment, a passive hostility that reflected the ambiguous neutrality of the Greek authorities, coupled with exploitative attempts by local traders to empty the soldiers' pockets and purses. As they marched past, although conscious of the antagonism palpable in the air, would the Tommies have suspected that amongst the onlookers there were spies, counting troop numbers and monitoring their movements? The nectar and ambrosia enjoyed by the gods on Olympus were clearly not on offer here.

After a five-mile march, they arrived at the 10th Division base depot on the outskirts of Salonika. The 10th (Irish) Division was one of those raised by Kitchener as a 'new army' establishment. It was composed of twelve 'service' battalions of existing Irish regiments. Battle-hardened in Gallipoli and organised into the 29th, 30th and 31st Brigades, they had served in Greece since October 1915 after having been withdrawn from the failed Dardanelles campaign. William was posted to the 30th Brigade, which was composed of the 6th and 7th Battalions, the Royal Dublin Fusiliers (RDF), the 1st Battalion, Royal Irish Regiment and the 6th Battalion, the Royal Munster Fusiliers.

The 10th Division had been the first British force to arrive in Salonika and had endured much hardship and privation in the sixteen months before William's arrival. There were sound strategic and geopolitical reasons why British troops were required there. Just fifty miles north of the port, the borderlands of Greece, Serbia, and Bulgaria conjoined within the ancient region of Macedonia to form a theatre of war where the Serbian allies of the Triple Entente were under threat from the Bulgarians, who had belatedly entered the war on the side of the Central Powers.

Complicating matters was Greece's conflicted neutrality; King Constantine, married to the Kaiser's sister, sympathised with Germany, whereas the Prime Minister Eleuthérios Venizélos favoured the Allies. Venizélos duly gave the British and French forces permission to land at the harbour and move up-country to support the Serbian army; his blessing was essential, as Salonika was the only feasible option for the Allies to land in the Balkans due to the dominance of the Adriatic by the Austro-Hungarian navy.

The Serbs were close to the point of collapse, having successfully fought off two efforts by the combined Austrian and Magyar forces to invade their land. They were reeling from an outbreak of typhoid fever and desperately needed support to fend off a third attempt by Austria-Hungary, who were now bolstered by German troops and, more recently, the Bulgarian army. Serbia appealed for military assistance in the form of 150,000 troops. As allies of the Triple Entente, their cry for help could not be ignored. The British and French were fully aware that the depleted Serbs would be unable to withstand this onslaught alone, so they both committed substantial numbers of troops to the campaign, although they had different views as to exactly what role they would perform.

Initially, the British had attempted to keep Bulgaria out of the war by promising them territory that would be won from Turkey. With that likelihood receding following the failure of the Gallipoli campaign, Bulgaria had considered their interests best served by entering into an alliance with Germany, Austria-Hungary and Turkey.

Britain now hoped that this combined show of strength with the French – the mere presence of this large Allied force – would be enough to dissuade the Bulgarians from invading Serbia. France was far more bullish; they had strong political and commercial ties with Serbia and wanted to take the fight to the Bulgarians, proactively supporting the Serbs in an offensive capacity. Straightaway, there existed a tension between the two allies. It's fair to say that there was no great enthusiasm on the part of His Majesty's Government or the British high command in this venture, some of whom considered Salonika to be very much a sideshow and a distraction from the main effort on the Western Front.

The Allies landed on the 5 October 1915 but failed in their initial objective. The Central Powers attacked Serbia the following day whilst the British and French were still busy establishing base depots and reception camps on the outskirts of Salonika, miles away from the action. It was all too little, too late: Serbia would ultimately fall, with what was left of their army retreating to the Greek island of Corfu to lick its wounds. Having initially moved north and crossed into Serbia, the French were forced to retreat southwards back towards Greece as the Bulgarians chased the Serbs westward, whilst the British 10th Division held the line further south near the border, northwest of Doiran, having relieved the French there on the 31 October.

Doiran was situated in the mountainous borderlands, the inhospitable climate of which came as a great shock to the men of the Irish regiments, many of whom were totally ill-equipped, through no fault of their own, to deal with the sub-zero temperatures accompanied by snowfall and blizzards experienced at that height above sea level. It was a failing of logistics and the supply chain, for they were still wearing their lightweight, hot-weather-issue khaki from the Dardanelles campaign, and although they had been provided with overcoats and balaclavas, the men were reporting sick with exposure and frostbite at an alarming rate. In addition, many were suffering the after-effects of dysentery and jaundice from their time at Gallipoli.

This put a great strain on the RAMC; the field ambulance units were almost overwhelmed with casualties. Medical staff described having to thaw out the patients as they arrived, dispensing hot cocoa and Oxo drinks liberally. The soldiers were presenting with the collars of their uniforms frozen solid to their necks.

In late November and early December 1915, twenty-three officers and 1,663 men from the Division were hospitalised in Salonika. Although they were not suffering battlefield casualties to the same extent as those in other theatres of war, they endured great hardship nonetheless.

Battlefield casualties were to come. On the 7 December 1915, the Bulgarians launched an attack against the 30th Brigade. A week previously, a request for reinforcements had been telegraphed by the Officer Commanding the Brigade who had feared such an attack on his depleted force. However, the decision to withdraw from Serbia across the Greek border had already been taken by the high command, and, therefore, any potential support was held at Salonika, far to the south, and all non-essential kit and stores had already been transported back to the base depots there.

When it dawned upon the General Officer Commanding (GOC) of the British Salonika Force (BSF) that the situation was critical, he belatedly sent reinforcements, to no avail. After this initial action and over the ensuing days, both the British and the French carried out orderly retreats from Serbia, reaching Greek soil on the 12 December. The British suffered casualties of 1,209 over this period, maybe not costly by Western Front standards but still significant enough to require time to consolidate and rebuild.

British politicians and the military high command were firmly of the opinion that the Salonika expedition should be abandoned, and they made representations to that effect at a series of conferences in France. However, they were outnumbered; the French, supported by Italy, Russia, and Serbia, argued that any withdrawal of Allied troops from Salonika would compromise the neutrality of Greece, possibly convincing them to throw in their lot with the Central Powers. In addition, it would show a lack of will and intent with regard to the Balkans as a whole, negatively affecting ongoing diplomatic moves to recruit Rumania to the Allied side. The British were forced to soften their stance. They agreed to remain, but only on condition that they would not be involved in any offensive capacity and would adopt a defensive posture to protect Salonika from any potential Bulgarian attack. The option of a complete withdrawal was left on the table. The defensive line chosen ran from the Gulf of Orfano in the east along a more or less straight line, linking the natural physical barriers of Lake Beshik and Lake Langanza, before it bulged in a north-westerly direction, creating a buffer zone surrounding the city of Salonika itself, then westwards to the east bank of the Vardar River, where the line turned left and dropped due south adjacent to the river, terminating at the Gulf of Thérmai. On a map, the shape of the front looked like a question mark that had fallen leftwards to a horizontal position. It was a strong and eminently defendable position, utilising the terrain to best advantage, with the bodies of water patrolled by naval gunboats and the higher ground giving the British an excellent view above the plains over which the enemy would have to advance at the mercy of artillery and machine gun fire.

Although the topography gave the advantage to the defending force, the problem facing the Allies was the road network – or, rather, the lack of one. Transporting large amounts of matériel and men to sites along what were fundamentally donkey tracks was a major logistical problem. Before construction of the substantial defensive earthworks could begin, these tracks had to be widened and suitably shaped and surfaced in order to bear the heavy loads that they would be required to support.

Work began in mid-December to construct the complex of front line and communication trenches, observation posts, machine gun nests, Regimental Aid Posts, and Battalion Headquarters for the whole length of the front. This was carried out in extremely variable weather – torrential rain, mist, biting wind, freezing snow, and oppressive heat, sometimes all together within the space of a few days; all these conditions were experienced during the winter, and the troops suffered accordingly. The work was harsh and uncompromising. The ground in the mountainous sectors in particular required hard labour with picks and shovels and dangerous blasting with explosives to excavate trenches into the solid rock that lay below a thin layer of soil. The whole front was heavily wired; hence, the Tommies christened it the 'Birdcage'. It was an entirely apt nickname for the fieldworks, as, although they had constructed an impressive fortified position, they had also set a physical limit on their military ambitions, effectively 'caging' themselves in the process. The Germans referred to it sarcastically as 'the greatest internment camp in the world'.

By April 1916, the 'Birdcage' was complete, and all was quiet on the Salonikan front. This state of affairs was not to the liking of the French high command; they were impatient for a more aggressive approach by advancing upon the Serbian border and taking on the Bulgarians and, more importantly, their German allies.

On their part, the Germans shared their frustration, and for more or less the same reasons. Both France and Germany wanted to tie down each other's armies in Macedonia, thereby leaving them unable to redeploy to the Western Front. But they were tethered by their respective allies. They shared the same idea, expecting the British and the Bulgarians, respectively, to take the lead in this theatre of war, thus freeing up their own men for the looming offensive at Verdun.

To this end, the French asked for more British troops – two whole divisions – to be despatched to the Balkans. The British already outnumbered the French in this alliance. At the turn of the year, the British deployment comprised five divisions – the 10th, 22nd, 26th, 27th and 28th – numbering 90,000 men compared to the three divisions of 60,000 men from France. Thus, the British took the leading role in terms of manpower, although they were nominally subordinate to the French Commander in Chief, General Maurice Sarrail. But the British would not countenance anything other than a defensive role and were determined that there would be no more drain on manpower there so that they could prioritise France and Belgium. The Bulgarians, likewise, had no appetite to carry the fight to the Allies; they were quite content with their success in Serbia.

Questions were asked in the seats of power on both sides of the Channel as to what was actually being achieved in Salonika by this largely immobile force. The answer was very little, other than a boom in the local economy fuelled by the enrichment of the local traders, suppliers, shopkeepers, and café and restaurant owners. The matter was debated by the French parliament in June 1916. The government won by a clear majority, endorsing the current strategy, but this did not quiet its critics. Georges Clemenceau, the future prime minister and a powerful and influential voice in French political affairs, referred witheringly to the troops as 'the Gardeners of Salonika'.

The Allies had previously met at a war conference in Chantilly in March 1916, where, as part of the overall strategy, it was agreed that summer offensives should be launched simultaneously on all fronts – in France/Belgium, Russia, and Italy, as well as actively engaging on the Balkan front – in an effort to stretch the Central Powers' forces and produce a decisive breakthrough. As a result, the French had wasted no time in moving their troops up towards the Serbian border and had already proved victorious in a skirmish with German troops at the village of Machukovo.

After four months of inaction for the BSF, a detachment from the Sherwood Rangers engaged with German cavalry southeast of Lake Doiran. This was the first British contact with the enemy since the withdrawal in December 1915. The momentum was now with General Sarrail, and the BSF were given approval by the British government to conduct limited operations in support of their allies, but only up to, and not beyond, the border between Greece and Serbia. Emboldened, Sarrail presented the man on the spot, Lieutenant-General George Milne, with an ultimatum. He was going to launch an offensive into Serbia in the summer of 1916 regardless of the BSF's involvement; Milne was either with him or agin him.

This ultimatum put Milne, the newly appointed commander of the BSF, in an unenviable position. Damned if he did and damned if he didn't, he would either be drawn into the offensive across the border contrary to his orders or be accused of backsliding by letting down an ally; he was entering a political and diplomatic minefield. Milne very cleverly came up with an alternative solution. He requested a sector of his own in which to operate, thus marshalling all of his forces on one continuous section of front. Thereby he would avoid the logistics and supply difficulties that would be caused by the alternative: a fractured deployment of the BSF serving in separate locations. Sarrail agreed, grasping the rationale behind the suggestion.

Although, obviously, Milne was tied to the French strategically, he had brilliantly manoeuvred himself into a semi-autonomous position whereby the BSF would not be in lockstep with them tactically. The British were given the easternmost part of the line, northwards from the mouth of the Struma River, where it flowed into the Gulf of Orfano, up the Struma Valley, and encompassing the vital supply route of the Serres Road. The advantages for Sarrail were twofold: Milne would maintain a level of operational activity that would keep the Bulgarians and Germans occupied, thereby preventing the reinforcement of enemy forces on the Western Front where the French were planning an offensive, with the corresponding bonus that the BSF's presence would relieve the *poilus* of any involvement in the Struma Valley and further strengthen Sarrail's forces for his planned attack.

The British relieved more Frenchmen in August when they took over the line westward up to the Vardar River, including Lake Doiran, and were now responsible for a continuous front of ninety miles. The two designated divisions for the extension of the line, the 22nd and the 26th, had an exhausting march northwards from the Birdcage ahead of them. Despite moving only in the evening or at night due to the heat of the Salonikan summer, the problem of keeping the men hydrated was a persistent one. Mule trains carrying water in leather bags struggled to keep up with demand.

Meanwhile, more troops were becoming available for Sarrail's grand plan. The reconstituted Serbian army of 120,000 men had disembarked in Salonika in readiness; a 5,000-strong brigade of Russians arrived at the end of July, and a division of Italians on the 11 August, followed a week later by a smaller contingent of Albanian partisans. Sarrail now commanded a multinational force of 320,000. And at last, Rumania declared war on Austria-Hungary on the 28 August, putting an army of 400,000 into the field at the Danube on the northern border of Bulgaria.

The offensive began on the 12 September, with the Serbian army at the forefront. They were fighting to reclaim their homeland and needed no greater incentive to motivate them in this brutal encounter. They fought in an uncompromising landscape where the exposed positions of both attackers and defenders on the mountain passes resulted in heavy casualties. It lasted three months and resulted in the recapturing of Monastir, an Allied victory, albeit a costly one, and hugely symbolic to the Serbs, for they had re-established a foothold on their own soil. Unfortunately, the Allies were unable to build on this. The Germans and Bulgarians were able to consolidate just north of the town, and they harassed the inhabitants constantly with well-aimed shellfire. The line stabilised here, with no significant progress being made until September 1918, when the decisive breakthrough was finally achieved that forced the Bulgarians to surrender.

The tension between King Constantine and Venizélos came to a head in late 1916 when relations between them completely broke down. What took place has been described as a revolution. The Greek political class fractured into two camps, the 'royalists' and the 'revolutionaries'. The conflicting allegiances of the king and the prime minister had been exacerbated by the invasion of neutral Greece by Bulgarian forces on the 17 August, when they had crossed into eastern Macedonia up to the Struma River. The ease with which this had been achieved and the positive response of Constantine's circle to this development seemed to confirm the fears of the revolutionaries that the Greek army's senior command had known of, and approved, the invasion.

Greek patriots and liberals rallied to Venizélos, and he removed himself from Athens, the seat of the government, eventually landing in Salonika on the 9 October and proclaiming the formation of an alternative 'provisional government' and a 'National Army' that would drive their old enemy, the Bulgarians, from Greece. The nucleus of the new force was made up of defectors from the king's army led by Colonel

Zymbrakakis, a hero of the Balkan Wars of 1912–13, and supplemented by a new rush of volunteers. They were able to field three battalions by mid-November that fought alongside the British on the Struma front. Greece was not to be united again until the 27 June 1917, after Constantine had abdicated in favour of his son Alexander, who received Venizélos as the acknowledged Prime Minister of all Greece and formally declared for the Allies.

The BSF had carried out a number of smaller-scale operations in support of Sarrail throughout late 1916, including during October and November when they crossed the Struma River in the east and successfully drove out the Bulgarians from a number of villages and other redoubts, extending the front line up to the Salonika-Constantinople railway. They had acquitted themselves well, with little recognition for their efforts, but by early December, these operations had ceased. This was to be the last significant action fought within this sector until late 1917.

When William arrived here in March 1917, he was initially posted to an entrenching battalion nominally attached to the 7th Battalion Royal Dublin Fusiliers. Entrenching battalions were formed to provide labour to carry out essential repair work, digging and maintaining trenches, and constructing other earthworks and road building. They had a high turnover of men as they were also used as a pool of troops to replenish and bring frontline battalions up to strength. William spent only two months at this kind of work before he was transferred to the 6th Battalion Royal Dublin Fusiliers on the 26 May. He arrived with a draft of sixty-two other ranks, bringing the fighting strength of the battalion up to thirty officers and 909 men, just as the 6th RDF was completing a stint in the Prosenik-to-Topolova outpost line adjacent to the railway. They were relieved by their sister battalion, the 7th RDF, and retired to Cuculuk behind the lines for rest and training.

The rest of William's time in the Balkans was relatively quiet, and apart from a few minor skirmishes with the Bulgarians, his main enemy was the mosquito. The British were deployed at the Struma River for most of the Salonika campaign, the low-lying terrain a complete contrast to the scree-laden mountain ranges that lay to the north, and the swamps and marshland that surrounded it were ideal breeding grounds for the malaria-carrying insect. Casualties stricken with malaria were ten times those from the battlefield; 162,517 men fell victim, many of them dying, and 34,762 were so badly afflicted that they were invalided home to a future of chronic and recurrent disease. In the autumn of 1917, twenty per cent of the BSF were hospitalised as a result of this condition.

Countermeasures undertaken included cutting down vast swathes of bush and undergrowth within 200 yards of their camps, the men carrying out the work dressed only in shorts and Wellington boots as they cut down everything in their path using billhooks and saws. They were issued with extra cigarettes for this work, the smoking of which helped mask the repulsive smell emanating from the black tortoises disturbed in the mud by all this activity. These creatures were collected in sandbags and released well away from the line, but more dangerous than a foul smell were the poisonous snakes that were also rudely interrupted, and the troops exercised great caution when cutting down the scrub that was their habitat. Other wildlife encountered included wolves, jackals, foxes, and the occasional wild boar that largely kept their distance.

Further measures included draining swamps and filling in pools, making the environment as inhospitable as possible for mosquitoes. The shirtless men were an inviting target for the mosquitoes, as well as horseflies, wasps, and hornets, and they were bitten and stung all over. The main preventative and treatment for malaria was quinine, the efficacy of which was questionable. It was also very unpopular with the men, who, although under orders to take a daily dose, would go to great pains to avoid it because the effects of taking it were considered almost as bad as the disease itself. The other main defence against the disease was the mosquito net, but, again, chronic supply problems led to late delivery of these essentials, and the season was well-advanced by the time they finally arrived.

In May 1917, the high incidence of the disease caused the GOC to order the withdrawal of the division from the low ground of the Struma Valley to a distance of four miles to the right bank of the river, giving up the gains won in late 1916. In all probability, this move saved William from contracting the disease. For their part, the Bulgarians mirrored the actions of the British, also withdrawing by a similar distance and thereby creating a nine-mile-wide no-man's-land between the opposing forces. It was an admission by both that the mosquito reigned supreme on this front.

As they retreated, the 6th RDF embarked on a course of demolition work, removing the front-line defences and filling in old Bulgarian trenches throughout May and June. On the 15 June, the 6th RDF war diary records that the 'Bulgars discovered our evacuation to right bank of Struma and pushed small posts forward occupying Hantazar previously held by 28th Division.' There followed a period of probing by the Bulgarian forces, with small patrols intermittently occupying villages previously held by the British. A game of cat and mouse ensued, whereby the 6th RDF, whilst holding the bridgeheads on the river, would send out detachments on raiding expeditions, engaging with and driving off these Bulgarian patrols. This state of affairs continued until the 4 July, when the 6th RDF was relieved by the 7th RDF and marched to a position known as Hill 439 on the Lahana and Turica Road for rest and training.

Although the incidence of malaria had been lessened by the withdrawal, the battalion was still depleted by the disease; on the 17 July, the war diary lists 102 other ranks sick with it. On that same evening, the 6th RDF was treated to a musical performance by the 10th Division band and pipers of the 5th Royal Irish Regiment (Pioneers), which lasted from 6:30 to 7:45pm.

Whilst they were enjoying this time out of the line, mostly engaged in physical training courses and schools of instruction in musketry, bombing, and gas attacks, a conference was taking place in Paris on the 25 and 26 July. In it, Lloyd George informed the Allies that the British intended to transfer a division from Salonika to the Egyptian Expeditionary Force (EEF) in Palestine. To say that this was poorly received by the other nations is an understatement; the French, Serbians, Greeks, Russians, Rumanians, and Italians were unanimous in their opposition to any weakening of the British forces in the Balkans. Nothing was resolved, and the Allies reconvened in London soon after, where a compromise of sorts was reached – the British refusing to reverse their decision but undertaking not to withdraw any further troops without consultation and only in exceptional circumstances – which was begrudgingly accepted.

Oblivious to these high-level discussions and unaware that the 10th was the division selected for the Middle East – possibly due to the fact that they were the longest serving on the Macedonian front – the 6th RDF went back into the line at Turica on the 1 August. They were to spend the best part of three weeks in the line, improving defences and observing enemy movements.

There were two events of note during this period. On the 9 August, William received a promotion to lance corporal (unpaid). On the 14th, an enemy patrol was espied approaching Cuculuk, one of the villages vacated by the BSF in the general withdrawal. Unaware that they were under surveillance, the Bulgarians entered the village into an ambush. However, the trap was compromised by over-enthusiastic Tommies breaking cover prematurely, and the Bulgarians escaped and fled north towards Kumli. The 6th RDF opened fire on them from a distance of 200 yards, killing two, wounding many, and taking one prisoner.

The 6th RDF was relieved in the line on the 19 August, returning to Hill 439, where they learned of their impending move to Egypt. The following day, they began their march to Lahana, where on the 24th they boarded a convoy of motor lorries and travelled to Uchantar camp on the outskirts of Salonika to prepare for embarkation.

The men of the 10th Division were departing Salonika with little regret. They were leaving behind not only comrades who had died and were wounded in action but also those who had suffered a range of illnesses and disease, from frostbite and exposure to dysentery, enteritis, and malaria – the non-battlefield casualties outnumbered those of the battlefield by a ratio of around twenty to one. In Kipling's words, it was 'fever, and not the fight … that slays'. On the 9 September, the battalion marched from Uchantar to English Quay, where they embarked on HMT *Aragon*; they were bound for the Holy Land.

CHAPTER THIRTEEN

# EGYPT AND PALESTINE

*On the rock-strewn hills I heard*
*The anger of guns that shook*
*Echoes along the glen.*
*In my heart was the song of a bird,*
*And the sorrowless tale of the brook,*
*And scorn for the deeds of men.*

SIEGFRIED SASSOON, *In Palestine* (January 1918)

It would have been a stately, three-day trip southwards on HMT *Aragon*, one of the Royal Mail's first-class liners turned troopship, negotiating the Greek archipelago en route to Egypt, had it not been for the ever-present threat of a torpedo attack. The trip included a stopover at Skyros to evade patrolling German U-boats.

One of William's fellow passengers was Captain Noel Drury, who recently returned from a year spent recovering and convalescing in Malta and Ireland after contracting malaria in July 1916. In May 1917, in preparation for his return to full duties, Drury had been stationed at Victoria Barracks, Cork. After a month there, he began badgering the authorities to send him back to Macedonia and his beloved 6th Battalion RDF. His wish was granted, but he'd not long made landfall in Salonika before he suffered a relapse and was promptly readmitted to hospital. He somehow wangled a discharge, probably not having fully recovered, and rejoined the battalion shortly before embarkation on the 9 September.

The *Aragon* arrived at Alexandria at 1745 hours on the 11 September 1917. As soon as the ship had berthed, it was surrounded by scores of small boats manned by local traders selling fresh fruit to the soldiers. The transactions were carried out by lowering bags of money to the vendors, who would replace the cash with bananas, dates, melons, and tomatoes for the soldiers to haul up. Local street urchins rushed to the dockside, and the troops amused themselves by throwing coins into the water for the boys to expertly dive after and intercept before they reached the bottom. The battalion disembarked and boarded trains that took them to the tented city of Moascar army camp at Ismailia, on the west bank of the Suez Canal. After all the hardships – the diseases and illnesses, the lack of decent food and kit, and the extremes of weather experienced in Salonika – the time at Ismailia was a very welcome interlude for the troops. It was also extremely hot in Egypt, but it was a dry heat, not the uncomfortable humid heat of Macedonia, and they had plenty of opportunities to swim in the lakes that formed part of the canal system, but not in the canal itself. Drury relates that:

> **We have had to read out to the men on parade a warning on no account to bathe or even wash in the fresh water canals, as they will get a disease known as Bilharziosis, or, as the troops call it 'Bill Harris'. It seems to be a bug which burrows through the skin and lays an egg which gets as big as a football. If you get more than six of these inside you, it is probably fatal!**

New kit was issued, kit that wasn't available in Macedonia, and they were far better equipped as part of the EEF than they were during their time in the BSF. Although the days were spent training, on route marches, undergoing inspections, and ceremonial parades, a wet canteen was provided for the men when the day's duties were done. Evening passes were available to visit the city of Ismailia itself, which had been founded in 1863 to house the engineers, architects, and builders that constructed the Suez Canal (which opened in 1869).

Laid out in a grid street system of thoroughfares running at right angles to each other, Ismailia was a picturesque development of houses built in a European style and set amongst wide avenues and squares. For the men of the 6th RDF, this was a Garden of Eden. They walked through the many parks and orchards – every green space populated with different species of palm and the spectacularly vivid scarlet blossoms of the flame tree, past houses with walls painted in alternating pink and white bands, like layer cake, and pierced by windows with intricate blue and green latticework, the dwellings punctuated by mosques and minarets – before browsing in the bazaars and buying embroidered souvenirs, carvings, leather goods, and marquetry for sweethearts and loved ones at home. William was right at home here as he haggled for the lowest prices – for what was a bazaar but an exotic version of the Bethnal Green Road market in the East End? The perfect finish to the day was a slap-up meal of steak and eggs or fresh fish for a few *piastres*.

It couldn't last, though. Towards the end of their stay at Ismailia, the 6th RDF, along with the rest of the 30th Brigade, was inspected by the Commander-in-Chief of the EEF, General Edmund Allenby, on the 20 September. Allenby was clearly impressed; on the 26th, he wrote to the Chief of the Imperial General Staff, Sir William Robertson, with his opinion of the troops: 'The 10th Division has landed, with the exception of one battalion and some details. I have inspected two brigades, and I like the look of them.'

General Allenby had taken command of the EEF on the 27 June 1917 following the failure of his predecessor, General Sir Archibald Murray, to defeat the Turks in the first two battles of Gaza. Prime Minister David Lloyd George and his Cabinet had wanted to replace Murray with someone who would show 'more resolute leadership'. Their first choice was General Jan Smuts, the formidable ex-Boer commander turned loyal servant to the British Empire and subsequently a very successful commander-in-chief of the British forces in East Africa earlier in the war. When Smuts declined the appointment, the post was offered to Allenby on Robertson's recommendation, with the expectation that Allenby would succeed where Murray had failed. In Lloyd George's memoirs, he recounts his instructions to Allenby:

**I told him in the presence of Sir William Robertson that he was to ask us for such reinforcements and supplies as he found necessary,**

and we would do our best to provide them. 'If you do not ask it will be your fault. If you do ask and do not get what you need it will be ours.' I said the Cabinet expected 'Jerusalem before Christmas'.

This put Allenby under intense pressure. Failure to take Jerusalem within this time frame would put him in a bad light and possibly blight the rest of his career, if not end it entirely. Very few British generals emerged from the Great War with their reputations enhanced, but it can be said that Allenby fared better than most, if not all, of them. Throughout his time on the Western Front earlier in the war, the reviews were mixed. During the retreat from Mons in 1914, he was criticised for his perceived mismanagement of the cavalry, but he earned some credit for his command in the subsequent First Battle of Ypres. He showed himself to be a competent, albeit unspectacular, leader during the Second Battle of Ypres in 1915 but was, again felt, to have fallen short in the Battle of Arras in April 1917, as it became yet another exercise in indecisive attrition resulting in huge casualty lists for no great strategic advantage.

But even where there were perceived failures, there existed certain redeeming features. At Arras, the initial advance on the first day had reached nearly four miles – an unimaginable gain within the general context of the Western Front at that stage of the war. Allenby had had tunnels excavated towards the enemy's front line from the existing underground complex of sewers, chambers, and natural caves under Arras itself. He amassed his troops in this subterranean network, and they took the Germans completely by surprise when they emerged from jumping-off points well into no-man's-land, giving them no time to react. Aided by a creeping barrage, the British overran the German positions. Allenby's reputation would have been assured had he been able to capitalise on his initial breakthrough, but it was not to be. Thus, the jury was still out when he arrived in Egypt for his latest challenge. He had everything to prove.

Allenby had an immediate effect on morale when he took command of the EEF. Both officers and men noticed the difference between Allenby's vigorous approach and Murray's lacklustre leadership, and they became energised. He moved the HQ of the EEF – previously situated well behind the lines in Cairo and before that, in Ismailia – much nearer to the front and was instantly visible and accessible to the troops, dropping in on them in their trenches and outposts. Bodily fit and 6ft 2in. tall, Allenby cut an impressive figure; he had a real physical presence. The other ranks could relate to him and respect him as a leader of men.

He also had some character defects, however. He was nicknamed 'the Bull' due to his explosive temper, and he didn't suffer fools gladly. His outbursts were legendary, so much so that a code was devised for him. 'BBL' ('Bloody Bull's Loose') was transmitted by semaphore to forewarn others when he was on the rampage. But, on the flip side, he was quick to move on and was always willing to change his mind on any given plan or tactic if his junior officers could convince him otherwise. He was able – and not too arrogant – to listen.

The other ranks always felt he had their best interests at heart. An anecdote that did the rounds illustrates this. When a consignment of beer was being delivered behind the lines to the general staff at El Kantara base depot, and Allenby became aware of it, he promptly ordered it to be redirected to the troops at the front. There was also a perception that he was not so profligate – as other leaders were seen to be – with the lives of those under his command in battle.

To take Jerusalem, the British would have to breach the Turkish defences that ran from Gaza on the coast to Beersheba inland to the east. This front line, unlike the continuous trench system on the Western Front that ran from the English Channel to the Swiss border, had an open flank at the eastern end, beyond which was a wilderness of rocks and sandy desert.

Having considered the previous failures of Murray's two attempts to take Gaza, Allenby decided to implement an existing alternative plan to attack the less-heavily defended settlement of Beersheba at the open end of the Turkish line, following which the British forces would outflank and 'roll up' the Turks westwards, finally seizing Gaza. To take the enemy by surprise, Allenby devised a feint attack on Gaza, including a combined bombardment from field artillery and naval guns anchored off the coast, whilst covertly concentrating his forces on Beersheba thirty miles away. To this end, an intelligence officer on horseback rode out towards the Turkish lines equipped with a dummy staff officer's notebook containing detailed plans for an attack on Gaza. The officer eventually found and managed to entice an enemy patrol to give chase, and during the pursuit he halted, dismounted, and took a shot at them before hurriedly remounting and dropping his intentionally blood-stained haversack before making his escape, giving the impression that he'd been wounded. It was a perfect example of Allenby's willingness to use deception and subterfuge in warfare.

Another strand of Allenby's open-minded approach was his readiness to embrace the opportunity that the Arab Revolt of 1916-1918 gave him to exploit the unconventional guerrilla tactics of the Hashemite Arab irregulars fighting against their Muslim brethren of the Ottoman Empire under the direction of Captain T.E. Lawrence – the fabled Lawrence of Arabia – and Emir Feisal. The Arab tribesmen were able to create mayhem within the Arabian interior beyond the open flank of the Gaza-Beersheba line, disrupting the Turkish supply and communication lines by demolishing bridges and sections of track of the Damascus to Medina railway, ambushing trains, killing Turks, and looting. Their contribution was crucial; by acting as a highly effective guerrilla force they occupied the attention of thousands of Ottoman troops who could otherwise have been deployed at the Gaza-Beersheba front or against the vulnerable open flank of the British as they advanced northwards.

On the 24 September, the 6th RDF's time at Ismailia came to an end. They set off on a two-day march eastwards to El Kantara, an advanced base depot, from where, on the 28th, they boarded trains for Rafah on the eastern border of Egypt with Sinai, arriving the following morning at 0700 hours. Here they pitched their tents and remained for most of the month of October, engaging in intensive training, including night exercises, and acclimatising to marching on soft desert sand, swiftly learning that it was impossible to keep in step. Whilst there, William was promoted to 'paid' Lance Corporal on the 7 October, having proved himself worthy of the modest rise in pay accruing.

The prearranged bombardment directed at Gaza began on the 27 October, signalling the start of the offensive. William, along with the rest of the 10th Division, left Rafah on the following day, advancing generally northeast and parallel with the coast to Shellal as part of a 40,000-strong force of infantry, artillery, and cavalry. The troops moved into the line at Wadi Ghuzzi in preparation for the first phase of what was to become the Third Battle of Gaza.

As the 6th RDF took up position with the rest of the 30th Brigade, forming the reserve for the main offensive, Lawrence and his band of Arab guerrillas were advancing on the right flank of, but not in touch with, Allenby's force, as they were well to the east of the EEF in the desert. Their mission was to go deep into enemy territory, bypass the Turkish left wing at Beersheba, and head northwards to demolish one or more of the railway bridges that crossed the Yarmuk River on a section of line that ran from the vicinity of Deraa (or Der'a) and extended to the southern point of the Sea of Galilee, an inland body of water also known as Lake Tiberias. This expedition, approved by Allenby, was conceived by Lawrence, who had calculated that carrying out the operation to coincide with the main offensive would fatally affect the enemy's ability to fight on for any length of time; with their vital artery severed, they would be completely cut off, with no prospect of reinforcement or resupply, forcing either a full retreat or surrender.

On the 6 November, the second phase of the Third Battle of Gaza commenced. This was a completely different war to the static one of attrition fought on the Western Front, no doubt reminding William of the war of movement that he had fought in South Africa. The cavalry, unlike in Belgium and France, played a full part by carrying out their traditional function, complementing the roles of the infantry and artillery. The 6th RDF was in support to the main attack. From his position,

Captain Drury was able to find some high ground from which he could watch proceedings:

> It was the most magnificent sight and I will never bother to look at a military review again.… I had a great view of two batteries of 18-pounders galloping up under heavy shrapnel. They tore along at top speed over the desert and, when they got to 50 yards of where I was, they wheeled round and got the guns into action like a flash.

Those who are familiar with the Royal Tournament or Trooping the Colour will have seen the present-day successors to those gunners that Drury describes, the King's Troop of the Royal Horse Artillery, who, during these displays, still use horse-drawn guns that were fired in anger during the Great War. Their swiftness and skill in deploying their guns have been honed over many years of endless training and conflicts fought around the world, and the displays are carried out with impressive élan and dash, just as Drury had witnessed on the field of battle.

The day went well for the EEF. All of their objectives were taken with great speed, and the Turks were driven out of their trenches by hordes of Tommies with fixed bayonets and forced to retreat north.

As the Third Battle of Gaza raged to his south, Lawrence, now well behind enemy lines and having considered various bridges as targets for his operation, was en route to the crossing point at Tell el Shehab, intending to blow it on the 7 November, a day when the EEF had, to all intents and purposes, taken the whole Gaza-Beersheba defensive line. Unfortunately, the weather and circumstances were against him, the rain turning conditions underfoot treacherous. As they approached the bridge in the darkness, one of the party under Lawrence's command, an Indian machine gunner, slipped and dropped his rifle, which clattered to the ground. A lone Turkish sentry opened fire, alerting the rest of the guard, who joined in with a volley of bullets. This prompted the Arabs carrying the sacks of explosives to ditch them in the gorge – understandably so, as a well-aimed round would have blown them apart, and they had to make good their escape.

Disappointed and demoralised, Lawrence felt this failure keenly. His hopes of contributing to the offensive had been dashed, but he could not bring himself to call off the escapade without accomplishing something. Likewise, the Arabs were not prepared to return empty-handed, without loot. They had managed to retain one sack of explosive and were determined to use it.

The same night that Lawrence's attempt on the bridge had failed, the 6th RDF were on the move to relieve the 60th Division, who had captured Sheria, roughly halfway along the Gaza-Beersheba line. The 'rolling-up' exercise was proceeding at pace, and the Turks were now in full retreat, leaving much of their ordnance behind. Allenby recorded forty-three artillery pieces being captured by the 8 November. The following day, the 6th RDF was engaged in securing these guns. The war diary records that they were 'employed salvaging enemy war material along Rushdi system'.

The day after that, the battalion carried out a gruelling nine-mile march to Karm, where they set up camp. It was a very hot day and many men fell out due to recurring malarial attacks – a hangover from Salonika. Allenby had previously noted the high incidence of malaria in the Irish regiments. On the 17 October he wrote, 'There is a lot of fever in the 10th Division – some 3,000 cases; but they came here strong, and I hope to have some 8,000 or 9,000 rifles on the day.' The extremes of temperature, combined with the taxing physical effort required to march on sand over long distances, were enough to bring on these relapses. That was not the only entry in the 6th RDF war diary that mentioned the collapse of 'considerable' numbers of men whilst footslogging across the desert.

On the 10 November, whilst the 6th RDF were resting at Karm, Lawrence had identified a suitable site for an attack on the railway at Minifir, halfway between Amman and Deraa, a place he knew well. He concealed his remaining thirty pounds of explosive in an eighteen-foot-high stone culvert. He used his last sixty yards of wire to connect the dynamite to a detonator, running it up the hillside to a small bush, which was the only cover within reach. He then lay in wait for a suitable target to appear. He missed a couple of opportunities that day, with the detonator failing on the second occasion, and he had to remove and repair it. Then at 10am on the 11 November, a troop train appeared, heading south at speed, en route to defend Jerusalem from Allenby. The train was made up of twelve carriages carrying 400 soldiers, pulled by two locomotives. He plunged the detonator as the leading engine passed directly over the mine, igniting a spectacular explosion that sent the engine plummeting into the valley below the tracks. He was knocked backwards and was fortunate not to have been badly wounded by the flying fragments and shards of metal from the shattered boilerplates. As it was, his right foot was injured, and he was bleeding from abrasions to his arm. The burnt and smouldering remains of a body – minus its lower half – landed just in front of him; clearly, sixty yards was not a safe distance from which to blow up a locomotive.

The second engine was thrown onto the first tender, and the second tender disappeared down the west side of the embankment. The first three carriages were badly damaged, and the rest were derailed. Whilst Lawrence scrambled back towards cover assisted by a rescue party, the Arabs shot over his head at the Turkish soldiers visible within the coaches, also providing covering fire for a looting party that had recklessly careered down the hill. The looters paid particular attention to the liveried carriage that carried the general of the Turkish Eighth Army Corps and his imam, putting heavy fire into it in an effort to claim a notable scalp. The Turks responded, about 200 of them having managed to detrain and deploy behind cover to return fire. The tribesmen stopped firing whilst one of their number broke cover and ran down the slope to rescue one of the wounded looters, successfully bringing him back to the safety of the gully. In the lull, the Turks began advancing up the hill towards them, and when they'd reached around halfway, the Arabs opened fire again, pouring bullets into them and forcing them back, killing twenty more. Lawrence and his men disengaged, ran to their camels, and made off as fast as their mounts could carry them, leaving behind the smoking wreck of the train, the twisted rails, the demolished culvert, and the Turkish troops to tend to their dead and wounded.

They arrived the following day at the sanctuary of Azrak. The Arabs were content that their honour had been satisfied, having looted sixty or seventy Turkish rifles as well as some prized pieces of luggage. The enemy had suffered significant casualties. The losses were described as 'heavy', but, although a minor victory, this was not the triumph Lawrence had wished for, as it did not have the significant impact on the Turkish forces that he'd hoped to achieve. However, Allenby was not displeased. The success of the main offensive and the swift breaking of the Gaza-Beersheba line had exceeded his expectations, and as the Turks were in full retreat northwards towards Jerusalem with the EEF in hot pursuit, the cutting of the supply lines assumed less importance.

Allenby knew a military genius when he saw one. He was an enormous admirer of Lawrence, and the feeling was mutual. The latter's marshalling of his Arab forces was remarkable. He had an understanding of the Arab psyche that few other Westerners possessed. In partnership with Feisal, he had to navigate forming and maintaining a fragile coalition of feuding tribes and clans, some with long-held rivalries and grievances, into a cohesive and effective fighting force. The thing that united them all was a resentment of the imperial yoke of their Ottoman masters. They justified their alliance with their British Christian allies by comparing it to the Turkish Moslem partnership with the German and Austrian infidels.

Lawrence had swiftly realised that imposing a Western concept of military discipline on nomadic Bedouin people was an impossible task, culturally unachievable. He and Feisal had to cajole, coax, charm, flatter, taunt, and chivvy those under their command, including by acting as referees, counsellors, prosecutors, and judges in inter- and intra-tribal disputes.

The qualities of the Arab warrior were most suited to the role of a guerrilla, but there was one occasion when Lawrence more than proved his worth as a conventional military tactician. At the Battle of Tafileh in January 1918, he organised his ragtag army of nomadic tribesmen, Arab deserters from the Turkish army, and armed locals, including Armenian settlers who had escaped the infamous genocide, into a body of men that defeated a supposedly superior Ottoman force of three infantry battalions, a cavalry detachment, two howitzer artillery pieces, and twenty-seven machine guns, in a masterly display of leadership and courage. For this impressive victory, Lawrence was recommended for a Victoria Cross; he was finally awarded the Distinguished Service Order (DSO), having not qualified for the higher award due to the lack of a British witness to this remarkable action.

There have been attempts over the years to debunk the 'myth' of Lawrence of Arabia; accusations of exaggeration and hyperbole have been levelled against both Lawrence's biographers and Lawrence himself. He was an incredibly complex character, almost as likely to underplay his exploits as to embellish them, and he refused honours that the King had attempted to award him personally. Thus, teasing out the truth is no easy task. But, disregarding the overenthusiastic writings of his admirers and his questionable postwar account of certain other events, government files have entered the public domain that corroborate the part he played in the raids and actions he had documented and also indicate that he may have even understated his role in those events.

For me, Lawrence's light remains undimmed; the descendants of those Arab tribesmen who rode and fought with him still speak of 'El Auruns' with respect and admiration. He was a constant thorn in the side of the Turks. There was, reportedly, a huge bounty on his head of £10,000 dead or £20,000 alive. His activities required that the Ottoman Turks had to deploy valuable resources in defending, patrolling, and repairing the vital supply lines from Damascus. He estimated that he was responsible for the blowing up of seventy-nine railway bridges, tying down as many as 50,000 troops that could otherwise have been deployed against the British. It doesn't take a mathematician or a military historian to deduce that far more of Allenby's men could have perished had thousands of extra Turkish rifles been ranged against them, and the Third Battle of Gaza might have been fought for far longer and harder or even lost as a result. Is it too fanciful to suggest that Lawrence just might have saved

William's life, along with those of many other soldiers of the EEF?

By the 17 November, William and his comrades were on the move again, marching from Karm and eventually reaching Deir el Belah the following day, to camp for just over a week. The war diary reported that the 'men show a great improvement in march discipline and turn out'. The small part that the 6th RDF had played in the Third Battle of Gaza was over; they had been kept in reserve or acted as support for most of it, having seldom been called upon due to the rapid success of the initial assault. Towards the end of November, the battalion was ordered to move north and then east to take up position in the Judean Hills around ten miles from Jerusalem. The Turkish 7th Army lay between the British and the Holy City, but Allenby was determined not to fight within its precincts or anywhere near it. The importance of this sacred site to the three great Abrahamic faiths was paramount in his thinking. The 6th RDF moved into the line on the 4 December and was soon subjected to enemy sniper fire. The following day they sent out a patrol to reconnoitre the front line. The war diary reports, 'Our patrol held up near El Tireh village by about 40 Turks with machine gun'. The detachment took cover until nightfall and retired under the cover of darkness. For the next few days they were subjected to 'slight' sniping and shellfire, generally meeting little resistance, before receiving orders for an impending attack in conjunction with the 74th Division. As it transpired, they were not needed. As they advanced on Jerusalem, news came through on the 8 December that the city had fallen and was already occupied by the 60th and 74th Divisions, as the Turks had evacuated during the day and were headed north towards Jericho and Nablus. Allenby had succeeded spectacularly quickly, where his predecessor had failed. Lloyd George had his Christmas present. The Bull's triumph was built upon the stoicism and fortitude of the men of the EEF. A biographer of Allenby paid tribute to them:

> During the race north to gain the western approaches to Jerusalem, the British had marched and fought too rapidly for their transport, existing for many days on half or quarter rations,

and for some on nothing at all; and yet a more buoyant, determined, or united force never marched on to victory. Thirst also was a serious problem, especially for the mounted forces. The men often sacrificed their sleep during a night halt where one or two deep wells would be discovered to draw water laboriously with a single bucket and line for from one to two thousand horses. Allowing three to four buckets per minute, daybreak often found the work uncompleted, and supplies frequently gave out. Waterless days, therefore, were not unusual for man or beast.

This was an understatement. Thirst became the mortal enemy of the EEF. The desert is a pitiless environment, and the needs of an army of men and horses on the move and frequently in combat are huge, but sources of water were scarce. The thirst drove some men mad, moving from delirium to unconsciousness and, in a few cases, death. Eating was impossible. Dry, swollen tongues rendered the army rations of bully beef and hard biscuit indigestible. The men were reduced to sucking on pebbles in an effort to produce moisture. Water was rationed to 2¼ pints a day per man, totally inadequate to sustain a soldier operating in the intense heat of the desert during such a rapid advance, punctuated by bouts of intense fighting. They depended heavily on the Camel Transport Corps (CTC) to maintain water supplies, and the native Egyptian drivers who shepherded those invaluable beasts of burden worked manfully to keep the troops hydrated. The fact that the men of the EEF were able to overcome such hardships makes their victory all the more remarkable.

Allenby's entry into Jerusalem at noon on the 11 December was perfectly and sensitively judged, proceeding on foot as a pilgrim rather than on horseback as a victor, paying homage and displaying a symbolic reverence and humility for the sacred ground he was treading. He gave Lawrence the honour of joining the procession, which included military attachés from France, Italy, and the USA as well as representatives from all of the regiments of the EEF, including the 6th RDF. The war diary details '2 representatives sent to join Divisional Party forming part of

General Allenby's bodyguard on his first entry into Jerusalem.' All of the holy sites were protected by sentries, and those that were of special significance to Islam – including elsewhere in Palestine, such as at the Tomb of the Patriarchs at Hebron – were guarded only by Indian Moslem troops with strict orders that no non-Moslems were allowed to pass through the cordons.

The advance of the British continued apace. They swept all before them, and they were ten miles north of Jerusalem by Christmas. However, William and the men of the EEF were not able to celebrate in style, as they had outstripped their supply lines, and the rapidity with which they'd progressed combined with the incessant seasonal rain ensured that there would be no turkey or plum pudding delivered in time for any festivities. Instead, they were on half-rations of bully beef and hard biscuit, a cup of rum the only consolation on a thoroughly wet and depressing Christmas Day.

There was to be no let-up. Allenby had the Turkish army on the run and was determined to press ahead, planning an attack straight after Christmas. But the Turkish had other ideas. Before he had a chance to put his plans into effect, the enemy counterattacked with the intention of retaking Jerusalem. From midnight on Boxing Day and throughout the 27 December, a bloody battle ensued, the 10th Division fighting in the rugged hill country to the west of the Nablus Road. Using fire and movement tactics, with each battalion taking it in turn to provide covering fire as they leapfrogged each other, they ascended the ridges and skilfully scaled the six-to-ten-foot-high terraces to drive the Turks from the peaks. William took part in the capture of Shamrock Hill by the 29th and 30th Brigades, with the 31st taking Kefr Shiyan. The Turkish counterattack had been repulsed across the entire front, and the pressure from the EEF was unremitting. It turned into a rout as the enemy retreated at speed. In a letter to Colonel Clive Wigram at GHQ, Allenby wrote that, 'by the evening of the 28th, not only had the enemy failed to take Jerusalem, but he was pushed 7 miles further from that city than when his attack started'.

From the taking of the Gaza-Beersheba line in early November, the British had advanced around sixty miles across deserts and rocky mountain ranges whilst experiencing extreme weather conditions. They were now in danger of overreaching and cutting themselves off in terms of both supplies and communications. A period of regrouping and consolidation was necessary before the race to Damascus could continue, and a programme of road building was begun to facilitate the efficient and timely delivery of supplies, constructing a link from the Nablus-Jerusalem Road to the coast. The 10th Division was ideally suited to this task, drawing on the expertise gained from their time in Salonika. For most of January and into February, the 6th RDF was employed in either improving defences or building roads under the supervision of the Royal Engineers.

Whilst engaged on such work, William suffered a serious injury to his right leg. His Casualty Form shows he was admitted to the Field Ambulance unit on the 12 February and then moved rearwards through the Medical Chain of Evacuation until he was admitted to the Citadel Hospital in Cairo on the 26th. He was treated here for a matter of weeks before being sent to the Convalescent Depot at Boulac, a sub-district of Cairo, on the 18 March 1918, where he continued his recovery for a week before being returned to the Citadel Hospital, this time suffering from a tonsillar abscess. This was a miserable time for William; he suffered injury and illness successively for six months, bouncing back and forth between hospital and convalescent depot. Meanwhile, throughout March, his pals in the 6th RDF continued to fight as part of the 10th Division's assault on Wadi el Jib, as the EEF advanced ever northward.

During William's period of sickness, another absentee from the battalion, Captain Noel Drury, was sitting on a train travelling towards Cairo via Ismailia for a week's leave when he encountered a 'peculiarly shabby looking fellow mouching along in an officer's tunic but without badges or regimental buttons, unshaven and with long hair.' Drury was outraged and was about to upbraid this miscreant when he was checked by one of his fellow passengers:

He looked such a disgrace that I was on the point of speaking to him when one of the 10th Division staff with whom I was sitting said to me 'Don't you think you might think first before blazing at him, and do you know who it is?' I said I didn't and he replied 'That's Colonel Lawrence.' He was probably just back from one of his wonderful stunts with the Arabs and had picked up any old gear to take him to Cairo.

Lawrence would, no doubt, have found the whole episode amusing had Drury confronted him. He was used to this sort of reaction at his appearance, especially when clad in his flowing Arab robes. It might be that he took a mischievous delight in provoking the hidebound attitudes of the conventional military mind; he had a laissez-faire approach to turnout dating back to his days in the Officer Training Corps at Oxford, and the army had been unable to knock this lack of discipline out of him as a result of his sideways route into soldiering and an absence of formal staff college training.

William's Casualty Form shows that he was 'Discharged to Duty' on the 6 April and sent to a Convalescent Depot at Abbassia, another district of Cairo, to complete his recovery. Whilst there, he was put to work on fatigues and other routine duties in an effort to build up his fitness. Unfortunately, his health deteriorated, and on the 23 May he was admitted to the Military Infectious Diseases Hospital at Choubra, in a separate suburb of Cairo, diagnosed with diphtheria, a potentially serious and sometimes fatal bacterial infection of the nose and throat. He was isolated here for a month before discharge to Boulac Convalescent Depot on the 23 June and thence to Abbassia again on the 4 July.

Whilst he had been laid up, events in France had determined the next phase of his war. On the 21 March 1918, as William was recovering from his leg injury at Boulac, the Germans had begun a massive offensive on the Western Front known as the Kaiserschlacht ('the Kaiser's Battle'), in an effort to smash through the British lines and end the stalemate, driving them into the sea and forcing an evacuation across the Channel.

The Germans were able to reinforce their armies in France and Belgium with 500,000 extra troops released from the Eastern Front due to the collapse of a war-weary Russia, aided by the Bolshevik Revolution in November 1917, and the subsequent negotiation – in reality more of an imposition – of the Treaty of Brest-Litovsk. This gave them a substantial numerical advantage of 192 infantry divisions against the combined Allied total of 169. The Germans now had a window of opportunity to make their superiority in numbers count before the US, having entered the war in April 1917, could fully mobilise their forces in Europe. They had to strike fast.

Over a million shells were fired in the first five hours of the offensive, at an average rate of about 3,000 a minute, a mixture of high explosive and cloying gas shells. The bombardment was followed up by elite regiments of storm troopers descending on the British lines in an onslaught that the Tommies were unable to resist, their efforts made more difficult by a dense fog that favoured the attackers. The Germans made spectacular gains and would eventually threaten Amiens, a major transport and logistics hub for the British, the fall of which would have been disastrous. One of the divisions that suffered most was the 66th (East Lancs) Division, a Territorial Force, who during the initial day of the attack, lost 711 men killed and over the first eight days sustained over 7,000 casualties, including killed, wounded, and missing.

It was a sledgehammer blow that drove the British back by up to eight miles, but stubborn resistance kept Amiens in Allied hands, and the first phase of the Kaiserschlacht – Operation Michael – ended on the 5 April with the Tommies bloodied and battered but defiant and unbroken. Over the coming months, the Germans made four more attempts to achieve a decisive breakthrough on different sectors of the front, from Ypres in the north to the Champagne region in the south, coming within sixty miles of Paris, but for all the territorial success – they had gained ten times the ground the Allies had won in 1917 – it was all to come to naught.

By the 17 July, the Germans had shot their bolt. They had suffered nearly a million casualties, and the Americans were arriving in their hundreds of thousands. Nevertheless, the substantial losses that the British had sustained during the great German offensive would have direct consequences for William and the men of the 6th RDF. On the 5 May 1918, Allenby wrote, 'Events in Europe overtop the little happenings in this theatre; and we watch, with keen eyes, the gigantic struggle on the Western Front.' He had to revise his plans and scale them back for the continuation of his offensive. He went on: '[M]y own projects have been modified, and the scope of my operations limited, by the requirements of the European battlefield. I have been called upon to supply battalions for France.'

The 6th RDF was one of the battalions chosen to transfer to France. As a result, the 10th (Irish) Division was effectively disbanded, and its constituent units were either absorbed by regular battalions from their respective regiments or redistributed to other divisions on the Western Front in dire need of reinforcement. The 6th RDF stayed intact and was one of four Irish battalions, along with the 5th Royal Inniskilling Fusiliers, the 5th Connaught Rangers, and the 6th Leinsters, that would be subsumed into the badly mauled 66th (East Lancs) Division.

Licking its wounds following the Kaiserschlacht, the 66th spent the summer rebuilding. In charge was a young, thrusting officer named Major-General Hugh Keppel Bethell, who had taken over as GOC on the 31 March. Along with other divisions that had been decimated during the German offensive, the 66th experienced a protracted, complex, and confusing period of reorganisation during which numerous infantry battalions were transferred in and out for short periods while others were disbanded and absorbed.

Complicating matters further was the need to grant much-deserved home leave – along with time spent acclimatising to the Western Front – for troops incoming from Palestine and Salonika. In such a state of flux, the future of the 66th was uncertain, and dissolution threatened. The fact that it survived was due to Bethell's determination to fight for its existence and convince the high command that he could forge it into a frontline force.

In early July, as William was being admitted to the Abbassia Convalescent Depot for the last time to complete his recovery, his pals were embarking on the SS Malwa at Gabbari Docks, Alexandria, bound for France via Taranto, Italy. He eventually returned to full duties over a month later and followed them on the 17 August 1918, setting sail on the HMAT Indarra, an Australian liner in its previous life. The Indarra formed part of a convoy of troopships, each of which would typically have carried anywhere up to 20,000 men. The convoy would have been escorted by a fleet of between six and ten Japanese destroyers to provide protection against the ever-present threat of U-boats.

William landed in France on the 20th and eventually rejoined the 6th RDF at Serqueux camp, around thirty miles inland from Dieppe, on the 4 September, whilst the battalion was in training along with the rest of the 66th Division. The division was undergoing its final reincarnation before going into battle again, being brought up to strength with its three brigades, each of which had now been reduced to three rather than four battalions due to a rationalisation of manpower, consisting of the 1st, 2nd, and 4th South African Infantry forming the 197th Brigade; the 6th Royal Dublin Fusiliers, the 5th Royal Inniskilling Fusiliers, and the 6th Lancashire Fusiliers forming the 198th; and the 5th Connaught Rangers, the 9th Manchester Regiment, and the 18th King's Liverpool Regiment making up the 199th. It was now the 'East Lancs' Division in name only, as the Irish and the South Africans provided two-thirds of the infantry component of its establishment, and, in fact, only two battalions remained from the original twelve that had arrived in France eighteen months previously: the 6th Lancs and the 9th Manchester.

Even though the Germans had been held at bay and, indeed, were now on the back foot, the feeling amongst the Allies – both the politicians and the generals – was that the war would drag on into at least a fifth year. Lloyd George had written off the idea that victory would come in 1918 and believed that Haig should keep his powder dry until 1919; Marshal Ferdinand Foch, the Supreme Commander-in-Chief of the Allied forces, also 'did not expect victory until at least 1919', and this filtered down to the commanding officers in the field. Lieutenant Colonel Walter Vignoles of the 9<sup>th</sup> Northumberland Fusiliers thought that 'we should settle him next year … if only the yanks had been fully trained and organised now, I think we could have finished it this year, but we'll give him something pretty hot next spring, I expect.' But the success of the Allies at the Battle of Amiens, which began on the 8 August – described by General Erich von Ludendorff as 'the black day of the German Army in the history of the war' – set in motion a series of successive victories that would gain impetus, a rising crescendo that escalated into larger offensives, during a period that became known as the 'Hundred Days', and the Allies' progress was to exceed all expectations, shortening the predicted length of the war.

Throughout August and September, the 66<sup>th</sup> Division was undergoing intensive training for the upcoming offensives, but the emphasis had switched from tactics that had been used during the stalemate of attrition, static trench warfare to those more appropriate for mobile or open warfare. The war diary of the 6<sup>th</sup> RDF described this variously as 'specialist', 'company', and 'platoon' training. It consisted of 'fire and movement' tactics designed for rapid advances over open ground. The division would attack with two brigades leading and a third in support, which would then leapfrog and take the vanguard after a set distance to refresh the offensive, and this sequence would be repeated as necessary. The fresh orthodoxies (although they were not wholly new as such, the remaining 'old army' regulars of the BEF were familiar with much of this style of fighting in one form or another) included advancing in 'artillery formation', arranged in single file as 'worms', rather than in traditional ranks lined up abreast and strung out across the battlefield, thus offering less of a target to incoming fire. Or the alternative of four sub-units or sections forming a diamond shape, often flanked by light trench mortar and machine gun sections. This diamond formation could be applied to either a company of four platoons or the smaller configuration of a platoon of four sections.

It was hoped that these tactics would reduce casualties to avoid the horror show of massed ranks of men being mown down in great swathes. Each sub-unit was allowed a degree of autonomy and was given the capacity to react to any given situation as it occurred – a flexible and resilient approach that had been largely denied the infantry during the battles of Loos and the Somme earlier in the war. Responsibility was devolved to platoon commanders, and in a combat situation, NCO section commanders – the sergeants and corporals – and even on occasion, privates – were encouraged to act on their own initiative. For the 'new army', this was an almost unprecedented level of delegation.

Embedded within these sections were four types of specialists: riflemen, bombers, rifle grenadiers and Lewis gun teams. When confronted with stubborn resistance, these specialists would be deployed to outflank and envelop a strong point or redoubt – whether a building or an earthwork, a machine gun nest or a pillbox, or simply a picket of soldiers fighting behind cover in a wood or in the open – and, using rifle, bayonet, and bomb, clear it from the rear. The men practised and perfected this new battle drill over and over again, completely unaware that the endgame was in sight, for in a matter of weeks, and after four tumultuous years, the war would be over, and William could look forward to returning home to the East End.

# CHAPTER FOURTEEN

# RETURN TO THE WESTERN FRONT

*'Tis not the bit of bronze and metal,*
*That tells the timeworn tale,*
*Of some act of heroism*
*Where bullets whine and wail.*

...

*They will tarnish with the weather,*
*In the plush or on the shelf,*
*For the real and lasting medal,*
*Is the soul within yourself.*

LEE CHARLES McCOLLUM Extracts from *The Medal*

William had been back with the battalion for only two weeks when he was granted leave to England, in line with the general policy of sending troops home who had served for a protracted period in the Mediterranean theatres of war and whose opportunities for leave had been practically non-existent compared to those of their counterparts serving on the Western Front. His leave commenced on the 18 September 1918, and his arrival at the door of 59 Russia Lane in Bethnal Green was a shock, albeit a happy one, for his widowed mother Frances. Like every other mother, she dreaded the knock at the door and the delivery of a telegram or letter with heartbreaking news. She had two sons serving in the BEF and was only too well aware of neighbours who had suffered loss and of the ever-increasing numbers of casualties published in the newspapers.

A grown man of thirty-six, battle-hardened and burnt brown by the Egyptian sun, William's appearance gladdened my great-grandmother's heart. Her joy at seeing her eldest boy in one piece and unharmed can only be imagined. For her and his sisters, his time at home flew by, and all too soon he was on his way back to France, rejoining the 6th RDF on the 6th of October at Ste Emilie. He was thrown back into the boiling cauldron of war just as they were making preparations for battle. The following day, they marched to Le Catelet to occupy the support trenches at the Hindenburg Line.

The Hindenburg Line was a heavily fortified trench system that had been constructed by the Germans in the winter of 1916 in response to the Battles of the Somme and Verdun, which had left them exhausted. The appalling losses suffered by the British at the Somme and the French at Verdun tend to obscure the fact that the Germans had suffered to a similar degree; in fact, and in terms of territorial gains – albeit small – the Somme was technically an Allied victory, although possibly a Pyrrhic one. After fighting so hard to defend their lines during these two titanic battles of 1916, the Germans had pragmatically withdrawn to more favourable ground, straightening their front. They had executed a scorched-earth policy on the land surrendered, poisoning wells, laying mines, and destroying anything that could be of use to the Allies when they subsequently occupied the land ceded. Ironically, this was to backfire on them when they themselves retook the same ground during the *Kaiserschlacht* in March 1918.

The Hindenburg Line had taken four months to construct, using hundreds of thousands of German workers and Russian prisoners of war. The fortification was an incredible feat of engineering, comprising reinforced concrete blockhouses and forts with an intricate system of deep dug-outs and chambers; these were in-depth defences that offered highly effective protection to their frontline troops, and it was considered impregnable. After the *Kaiserschlacht* series of offensives had failed, and after their subsequent defeat at the Battle of Amiens in August, followed by a sequence of further defeats at the hands of the Allies, the Germans were forced to retreat yet again to the safety of the Hindenburg Line, giving up all the ground they had won throughout the spring and early summer of 1918 but secure in the knowledge that their defences were practically impenetrable.

That makes the achievement of the 46th (North Midland) Division, when they broke the Hindenburg Line at Bellenglise on the St Quentin Canal on the 29 September 1918, all the more remarkable. It was the defining moment in the war, the long-wished-for breakthrough that would win it for the Allies, as it eventually prompted a request from Austria, Germany, and Turkey for an armistice. The 46th took 4,200 prisoners, 70 artillery pieces, and over 1,000 machine guns, giving the BEF an opportunity to free up the battlefield for the open warfare that it had so assiduously trained for and to force the Germans into a full-blown retreat – pursued by what would be an unstoppable and irresistible force, including William's battalion as part of the 66th Division, who were to play a prominent part.

And so, just over a week after the breaking of the Hindenburg Line, at 0100 hours on the 8 October, the 6th RDF crossed the St. Quentin Canal over a bridge just west of Le Catelet, five miles north of the 46th Division's breakthrough at Bellenglise. They gathered at the assembly tapeline and straightaway came under intensive fire from machine guns and gas shells, suffering a hundred casualties, including four officers, before the advance had even started.

They endured the enemy bombardment for over four hours before zero hour. And then, at 0510, the British artillery opened up, putting down an awesome barrage. The battalion advanced over a front measuring 600 yards. They captured their first objective, an unnamed farm, within ten minutes – thirty-five minutes ahead of schedule – and they took forty prisoners.

The 6th RDF relished this type of warfare. Drury noted that 'The enemy are now driven into the open country, and those of us who have been accustomed to open fighting feel much more at home than in the trenches.' Their next objective was Petit Verger farm. They came under heavy machine gun fire from their left. A platoon was dispatched to deal with them, and by 0600 they had captured this farm also and taken another fifty prisoners. The attack continued but was temporarily held up by three machine guns and snipers from a position 200 yards west of Marliches Farm. Drury was champing at the bit: 'We were all itching to get on fast but were told we must conform to the other troops, who were not used to open fighting.' A smoke screen was laid down by the artillery, and a company under Captain Shadforth of the 6th RDF was able to push on undetected and assault a sunken road adjacent to the farm, taking a further forty prisoners. They went on to take the farm but were driven back by machine gun fire from the rear and their left flank and had to withdraw to the sunken road, where the heavy machine gun fire continued. Further to their left, their colleagues were able to outflank the machine gun nests, and they managed to take and clear the village of *Villers-Outréaux*, leaving the German line untenable, thus causing the enfilading machine gun teams to retreat.

They continued to advance, reaching Lampe Farm at 1300 hours, where they established outposts and consolidated their position. The 6th RDF had suffered 271 casualties during the day, taking 170 prisoners and capturing a substantial amount of the enemy's ordnance including fourteen field guns and forty-one machine guns.

The following day, the 6th RDF was ordered to continue the advance. This period, from the 9 to 11 October, was officially titled 'The Pursuit to the Selle' by the authorities, although the preceding day, the 8th, is so inextricably linked that the pursuit can justifiably be claimed to have started then. This operation was a fast-moving episode in the closing stages of the war, the enemy doggedly fighting a rearguard action with the BEF snapping at their heels. However, it was not a rout. The Germans managed to retreat in relatively good order, the machine gun teams in particular making the Tommies fight hard for every yard of ground taken. They were not beaten yet, and they fought fiercely; in their eyes, they were fighting in defence of their homeland. And as they were forced back eastwards towards the German border, they were not just fighting for each other; they were protecting their families and homes. The Germans' objective was to withdraw with their corps and ordnance mainly intact to the River Selle, where they would make a stand. They had, with an efficient thoroughness and foresight, already accounted for the breaking of the Hindenburg Line by planning and preparing the construction of the Hermann Line, a fallback position adjacent to the east bank of the Selle. Their defence strategy included occupying the high ground of the railway embankment at Le Cateau and using the river as an added barrier for the Tommies to negotiate. Although it was nothing like as heavily fortified as the Hindenburg Line, with hastily dug and incomplete trench systems, it was well organised nonetheless. Heavily wired and with well-appointed machine gun posts and battery positions, it was another formidable obstacle to be overcome by the BEF.

The 6th RDF recommenced their advance at 0520 hours. In conjunction with the 5th Royal Inniskilling Fusiliers, they took the village of Elincourt and captured eleven prisoners. The rest of the German garrison had fled in a hurry; plates of still-warm food had been left uneaten on tables within their billets. By 1200 hours, the battalion had reached a position known as Iris Copse, whereupon they halted.

Early the next morning, at 0330 hours, they were on the move again and advancing at a punishing rate, pushing on along, as well as north of, the Roman road through L'Epinette and Maretz before reaching Reumont at 0630, where they came under artillery fire whilst following up the 5th Royal Inniskilling Fusiliers and the 6th Lancashire Fusiliers. They continued advancing in artillery formation, leaving Reumont behind, under 'considerable hostile shelling' before crossing the Cambrai to Le Cateau road and digging in just west of the River Selle and to the northwest of Le Cateau town itself.

On the morning of the 11 October, the last day of the official 'Pursuit', the 6th RDF was ordered to relieve the 6th Lancs in their outposts, preparatory to an assault on the Hermann Line. By the evening, this order had been cancelled, and they were moved back behind the lines to billets in Maurois just west of Reumont. On the way, they suffered three more casualties, and one of them happened to be William. However, it must have been a slight injury; unlike his wound at the Somme, his Casualty Form records this incident as 'Wounded in Action – at Duty', signifying that after treatment and the application of a field dressing he was able to continue soldiering. This is emphasised by his subsequent promotion to (paid) Corporal just two days later on the 13th.

The total casualties sustained by the 6th RDF during the Pursuit to the Selle were listed as 318, including forty-two fatalities. The 66th Division as a whole had performed exceptionally well over the course of the advance. Walter Guinness, one of the divisional staff officers, noted that:

> During the three days' fighting the Division advanced fourteen miles on a two-mile front, the actual time taken up being only 53 hours. We took prisoners from eight German Divisions, 26 officers and 1,031 other ranks; also material, sixty-two 7.7cm guns and four 21cm Howitzers, three 8.8cm Howitzers, three 5.9cm Howitzers, one anti-aircraft gun, fifteen trench mortars, six anti-tank rifles, 126 machine guns and two motor cars.

The 6th RDF had retired to billets in order to prepare for and take part in a fully coordinated attack, for it was clear that the advance had to pause. The assault on the Hermann Line could not be carried out ad hoc. Intelligence gathered from enemy prisoners, local villagers, and aerial and infantry reconnaissance had indicated that the Germans were strengthening their defences, bringing up reinforcements, and improving the trench system on the east bank of the Selle.

Although the high command had wanted to maintain the momentum of the 'Pursuit', this battle could not be rushed. They were also aware that the Germans were preparing another defensive line still further east on the Sambre-Oise Canal, known as the 'Hermann II', in the event of the Hermann Line being breached. The coming battle would require meticulous planning involving accurate artillery work and a determined infantry executing a swift crossing of the river in sufficient numbers and at various points in order to overcome stiff resistance.

The 66th Division, as part of the Fourth Army, was at the vanguard of the Allied charge across the whole Western Front. Initially, Haig had been keen to exploit their success and felt that risks could be taken to press home the advantage. However, after consulting his army commanders, wiser counsel prevailed, and he was convinced of the need to delay the battle. Subsequently, the date of the assault on the Selle, which had been planned for the 14 or 15 October, was postponed by Fourth Army HQ until the 17th.

The 66th Division was set the objective of crossing the river to the north of, as well as adjacent to, Le Cateau, to secure the Hermann Line on the eastern fringe of the commune atop the railway embankment and clear the town of enemy troops. Two companies of the 6th RDF were detailed to initially support the 4th South African Infantry north of Le Cateau before peeling away to enter the town itself from the northeast. The remaining two companies were tasked with penetrating it from the west, with the intention of gaining touch with their fellows from the north in a 'pinching-out'-type action after having 'mopped up' the Germans.

The artillery bombardment was to commence forty-eight hours before zero but would not include the town itself, which had a peacetime civilian population of between 10,000 and 11,000. In conjunction with smoke bombs and shelling specifically directed well to the north by the Third Army, this would deceive the Germans as to the precise location and time of the attack. Facing the 66th Division were the 17th and 44th Reserve Divisions of the German Army, both considered elite divisions – the former rated the best of the eleven German divisions that fought at the Selle – and, as such, their morale and fighting spirit were higher than that of less-accomplished troops. They had a slight superiority over the 66th in terms of manpower: 11,750–12,200 infantry as opposed to 10,000–10,500.

The Royal Engineers were the unsung heroes during the 'Hundred Days'. By the 24 October, when the Battle of the Selle came to its end, they had erected nineteen pumping stations and laid miles of pipe; supplied hundreds of thousands of gallons of water for men and horses by motor transport; constructed and maintained hundreds of miles of roads and tracks and built scores of bridges; and removed tons of mines and explosive booby traps across the whole front, all since the offensive had begun in August. As impressive as these statistics are, their most astonishing feat was constructing and transporting a large number of bridges to within metres of the Selle to enable the infantry and artillery to cross it unscathed – right under the noses of the enemy.

The Germans had destroyed or partially destroyed all of the bridges across the Selle. Crossing the river would be crucial to the outcome of the battle, and the topography of the battlefield favoured the defending force. The Selle lay in a half-mile-wide valley between 200-foot-high ridges. In certain sectors, this meant that the 66th Division had to advance down the western slope with precious little cover in full view of the enemy, cross hundreds of yards of exposed flood plain that flanked each side of the Selle, negotiate the twenty-foot-wide river itself, and ascend the steeper eastern slope where the German troops awaited them. Once there, they had to not only break the line but also carry on, pushing eastwards over a plateau with plenty of natural and man-made obstacles affording cover to the German withdrawal. The potential for heavy casualties was very high.

The two companies of my grandfather's battalion tasked with tackling the western approach to the town of Le Cateau itself had to cross the river between two brick-built banks before clearing the streets and buildings in an urban warfare-type environment. The houses and cellars were infested with machine gun nests and pickets of troops waiting to ambush them from the rear and with enfilading fire.

Three types of bridge were needed for the assault: footbridges for the infantry; more substantial structures for the artillery; and some stronger still for the largest and heaviest transport vehicles. These had to be built in quantity; building too few would lead to pinch points that would enable the Germans to concentrate their fire and cause heavy casualties. The footbridges were constructed as rafts – wooden duckboards tied to petrol cans – and were easily portable. They were stress-tested behind the lines by cramming as many men on to them as possible.

The Royal Engineers had begun their work on the 13 October at dusk, four days prior to the battle, erecting two bridges across the Selle near Montay, to the north of Le Cateau. On the afternoon of the 16 October, the day before the battle, the Royal Engineers and attached pioneers carried more preconstructed bridges to within 1,300 yards of the river, and by 2230 hours had moved them closer, to around 500 yards, in the process risking life and limb from enemy fire.

On the eve of the battle, a hundred sappers from 431 and 432 Companies Royal Engineers, with the assistance of the 9th Gloucestershire (Pioneers), constructed four more footbridges and deployed them in a valley to the north of the town, under fire, and without suffering a single casualty. A 'bridging group' was assigned to each battalion for the actual crossing, composed of sappers and pioneers, headed by an officer from each corps. Each group was subdivided into teams of two sappers and six pioneers that were responsible for each individual bridge. In the early hours of the 17th, these bridging groups quietly led the infantry through to the crossing points. The Germans were totally unaware. Five minutes prior to zero hour, some of the bridges were already in place. The rest were installed within a minute of the barrage 'lifting' on to the Hermann Line itself. As a result, the infantry were able to cross the river swiftly with minimal casualties. It was a remarkable achievement.

Noel Drury was attached to the South African Brigade as a liaison officer for the duration of the battle, much to his disgust. Not through any bad feeling towards the South Africans – on the contrary, he held them in high regard – but by being separated from his beloved 6th RDF, he was relegated to the sidelines and unable to take an active part in the assault. He described the initial events of the 17th:

> The South African attack went on fast and up to time, and they got to their objectives quickly although the Bosch put up a stiff fight. The River Selle is a great barrier as it is too wide to jump and too deep to ford. The plans said it was four feet deep but at the part near the Seydoux factory where I saw it, the river was about 25 feet wide and about ten feet deep and the water was only eighteen inches below the level of the meadow. Pontoons have been ordered up to bridge the river at some points including this, but ours had been burst up by shell fire. Presently some tanks appeared and one

was driven down into the river and the men were able to run over on its back which was like a half-tide rock. I heard that another tank was driven over the river on the back of the sunken one.

At 0715 hours, B and C companies of the 6th RDF crossed the river to the north of Le Cateau in support of the South Africans. They came under intense heavy-explosive fire and gas shelling during a thick fog and were drawn into the fighting alongside the South Africans. One of the platoons from Captain Shadforth's B Company made for the railway crossing on the other side of the town in an attempt to intercept the enemy fleeing Le Cateau, but he and some of his men became isolated and had to take shelter in a house adjacent to the railway. They used furniture as a makeshift barricade before eventually making their escape from a shell hole at the rear of the building at 1300 hours.

Lieutenant Colonel William Benjamin Little, CO of the 6th RDF, became concerned that the mopping-up operation was not proceeding at a fast enough pace, partly due to the fact that two platoons of B Company were still embroiled in the fighting with the South Africans and had been unable to extricate themselves. He withdrew D Company from their allotted task and ordered them to reinforce B Company. He then ordered a platoon from A Company to cross the Selle from the west bank into the town itself and work their way up to the church, where they would gain touch with B and C Companies coming from the northeast. They successfully crossed the river and swiftly captured a machine gun post and nine men. Encouraged by this, Little sent a second platoon to assist, soon followed by the remaining two platoons of A Company. The 6th RDF war diary contains an account of what happened next:

'A' Company met with considerable opposition from all quarters by machine guns and snipers. The enemy were a very brave and stout lot of fellows, and I regret to say treacherous. About 11:00 one platoon had just taken two snipers when a runner reported that another platoon was held up and the platoon officer and others killed. Lieut. Hannin and a Lewis Gun section immediately put a screen of prisoners in front of them and proceeded direct along the street and called on them to surrender. Ten came out with their hands up apparently for this purpose, but instead of surrendering opened fire with a machine gun killing some of our men and taking cover. Needless to say the prisoners in possession were promptly despatched to another world. Our party then quickly fell back to cover and erected a barricade in front of two Lewis guns which were turned on to the house and good street fighting began. Half an hour later CSM Cooke reported to his company commander, Capt. Hayes, that there was another strong party of about twenty in a house with machine guns in another street, and that he had captured four. Lieut. Whyte, who speaks German fluently, instructed one of them to go down the street and tell his comrades that if they would surrender they would get a safe conduct through our lines, and that if he himself, who was covered with rifles, did not return, his other three comrades would also be shot. This prisoner did as he was instructed, but the reply he got was 'No surrender'. Curiously enough this man was allowed by the party referred to, to return safely to us. On hearing of this obstinacy I despatched a platoon of 5th Royal Inniskilling Fusiliers, who had come up, round to the south of the town for the purpose of enveloping these parties. This was successfully done.

Although, by today's standards, the use of German prisoners in this way as a 'human shield', might seem brutal, context is everything. The Geneva Convention that formalised the acceptable treatment of prisoners of war would not come into force until 1929, and this type of practice was commonplace; indeed, the Germans had gone even further. Reports of civilians being used in such a way dated back to the early years of the war during the invasion of Belgium.

One such atrocity took place during the Battle of the Selle itself, as Gunner Alexander Caseby discovered after crossing the river to the north of Le Cateau to find that the Germans had cynically and cold-bloodedly herded many of the locals into the trenches on the railway embankment, knowing full well that it would be a primary target for British shelling. The horrors that Gunner Caseby saw there would stay with him forever: 'Boys, girls, old men and women lay mangled in heaps, and groaning children lay everywhere. In one sad case a woman lay dead and two small children were trying to make her speak.'

At 1210 hours, the CO issued an order to the effect that all available units from the 6th RDF other than those already involved in the fighting to the north of Le Cateau were to concentrate on the clearing and defending of the town itself. By 1227 hours, A Company had cleared the enemy from the west side of the town and had reached the church over to the east.

Meanwhile, Drury had been dismissed for the day from his duties as a liaison officer by the General of the South African Brigade and told he might be of more use to his battalion. He takes up the story:

> I got down into Le Cateau about 15:00 and found that the mopping up was a tremendously difficult business and it seemed to me that at least two battalions would have been required. The main difficulty was the inter-connected cellars. As soon as we had cleared one street and driven all the Huns out of it and started down the next street, machine gun fire would be opened on us from the very houses we had first cleared. The big church … was cleared three or four times and yet the Hun fired from the tower (which is 180 feet high). [Major] John Luke [commanding C Company of the 6th RDF] was having the devil of a time clearing the street leading from the church out under the railway towards Bazuel. Bullets were whizzing about from all directions and it was not a bit safer under the walls than in the middle of the road.

By 1730 hours, the southern sector of the town had been cleared, leaving only the northern fringe with a significant German presence – where

Captain Shadforth was still involved in heavy fighting with detachments from B, C and D Companies. By 1900 hours, to all intents and purposes, the town was under the control of the British, and the streets were being heavily patrolled by the Tommies. The 6ᵗʰ RDF had fought long and hard to secure the town. Having earned a well-deserved rest, they were relieved by the 6ᵗʰ Lancs on the 18 October and went into reserve trenches before going into billets in Maurois on the 20th.

They had gone into battle on the 8th with a fighting strength of 41 officers and 806 other ranks. By the 22nd, they had been reduced to 20 officers and 240 other ranks.

Although they didn't know it, in just over three weeks' time it would all be over. The Battle of the Selle was the last major action of the war that the 6ᵗʰ RDF was involved in, and although it is rarely mentioned, it has been described as one of the greatest military victories in the nation's history. The 6ᵗʰ RDF, as a constituent part of the 198ᵗʰ Brigade, had performed superbly. The Brigadier General Commanding wrote this about the Brigade on the 21 October:

> The BGC wishes to congratulate the Brigade on their performances of the last 12 days. During that period they have advanced 13¾ miles on 10½ of which they were actually in touch with the enemy, have captured 484 prisoners, 23 field guns, 3 heavy howitzers and a large number of machine guns, in addition to inflicting heavy casualties on the enemy. Their final effort was to clear the town of Le Cateau, east of the River Selle, so liberating over 1,000 French civilians who have been under German domination for four years. This result has been attained by the hard work and unselfishness of all ranks, coupled with a determination to do their duty and get to grips with the enemy in spite of all deterrents. The BGC regrets the casualties sustained in fighting a stubborn enemy, but he knows that now the Brigade has got the measure of the enemy and that he can rely on them in future operations to do equally good work in bringing the war to a speedy and victorious conclusion.

In fact, the 66th Division as a whole were ranked as the most successful infantry division within the Fourth Army during the last 'Hundred Days', having carried out ten attacks with a hundred per cent success rate, and they were rated joint first in the whole of the BEF. It was an achievement to be considered all the greater when the quality of the opposition they faced is taken into account; the finest of all of the troops ranged across the whole Selle battlefront were their opponents, categorised by the Germans as 1st Class/A.

There are a number of factors that might explain the outstanding success of the 66th Division. One is leadership. The Divisional GOC was the aforementioned Major General Hugh Keppel Bethell. Young, energetic, and proactive, he was thirty-six years old at the time, over eight years younger than the average age of the seven other major generals in command of British divisions at the Selle. In fact, he was the youngest divisional commander of either world war. Bethell has been described as a 'thruster in a class of his own' and 'like quicksilver'. This mercurial character was impressive and maddening in equal measure and infamous for his disregard for rules and protocol. He would procure equipment and recruit talented officers and whole battalions of men from other units by fair means or foul. He was a hard taskmaster and didn't suffer fools gladly; his staff found him a nightmare and were barely able to keep up with his scattergun orders, the most recent of which would often conflict with the one that had immediately preceded it – and some of them unrealistic if not unachievable.

One of Bethell's staff officers, Walter Guinness, describes a point in 1917 when he could tolerate Bethell's Vesuvius-like rages no more. Guinness had been the object of his CO's ire when he was accused of losing a document, only to find it had been nestling in Bethell's tunic pocket throughout. There had been other instances of subordinates being unfairly and inaccurately accused of misdemeanours, as well. Guinness confronted Bethell about his behaviour, pointing out that the dynamism and enthusiasm that he brought to his command were being cancelled out by the petrifying effect he had on his staff. Bethell, to his credit, seems to have taken this advice on board and was the better for it. But he never stopped being a thorn in the side of the pen-pushers and bureaucrats; he was described as 'a wonderful fighting soldier, but a terror to the administration of an army'. He can be seen as a younger version of Allenby, and the fact that he has been described as a 'young bull' reinforces the comparison.

But Bethell himself had no doubt as to the main reasons behind the 66th Division's success at the Battle of the Selle. In a Special Order issued on the 24 October, he listed those reasons, the top two of which were 'the drive, marching and staying power of the men', and the 'foresight and initiative displayed by junior officers and NCOs'.

What makes the achievement of the men of the 66th exceptional is the fact that the Battle of the Selle seems to have been an anomaly within the 'Hundred Days' offensive that ended the war. The Selle was not the all-arms combination of air power, tanks, and artillery in support of the infantry that was seen as the overriding factor behind the BEF's success in this period. The prevailing weather conditions, an unsympathetic terrain, limited availability of ordnance, and inaccurate intelligence significantly reduced the ability of those arms to support the 66th. Rather, it was down to the skill, professionalism, tenacity, and resilience of the foot soldier, the 'poor bloody infantry', that this battle was won. They were a perfect combination of grizzled veterans from the Irish regiments that had served in Gallipoli, Salonika, and Palestine; of South African warriors who had experienced the hell of Delville Wood in 1916; and the battle-scarred Lancastrian remnants of the original, shattered 66th Division whose ability and proficiency now equalled that of their regular brothers in arms. And Bethell made special mention of William's battalion, thus: 'The 6th RDF of 198th Bde were detailed to mop up Le Cateau by a concentric attack. This difficult work was most thoroughly accomplished with great dash.'

The 6th RDF spent the next two weeks reorganising and training, a period that included marching to the old battleground on the 25th to bury their dead and salvage ordnance and matériel. By the 31st – the day that Turkey signed an armistice following Allenby's stunning success in the Middle East – they had increased their strength to thirty-one officers and 472 other ranks. On the 3 November, the battalion paraded at Le Cateau, where the Officer Commanding 198th Brigade presented the Military Medal, the third-highest award for bravery, to a number of NCOs and men of the battalion. This ceremony might have included William, although it's possible his medal could have been presented to him after the armistice, on the 14th, when a further six were awarded, at Soire-le-Château. It is deeply frustrating that I'll never know what act of bravery or gallantry my grandfather performed to earn this award, or exactly when it happened; was it during the early days of the 'pursuit' taking out a German machine gun nest? Was it when he was wounded in action a couple of days later? Or was it during the clearing of Le Cateau? Unlike the Victoria Cross and the Distinguished Conduct Medal, the two higher awards, there is no citation published that details the specific act. The Military Medal warrants no more than the recipient's name being listed in the London and the Edinburgh Gazettes.

The following day the battalion was on the move, and by the 8th it was back in the front line at Le Jonquière farm, taking part in an attack supporting the 6th Lancs. They were held up by heavy machine gun fire, and a platoon from B Company took up position on the Lancastrians' left wing as reinforcement. However, the attack was discontinued when darkness fell at 5pm. The following day, the 6th RDF were ordered to take over the offensive at 6am to capture the town of Semousies, the final objective, but found that the enemy had evacuated their lines and retreated during the night.

On the 11 November, the men were engaged in repairing a road, filling in a mine crater at Dompierre, when news came through at 8:30am that hostilities were to cease at 11am. The bearer of these tidings was the battalion's CO, Colonel Little, who, in a very low-key manner, remarked, 'Well, we stop today.' Captain Drury took this to mean that he was calling a halt to the road works, until the CO mentioned the signing of the Armistice, and he realised it really was all over.

For many, this report was received with a sense of anticlimax – no wild cheering, celebrating, or 'mafficking about'. Some were stunned; no doubt, some were relieved and others frustrated; it was just a brief hiatus before carrying on with their work. Drury describes how his men took the news: '[T]hey just stared at me and showed no enthusiasm at all. One or two just muttered, "We were just getting a bit of our own back." They all had the look of hounds whipped off just as they were about to kill.'

There might have been a celebratory cheer at 11am when the time came, but for these men, everything they had come to know as normal – all that they had experienced, in some cases, for four years – was about to change. The earth was shifting beneath their feet. An uncertain future awaited them. The incredibly strong bonds with their comrades that had been forged in the fire of war were about to be broken, and they were to be cast amongst a civilian population largely fed with media propaganda and a complete lack of understanding of what they had been through. No doubt the old soldiers like William carried on their duties with a detached cynicism, using humour as a coping mechanism and exuding a fatalistic air, muttering 'San fairy ann' (slang for 'Ça ne fait rien' – 'It doesn't matter') as they shovelled hardcore into the gaping hole of a mine crater.

Following the Armistice, the battalion headed east, crossing from France into Belgium on the 17 November. The official 'March to the Rhine' commenced on the 19th, with the 6th RDF forming the advance guard to the 66th Division. The Divisional GOC, Major General Bethell, had issued the following Special Order in tribute to his men:

> To it [the 66th Division] fell the honour of retaking Le Cateau. Forming part of the Fourth Army Advanced Guard, it was the last Division of this Army to be in action with the enemy. At 11:00, 11th November 1918, on the termination of hostilities, it was holding the Fourth Army front, and in close touch with the enemy. It is now about to advance to the Rhine on the right of the British Army. South Africans, Irishmen and Englishmen, you have proved yourselves all to be magnificent infantry.

William was posted to the 66th Division Traffic Control. It would be three months before he would be formally demobilised. During this period, he carried out routine work, including improving and repairing roads, cleaning captured German guns, and repetitive ceremonial drill and parades. There were also many comings and goings, officers sent on and returning from leave, and attending courses. A fresh draft of 199 men arrived on the 21 December, and many more were to go the other way as the process of demobilisation began. Men were sent home on a sporadic basis in groups of varying size throughout December and into January.

William returned to the UK on the 26 January 1919.

The remaining troops still had time for recreation. On the 13 February, the 6th RDF played in the Divisional Football Cup, losing 2-1 to the 5th Royal Inniskilling Fusiliers in the semi-final. However, the battalion practically ceased to exist by the end of February, when a large number of the men were sent home – 500 on the 21st and fifty-two on the 26th.

Although he was already back in the UK, William remained officially a soldier until he was 'transferred to Class "Z" Army Reserve' on the 23 February 1919. His 'Certificate of Transfer to Reserve on Demobilisation – Army Form Z.21' details the awarding of four blue chevrons and two wound stripes. The chevrons represent the number of years he served overseas in the Great War, and the wound stripes signify his injuries on the Somme in August 1916 and at the Selle in October 1918. His medical category is listed as A1. And, as a nominal member of the Army Reserve, he is directed to report to the nearest infantry depot in case of emergency.

He finally said goodbye to the military, this time for good, and walked away from the army depot in his cheap demob suit to pick up the pieces of his old life in Bethnal Green.

In 2018, a hundred years after these events had taken place, we decided that our annual pilgrimage to the Western Front would concentrate on the final 'Hundred Days' of the war. Over the previous four years, from

2014 onwards, we had consciously tied in each individual battlefield tour with a thematic exploration of events that had occurred exactly a hundred years previously, marking each centenary accordingly. This, the last of the five-year run, was perhaps the most significant of them all, the end of the 'Great War for Civilisation', and, of course, I ensured that this trip would cover the Battle of the Selle.

None of our previous bases for exploring the Western Front, Ypres, Arras, or Amiens, were suitable for researching the breaking of the Hindenburg Line at the St. Quentin Canal or for walking the Selle battlefield and Le Cateau. Thus, we chose the town of Cambrai as our battlefield tour HQ. Cambrai is around fifty miles northeast of Amiens and about twenty-five miles southeast of Arras and is itself an important Great War site. It was where the first major use of tanks in battle took place, in November 1917. It is less popular than the Ypres and Somme sectors for the general battlefield tourist – understandably so – but is worthy of attention in its own right. The town is of a similar size, in terms of population, to Ypres and Arras, and, like both, it has a charm of its own, with a magnificent main square and scores of architectural and historical gems. Although nowhere else touches Ypres for the almost-spiritual significance and emotional pull that it has for the British, I immediately warmed to Cambrai and will return if I get the opportunity.

By this time, our party had grown to sixteen strong, some of us veterans of fourteen trips. We were travelling in a four-car convoy, and the size of our group brought with it a growing logistical challenge to find a place to stay, restaurants, and parking spaces that would accommodate us all. Having successfully managed to fulfil all these needs, after our customary early Friday morning crossing on the Eurotunnel service, we checked in at our hotel and then set off for the front. It was a beautiful sunny autumnal day, unseasonably warm for October, hot even – yet again, we had been fortunate with the weather – and we drove due south to Bellenglise, a small village nearly twenty miles away that had been adjacent to the German fortified trench system in 1918. After parking the cars, we began to walk the ground, tracking the Hindenburg Line. We joined the footpath, which eventually climbed high up on to the west bank of the St. Quentin Canal, varying in height between thirty and fifty feet. We tramped northwards, welcoming the protective shade of the woods as we walked, each deep in our own thoughts, imagining the scene a century ago when this cutting was largely bare of trees due to constant shelling.

After a mile, we reached the Riqueval Bridge, the northernmost point of the 46th (North Midlands) Division's frontage and the sector where the Hindenburg Line had been broken. The scenes following this remarkable victory three days later were recorded in a series of photographs, the most famous of which shows Brigadier J.V. Campbell VC on the parapet of the bridge, addressing the massed ranks of his victorious 137th Brigade, who were covering the east bank of the canal as if they were fans on the terraces at a football match.

We had intended to recreate the photograph – our much smaller party of sixteen sitting on the bank in a similar pose – but the now heavily wooded, steep slope defeated us. We carried on northwards towards the entrance to the Riqueval tunnel, where the canal goes underground for 5,670 metres, and where the American 30th Division subsequently broke through the German line following the success of the British further south. The tunnel had been adapted by the Germans to form part of their defensive fortifications, excavating the walls of the structure to form chambers that were used as medical posts, offices, and storerooms, and installing electricity to provide light and heating. The tunnel's ventilation shafts were used to access strategically placed machine gun posts above ground. Barges moored within the tunnel were used as billets for the troops. Crossing the canal here, we made our way back south on the east bank footpath and returned to the cars to complete an easy four-mile walk. We looked forward to a pleasant evening sampling the restaurants and hostelries of Cambrai.

I awoke on Saturday morning with an eager sense of anticipation. Fortified by a breakfast of fresh rolls and coffee, we were on the road just after nine o'clock. It was another gloriously sunny day. We headed south-southeast through pleasant countryside on the D960, passing through Walincourt-Selvigny, and halted at the crossroads with the old Roman road, the present-day D932. The intersection was just south of Elincourt, the commune that had been cleared of Germans by William and the 6th RDF during the morning of the 9 October 1918 – the first day of the official Pursuit to the Selle. On previous tours, we had generally walked the ground of each particular battlefield – and on a couple of occasions, we'd hired pushbikes and cycled them – as this was the best way to gain an understanding of what took place in each battle and the challenges presented by the terrain. And a good yomp in our modern walking boots increased our appreciation and admiration for the men who'd marched far greater distances in far less comfortable army-issue boots, carrying anywhere between fifty and eighty pounds of kit. However, this time we travelled in the cars, as the 6th RDF had advanced at such a rate during the Pursuit to the Selle that to literally follow in their footsteps would have taken up far too much of our time.

Travelling by car also highlighted how remarkable their progress had been. On previous occasions, when exploring the attritional battles at Ypres and the Somme, we spoke of ground won in terms of yards; in contrast, here at the Selle it was *miles*, and all in a single day. Heading northeast along the Roman road, we stopped briefly at Maretz and Reumont en route to Le Cateau – orientating ourselves at these significant landmarks on the original march to increase our understanding of the 6th RDF's feat of arms.

We stopped briefly at the International Cemetery to the northwest of Le Cateau, so called because of the mixture of British, German, and Russian soldiers buried there. The cemetery overlooks the town and provides a convenient vantage point from which to appreciate the topography of the battlefield, not far from where the 6th RDF commenced their attack on the 17 October 1918. Thence down into the town itself, where we found a convenient parking spot, an area of hard standing adjacent to the Pont Fourneau, one of the bridges crossing the River Selle, and began our short walking tour of the town, hugging the west bank of the river and heading northwards along the Rue des Digues, until we reached the main bridge carrying the N43 into the town from the west. We took a right turn and crossed over the river into Rue Charles Seydoux, passing a magnificent building housing the Matisse Museum on our left as we walked uphill into the centre of town. We came to a crossroads and posed for a group photograph by a commemorative horse trough, which bears the inscription:

**In memory of those of the 66ᵗʰ Division of the British Expeditionary Force who fell in the liberation of Le Cateau from German occupation in October 1918.**

Then we about-turned and headed towards the church mentioned in the 6ᵗʰ RDF war diary, where A company, approaching from the west, was to rendezvous with B and C companies coming from the northeast to complete the mopping-up operation. The Eglise Saint-Martin is an imposing structure, a former Benedictine abbey built in the seventeenth century. We gathered in the courtyard in front of the church, and I ran through the events of the 17 October, quoting extracts from the war diary for the benefit of the group.

Afterwards, I took a moment for myself. Facing away from the church door, I gazed down the Rue Pasteur towards the river, letting my imagination run and travelling back in time a hundred years. I could see the men of the 6ᵗʰ RDF methodically clearing the street, house by house; I could hear sporadic bursts of machine gun and rifle fire, with the occasional report of a lobbed Mills grenade punctuating the proceedings, followed by German prisoners being dragged out of doorways by the scruffs of their necks.

And then I saw a familiar figure, just as my father had described him. I recognised the slightly bowed legs and the way he carried himself as he led his section up to the church, his Lee Enfield at the ready, finger poised inside the trigger guard, steel helmet slightly angled, his face streaked with grime and sweat, his blue eyes focused, and scanning the line of buildings from left to right and back again. I heard his cockney accent contrasting with those of his Irish brothers in arms. He broke free of the street and crossed the road towards the church – towards me – and I smiled.

But he saw nothing, for I was but a ghost from the future.

CHAPTER FIFTEEN

# BERMONDSEY

*There are strange Hells within the minds War made*
*Not so often, not so humiliatingly afraid*
*As one would have expected – the racket and fear guns made.*

IVOR GURNEY, from *Strange Hells*

On his return to civilian life, William was able to pick up where he left off and go back to his pre-war job with the vinegar brewery – now trading as Champion & Slee (eventually to trade as Sarson's) – which had relocated operations from the City Road in Hoxton to south of the Thames in Bermondsey, adjacent to Tower Bridge Road. He now had farther to walk from Bethnal Green, but his commute would not prove to be long-lived; his circumstances were about to change dramatically. The workplace move from Hoxton to Bermondsey was key to what followed.

An old army pal introduced his cousin, Florence Gilbey, to William, and there was an instant attraction that developed into a whirlwind romance. A matter of months later, on the 11 April 1919, they were married at the register office of St. Olave's, Bermondsey. It is clear from my Uncle Charlie's birthdate why the marriage was so hastily arranged.

Florence, known as Florrie, or Flo, was a twenty-nine-year-old war widow with two young children: a boy also named William, aged six, and a girl named Ethel, aged four. She had been pregnant with Ethel when her first husband, William Edward Gilbey, was tragically killed whilst serving in the navy during the early days of the war. Able Seaman 221975 William Gilbey was serving on HMS *Pathfinder*, a scout cruiser of the Eighth Destroyer Flotilla, when a German U-boat sank it on the 5 September 1914, with the loss of 260 men. It was the first successful submarine operation of the war. The planets had aligned on that day; it was the very same day that my grandfather had re-enlisted at Finsbury Barracks. As Florrie lost one husband, her future spouse was taking the first step in a course of events that would lead to their fateful meeting.

The newly married couple lived at 4 Perseverance Street in Bermondsey, the tenancy of which had passed on to Florrie after her parents had died. It was a small, terraced house in the heart of south London's docklands, just a stone's throw from the vinegar works. William's life was entering a new phase. Many of his fellows within the ranks of the demobilised masses were not so fortunate. With a new wife, a roof over his head, and secure employment, my grandfather was one of the lucky ones. The same could not be said of hundreds of thousands of his brothers in arms.

On the 23 November 1918, whilst my grandfather was still in Belgium at a place named Rosée on the route of the March to the Rhine, the British Prime Minister, David Lloyd George, was in Wolverhampton, attending a meeting in the run-up to the general election. There he made his famous speech, promising a better life for those who had served and suffered during the war: 'What is our task? To make Britain a fit country for heroes to live in.' Those words would come back to haunt him when he was unable to make good on his promise. It was well intentioned, but he would eventually abandon his progressive principles in an attempt to appease his Conservative colleagues in the coalition government, who looked nervously over their shoulders at the disapproving Tory faithful and at Lord Rothermere, the right-wing newspaper proprietor who waged a 'war on waste' and to whom any hint of a collectivist approach – such as subsidised council housing – was anathema. The result was that the coalition government failed to meet the hopes and aspirations of the returning men and their families.

The Britain that the troops came home to was a different place from that which they had left four years earlier. The economic and industrial landscape had shifted, including the trading relationships with the rest of the world. Whilst Britain's economy had been placed on a war footing, foreign investors had looked elsewhere, and the growing influence of

America as a major financial and banking power had filled the void. Britain's place as one of the world's largest manufacturers and producers was under threat, and its major industries suffered accordingly. Coal, shipbuilding, textiles, and steel declined, causing unemployment and much hardship. The returning soldiers faced huge challenges in finding work. Many had given up good positions to fight for their country; apprenticeships had been interrupted and careers prematurely stalled. And now, their training incomplete and without qualifications, they found themselves frozen out of the job market.

By 1920, 250,000 ex-servicemen were unemployed, and this figure was to soar to something in the region of 600,000 to 800,000 by the mid-1920s. The plight of the jobless ex-soldier is bleakly painted by Ivor Gurney:

> *Where are they now on State-doles, or showing shop patterns*
> *Or walking town to town sore in borrowed tatterns*
> *Or begged. Some civic routine one never learns.*
> *The heart burns – but has to keep out of face how heart burns.*

Lloyd George's promises would be seen as another lie, a deceit to rival the 'old lie', 'Dulce et decorum est pro patria mori' ('It is sweet and proper to die for one's country') – the Roman poet Horace's exhortation or call to arms that Wilfred Owen took and twisted, and that was recycled and juxtaposed by Ezra Pound:

> *Died some, pro patria, non 'dulce' non 'et decor'…*
> *walked eye-deep in hell*
> *believing in old men's lies, then unbelieving*
> *came home, home to a lie,*
> *home to many deceits,*
> *home to old lies and new infamy;*
> *usury age-old and age-thick*
> *and liars in public places.*

The reality was that many of the demobilised soldiers were returning to the inadequate and insanitary pre-war slum dwellings. The Unhealthy Areas Committee, reporting on the 14 January 1920, stated, 'That it is a gigantic problem … that there are 600,000 people living in London under unsatisfactory conditions as regards housing.' In Bermondsey alone, 10,000 houses were formally condemned as unfit for human habitation in 1930. As late as 1935, across the whole of the country, there were around 250,000 such houses still standing and occupied.

For the even more unfortunate, homelessness awaited – or the workhouse, which survived in one form or another until the passing of the National Assistance Act 1948. The national programme of housebuilding and slum clearances announced by the government in 1919 failed due to spiralling costs, inefficiency, and misadministration, and although it might have survived with more competent management, politics was the decisive factor. If Lloyd George were to survive as Prime Minister, he needed the support of the Tories. Thus, the 'Homes Fit for Heroes' scheme fell victim to political ideology and personal ambition.

After Uncle Charlie's birth in 1919, William and Florence went on to have two more children, my father George, born in 1922, and my Aunt Florrie, born in 1926. Along with young William Gilbey (known to the family as Bill) and Ethel – my grandfather's stepchildren – the family was now complete.

In 2009, when my Aunt Florrie wrote to me with some of her memories of growing up in Bermondsey, she emphasised that my grandfather had cared for Bill and Ethel as if they were his own – and they loved him for it. After years of bachelorhood and soldiering, he had taken to family life surprisingly seamlessly; he always had time for the children, playing games with them after work, and he shouldered his share of household chores. My father and Uncle Charlie played in the street, and at the same time every day, they would run to meet him coming home from work.

Aunt Florrie recalled that the house was always full of people. I remember my father telling me that, come teatime, whichever of the neighbours' children who happened to be playing with them outside would be swept up and sat at the table to be fed with the family. And the favour would be returned – an example of working-class altruism and community spirit.

My favourite anecdote was one that my father told me – one that I constantly asked him to repeat, as he was an engaging and skilful raconteur – involving a period of my grandfather's life when he was working with horses. This cameo would fit well within the pages of *Black Beauty* or, perhaps more aptly, *War Horse*. During his career at the vinegar works, in the period before motorised transport supplanted horsepower, William used to work at the company's stables, not only as a stableman and groom but also as a tracer. The tracer's duties involved attaching an extra horse, known as a trace-horse, to the horse-drawn vans heavily laden with full crates of vinegar as they left the works in Tower Bridge Road to head over the bridge into the City of London and all points north. The horses had to negotiate a steady incline up to the crest of the bridge where the two bascules met, and their hooves would slip on the stone-paved road as they struggled to pull these heavy loads. The trace horse, attended by my grandfather, was there to lend its muscle power to make their task that much easier. Once they were over the crest and on the downward slope, he would detach the animal and return to his station at the gates of the vinegar works in readiness for the next van.

On the day in question, my grandfather saw a driver (not associated with the vinegar works) cruelly whipping an exhausted horse that was clearly pulling a load too heavy for it. I got the impression from my father's stories that William, when his official duties allowed, had a sideline in hooking up his trace horse to other horse-drawn traffic for a few extra pennies. He was certainly a familiar face to all of the regular drivers passing over Tower Bridge. However, this particular driver was obviously determined not to pay the fee, and his horse was suffering for it. Incensed, my grandfather leapt into action. He pulled the driver from his seat and administered a blow that left the miscreant on his backside in the middle of Tower Bridge Road, nursing a sore jaw. (My father used more colourful language than this when he told the story.) He then hooked up the trace horse free of charge, for the sake of the beaten animal, escorted the suitably admonished driver to the apex of the bridge, and then sent him on his way with a flea in his ear and a stark warning as to his future health and well-being if he were ever to see him mistreating a horse in that way again.

I admit that I took a boyish satisfaction from the summary justice meted out by my grandfather. And from all that I had learnt, this was totally out of character for him, revealing the depth of feeling he had for the welfare of horses, something that had obviously been kindled during his time in South Africa. This is the only instance that I'm aware of when he acted in such a way. My father and my aunts and uncles have all said that they had never seen him lose his temper – not once. Rather, they said he remained calm and measured under all circumstances and was able to handle any given situation with equanimity. This insight into his mental state indicates that the war had not affected him as profoundly as it had countless others. If he did, indeed, suffer from Gurney's 'Strange Hells', he hid it well. There is nothing to suggest that he had experienced after-effects such as those suffered by Rifleman Fred White of the 10th Battalion, King's Royal Rifle Corps:

> Us fellows, it took us years to get over it. Years! Long after when you were working, married, had kids, you'd be lying in bed with your wife and you'd see it all before you. Couldn't sleep. Couldn't lie still. Many and many's the time I've got up and tramped the streets till it came daylight. Walking, walking – anything to get away from your thoughts. And many's the time I've met other fellows that were out there doing exactly the same thing. That went on for years, that did.

To gain an understanding of why he might have been able to cope with the psychological effects of war more rationally than others, we should turn to Lord Moran's *Anatomy of Courage*. As a veteran of the Boer

War and a seasoned soldier accustomed to army life prior to the Great War, William had the resilience, self-discipline, and mental toughness that made him, in Moran's words, 'more than usually resistant to the corroding effects of strain and battle.' Men like William, professional soldiers who had served in South Africa and India, were already battle-hardened; having previously experienced being shelled and shot at, the trauma of the Great War for them was less dramatic than that suffered by many of the volunteers and conscripts of the great citizen army who had joined after 1914.

Earlier in these pages, I posed the question, Was my grandfather one of the Lost Generation? In other words, was he traumatised? 'Lost' to his family, to his community, to society? The evidence suggests not.

William and Florence celebrated their tenth wedding anniversary in 1929, the same year as the Wall Street Crash, an economic crisis caused by excessive speculation on the American stock market that had created an unsustainable bubble that collapsed when investors panic-sold stocks and shares. The crash precipitated the Great Depression of the 1930s, a devastating economic slump that spread around the globe like wildfire. Trade and industry suffered profoundly, leading to a commensurate drop in prices and profits, affecting personal income and tax revenues, and resulting in record unemployment levels. In the UK, nearly three million were out of work by 1932, a catastrophic year for the working class in particular.

Britain was still recovering from the huge expense of the Great War when the financial storm broke: there was a run on gold reserves as foreign investors withdrew their assets from the Bank of England. The Labour Prime Minister, Ramsay MacDonald, relied on the unimaginative economic orthodoxy of balancing the books through tax hikes and spending cuts, including reducing unemployment benefit by twenty percent; in a word, 'austerity'. The unemployment benefit cut split the cabinet and was completely unacceptable to the Labour Party at large; it was a betrayal of all they stood for.

A substantial cut in the unemployment benefit was seen by MacDonald and the Tories as preferable to coming off the gold standard, the historic monetary system whereby the currency's value was linked to a fixed quantity of gold. Such a fixed exchange rate mechanism gave governments little room to manoeuvre when it came to economic and fiscal policy in a crisis, and the incumbents at the time chose the blunt instruments of cutting public spending and raising taxes. MacDonald was not prepared to abandon the gold standard and suffer the devaluation of sterling that would follow.

Without the full support of his cabinet, MacDonald felt compelled to offer his resignation to King George V. He was granted an audience with the King, who preempted him by stating that he expected MacDonald to stay in office and see the nation through to the end of the crisis as the head of a national, all-party government. He duly accepted, offering the resignation of the Labour Government and forming a coalition of all three parties that would remain in office until the storm was weathered. As a result, he was, along with the few Labour MPs that supported him, expelled from the party and thereafter demonised by the left. The general election of 1931 saw MacDonald and his national coalition government win a landslide victory, but the economic crisis was still unresolved. The measures they'd taken came to nothing, and the government's position proved unsustainable. As the pound came under severe pressure, they were forced to abandon the gold standard anyway – on whose altar the massed ranks of the unemployed and effectively the Labour Party had been sacrificed – and the breaking of the chains of this fixed exchange rate set the country free to pursue economic recovery. Fears of the consequences of devaluation proved to be groundless.

But this recovery would take a while to trickle down to the man in the street. The country would suffer for a while yet. Throughout the crisis, the world's major economies, including Britain, had seen their GDPs fall by a quarter, commodity prices halved, consumer prices fall by a third, a quarter of male workers put out of work, and wages cut by a third. This last issue, reduced pay, was the major concern of workers like William.

He had a wife and five children to support, although by 1932, Bill and Ethel were of an age to seek employment and, thus, could also contribute to the household finances.

I alighted from the train at London Bridge Station and travelled down the escalator to the impressive lower ground concourse of the recently updated terminus, exiting the station to the south, on to St Thomas Street, then turning east. On my left was the freshly cleaned brickwork of the railway viaduct that supported the Southern and Southeastern railway tracks above. The warm, sunny day matched my mood as I made my way to the site of my grandfather's workplace. I hadn't passed this way for at least two years. As I walked, my attention was immediately drawn to the rich yellow-coloured hoarding advertising Vinegar Yard to my right, on the south side of the street, and the thumping of the sound system coming from within.

Established in April 2019, what was once a patch of waste ground is now a vibrant and popular culture and events hub of shops, bars, and street food stalls complementing Borough Market nearby and bringing life and colour to a previously nondescript part of Southwark adjacent to the railway tracks. This whole area was undergoing a regeneration process to match the bright, shiny new station and the towering Shard that were at its centre. There are plans to eventually erect a nineteen-storey building here, with Vinegar Yard set up to move into and manage the whole ground floor, curating a similar mix of eateries and independent retail outlets. The current site also hosts a weekend market selling vintage clothes, vinyl records, and books, and it boasts a huge contemporary artwork consisting of a decommissioned railway carriage swarming with giant red ants raised up high above street level. I wondered what my grandfather would have made of it all.

I continued winding my way east until I emerged onto Tower Bridge Road and located the site of the old Sarson's vinegar works. The brewery consisted of two rows of buildings, eastern and western, bounded by the railway arches to the north and Tanner Street to the south. Today, most of the eastern buildings facing onto Tower Bridge Road survive from the works, the exception being a large warehouse that was demolished in 1982 and replaced with a modern building on more or less the original footprint.

The company sold up in 1992 and moved to Manchester. The old Sarson's site, now a mixed-use development named Maltings Place, is occupied by multiple businesses and residential flats. In its previous life, the surviving buildings on the east side included another warehouse, the general office, the laboratory, and the acetifier house. I entered the complex from the Tower Bridge Road entrance and walked into the narrow yard between the east and west sections of what was the brewery. I saw that all of the western buildings, some dating back to the 1820s, were intact. These buildings have now been granted Grade II listed status.

I found myself transported back to the early twentieth century. Whatever *exhaust* is left behind when a person vacates a physical space – whether it be molecular or ethereal, real or imagined – William had left his in this place. Using my mind's eye, I envisaged him here at work, the yard bustling with activity as the crates of vinegar were manhandled from the bottling store to the loading bay adjacent to the gated entrance.

I scanned the old buildings and was able to identify which of them housed the fermentation vats and bottling store, the malt store, the brew house, and the coal store. Most importantly to me, I could identify the boiler house and the engine house where William worked as a stoker and a stationary engineman, respectively. Here, I had my 'sense of place' again, and then some.

I walked to the top of the yard, where the railway arches stood. Now empty and cleaned up as part of the London Bridge station regeneration project, they were cavernous. The brewery had had a leasing arrangement with the railway and had occupied the southern half of all of the arches that ran along the northern edge of the works. A sawmill and cooperage had been established there, and those at the eastern end adjacent to Tower Bridge Road had been employed as stables, where William would have tended to his horses. I recalled my Aunt Florrie telling me of an old photograph she'd once seen of him flanked by two horses, their bridles gripped in his hands. It's not known if it still exists or who might now possess it. That photo had surely been taken here, in front of these arches.

I left the old vinegar works and carried on eastwards along Tanner Street, passed through the railway arches, and into Druid Street, towards the Arnold Estate, where Perseverance Street once was. My grandfather's house was pulled down in the slum clearance programme of the 1930s, not long after his death. The linear street plan lined with rows of two-up, two-down terraced dwellings had disappeared completely. It had been replaced by a snaking estate road weaving through the individual, angled blocks of low-rise flats, which made it difficult to orientate myself. I attempted to make an informed guess in my mind as to where he might have lived by overlaying the replica Ordnance Survey map of 1914 Bermondsey that I had been using as the basis for my exploration onto the current street plan.

I didn't dally for long; without any contemporaneous buildings or street furniture to anchor me in my musings – no backdrop, no physical context – I moved on, joining Jamaica Road, and continued heading east just a few hundred yards south of and parallel to the Thames, the Dickens Estate blocking the river from view. I passed a couple of familiar landmarks on my right: the mock Tudor façade of the Gregorian pub, overshadowed by the magnificent spire of St. James – modelled on one of Wren's churches in the City – which has dominated the area since the mid-nineteenth century.

As I walked, my mood changed, for I knew that this was the final leg of my odyssey; I was metaphorically approaching Graham's 'grey wooden cross' and the end of my grandfather's life. I carried on past the railings of Southwark Park to my right, in my grandfather's time a pleasure ground for the families of the dockers and stevedores, the lightermen and watermen, the tanners and leatherworkers, the biscuit, jam, and vinegar makers that constituted the local Bermondsey economy. Reaching the roundabout at the eastern end of Jamaica Road, I headed south in Lower Road until I reached a turning on my right into a modern residential estate named Ann Moss Way. The estate was built on the former site of St. Olave's Hospital, where my grandfather's life ended, and which had closed in 1985. But there was a small remnant of the hospital still standing: the southern gatehouse on the corner of the old entrance to St Olave's adjoining Lower Road, now the main access road to the estate. A blue plaque adorns the wall of the gatehouse, celebrating the birth of the actor Sir Michael Caine at the hospital in 1933 – the year following William's demise. (In another curious case of synchronicity, Caine would also serve with my grandfather's battalion, the 1st Royal Fusiliers, during the Korean War of 1950–53.) It was a reminder of the remorseless nature of life and death; that as one journey ends, so another begins.

It was the day before little Florrie's sixth birthday, the 18 February 1932. She would be celebrating it in the children's ward of St. Olave's Hospital, having been admitted with a persistent eczema-like skin condition a few months prior. She was looking forward to visiting time and seeing her mum and dad. That always made her happy. But today it was not to be. William came home from work that day feeling ill. My grandmother told him to go straight to bed, and she would make him a hot drink. As she was making it, she heard a dreadful moaning. She rushed to the bottom of the stairs and saw William bent over the bannister, sweating profusely and clearly in agony. She swiftly called for young Bill and sent him running full pelt to fetch the doctor, who was fifteen minutes away.

When the doctor came, he immediately sent for an ambulance. Upon arrival at St. Olave's, William was admitted to the ward immediately below his daughter's, but it was all to no avail; he died that night on the operating table from a perforated ulcer. Bill and Ethel visited young Florrie in the children's ward, and straightaway she sensed something was wrong, asking where her daddy was. Bill and Ethel, only teenagers themselves, told her that he couldn't come that day as he was working hard, but Florrie wouldn't give up. Eventually they had to tell her and broke the news as gently as they could, using these comforting words: 'Daddy has gone to heaven with the angels, and you must be brave because he will always be with you and looking down on you, and to remember, he will always love you.' My grandmother was heartbroken. Now forty-two years old and twice widowed, she would never marry again.

My grandfather's experience is echoed in Michael Longley's poem *In Memoriam*. Longley's father, also a veteran of the Great War, contracted cancer and suffered agonising pain as well. The similarity between the two's last moments is striking:

> *Which ended with the ambulance outside,*
> *You lingering in the hall, your bowels on fire,*
> *Tears in your eyes, and all your medals spent…*

William had lived an eventful life, full of far more adventure and travel than a typical East End boy could ever hope to experience, overcoming poverty and war. Whether soldiering or labouring, he had fought hard for his country and just as hard to provide for his family. 'Lions led by donkeys', the apocryphal phrase used to describe the ordinary soldiers of the Great War, was referenced in the title of Alan Clark's damning indictment of the generals (*The Donkeys*). Siegfried Sassoon was just as scathing in his famous poem *The General*.

But it wasn't an incompetent or callous commanding officer – a 'butcher' or a 'bungler' – who caused the death of this particular 'lion'; for William, it wasn't an officer who 'did for him' with his 'plan of attack'. His own body failed him. Just as the economy was showing the green shoots of recovery; just when his quality of life might have improved. There was one consolation: he never had to witness his boys, Charlie and George, march off to serve in another world war. The Great War – 'the war to end all wars' – had been but a prequel to the next, equally (if not more) catastrophic and inextricably linked global conflict.

CHAPTER SIXTEEN

# REMEMBRANCE SUNDAY, 13 NOVEMBER 2005, CHURCH OF ST. SEPULCHRE-WITHOUT-NEWGATE, HOLBORN VIADUCT, LONDON

*And you, the soldier:*
*you who are dead: is it not so with you?*
*Love: devotion: sacrifice: death: can we call you unknown,*
*you who knew what you did? The soldier is crystal:*
*crystal of man: clear heart, clear duty, clear purpose.*
*no soldier can be unknown. Only he is unknown*
*who is unknown to himself.*

CONRAD AIKEN *The Wars and the Unknown Soldier*

I looked to my right, towards the south aisle of the church, at the pew immediately adjacent to mine, as the St. Sepulchre's Singers began the opening hymn of the service.

*O valiant hearts, who to your glory came*
*Through dust of conflict and through battle flame;*
*Tranquil you lie, your knightly virtue proved,*
*Your memory hallowed in the land you loved.*

I scanned the row of much-loved and familiar faces, their eyes fixed on the Order of Service in hand and their voices adding to that of the choir, and I felt a rush of emotion. For on this day, at this moment, what was taking place was nothing less than the righting of a wrong. Three generations of the family, with Aunt Florrie as the guest of honour, were here to celebrate the life of the man who had begotten us all.

*Proudly you gathered, rank on rank to war,*
*As who had heard God's message from afar,*
*All you had hoped for, all you had, you gave,*
*To save mankind – yourselves you scorned to save.*

In this place stood his daughter, grandchildren, and great-grandchildren, who owed their very existence to his prowess as a soldier; his remarkable ability to survive and withstand all that had been thrown at him throughout two conflicts – and naught more deadly than the *Storm of Steel* that took the lives of so many of his comrades during the Great War. So many 'there but for the grace of God' moments when bullets missed him by inches, when shells landed close by and either failed to detonate, or when they exploded, hurtled deadly shrapnel that miraculously passed him by.

*Splendid you passed, the great surrender made*
*Into the light that nevermore shall fade;*
*Deep your contentment in that blest abode,*
*Who wait the last clear trumpet call of God.*

Here we were, honouring a man whom only one of us had actually known – a man whom we would always view as legendary. But not mythical, for we knew of his deeds, made real by virtue of his medals, evidenced through army records and oral testimony – primary sources that documented and authenticated his life.

*O risen Lord, O shepherd of our dead,*
*Whose cross has brought them and whose staff has led –*
*In glorious hope – their proud and sorrowing land*
*Commits her children to Thy gracious hand.*

As the final words of the hymn echoed throughout the church, I fixed my gaze on the oak panelling alongside the pew occupied by my family.

There, engraved into the wood and picked out in freshly applied white lettering, was the following inscription:

**Corporal William Charles Blumsom MM**
**Royal Fusiliers**
**Died 18 February 1932**

His name had been added to the memorial wall of the Royal Fusiliers. A roll of honour, listing officers and men who had served with the regiment, lined the south wall of the church of St. Sepulchre's, the south aisle of which had been dedicated in 1950 as the Royal Fusiliers Memorial Chapel. Hanging above the pews are the regiment's Colours, the oldest of which is the 1st Battalion's, dated around 1789, along with the tattered remains of the 2nd Battalion's, which, in August 1880, was the last to actually be carried into battle. Also represented are the 3rd and 4th Battalions' Colours and those of a number of militia, territorial, and service battalions. During his two spells with the regiment, William had served under no less than four of them.

This was a special moment, a fitting and worthy memorialisation of his life that superseded what had been provided him by the state: a common grave in Nunhead Cemetery, unseen and unvisited, marked by an inadequate headstone that had lain flat for seventy years buried in the undergrowth. Now, looking at his inscribed name, I couldn't have been prouder.

Our attendance here today was the result of a conversation I had had with the Rector on a visit to the church in early 2005. He confirmed to me that my grandfather qualified for a commemorative inscription on the memorial panelling. He told me to contact the regimental HQ at the Tower of London for further advice. After corresponding with Major Bowes-Crick and making the necessary arrangements, we were invited to attend the Regimental Remembrance Day Service, traditionally the day when newly engraved memorial inscriptions are dedicated.

The day's proceedings began with a march by the regiment's band, sporting ceremonial bearskins more familiarly associated with the Guards, and detachments of past, present, and future Fusiliers – smartly attired veterans in blazers adorned with rows of medals, serving soldiers, and cadets, many sporting the regimental red and white hackle on cap or beret – to the Royal Fusiliers war memorial at Holborn Bar, at the boundary of the ancient City of London around 400 metres west of the church. It was a bright, crisp autumn day. The fragile rays of the sun shone on the guard of honour as they formed up on the four corners of the base of the memorial. Sculpted by Albert Toft and erected in 1922, the memorial is a large bronze representation of a Great War soldier, right leg raised and placed on a rock, left leg straight and firmly planted on the ground, rifle held in his right hand pointed forward with bayonet attached, his left arm by his side with his fist clenched. His torso is twisted as he looks behind, seemingly urging his colleagues on, and he is poised, ready to advance. The sculpture portrays a steely resolve and an unyielding attitude.

Our family group took up position on the north side of Holborn at the junction with Brooke Street, where we had a good view of the ceremony, one of many taking place throughout the land on this Remembrance Sunday. The Rector stood facing the memorial on the west side with the current cohort of serving fusiliers behind him. The band took up position to the east of the monument, and the detachment of cadets lined up to the south with the veterans on the north. The whole scene was framed by the familiar backdrop of an iconic London landmark, Staple Inn, a striking Tudor timber-framed building that has stood here for over four hundred years.

Eventually we came to the most poignant moment of the ceremony, the playing of the *Last Post* by a lone bugler. As the closing note faded into the fresh autumn air, the veterans of the Fusilier Association formed up, standards unfurled, ready to march back to the church for the service. They set off, leading the band, the serving soldiers, and the cadets in that order.

Our party followed, making our way back to the church, where the Major was waiting to greet us and show us to a pew reserved for us adjacent to William's memorial inscription. On the seat was an A4 sheet printed 'Reserved for family of Cpl Blumsom', which I swiftly tucked into my Order of Service as a keepsake. The pew couldn't accommodate us all; thus, I gave up my seat and moved to the central pew across the aisle, which gave me the opportunity to see the reaction of my kin to this special moment. After a couple of hymns and the reading of the first lesson, the Rector made his way from the pulpit, stopped alongside our pew, and performed the dedication ceremony, his voice resonating throughout the church: 'In the faith of Jesus Christ, we dedicate the inscriptions on these Memorials to the glory of God, in the name of the Father and the Son and of the Holy Ghost, and to the memory of Corporal William Charles Blumsom MM.' I could see that Aunt Florrie was transfixed, and I can only imagine the emotion that she was feeling. It was deeply moving.

For me, the latter part of the dedication was what this day was all about: '…to the memory of Corporal William Charles Blumsom MM'. William's name is now etched in perpetuity alongside his brothers in arms, including his former commanding officer, Colonel Guy du Maurier. This is where it belongs – where future generations of the family can pay their respects and where he will be remembered. When the ceremony was finally over, we emerged from the church, blinking, into the weak autumnal sunshine.

There was one more thing that had to be done. The family party decanted into two cars and set off, travelling in tandem past St Paul's Cathedral and through the City of London, across the Thames over Tower Bridge, heading south via the old Sarson's vinegar works into Bermondsey, the family's heartland, and thence, via Deptford and Peckham, to the gates of Nunhead Cemetery in Linden Grove.

Our little group passed through the entrance into the necropolis and headed towards the roofless chapel, retracing my steps taken earlier that year. We turned left, took the left fork where the path split, and arrived at William's grave. We gathered around, and Aunt Florrie laid flowers by his headstone before gently placing her hand on his engraved name.

After seventy years, the daughter was finally reunited with the father.

Aunt Florrie wrote to me a few weeks later. 'I still look back on the 13th November as a wonderful day. I still see so vividly the whole ceremony…' She thanked me for 'all your efforts, to make that day – and indeed the future days something I can remember always … you gave me a gift I never thought I'd have – and for me that has meant everything.… I know your dad would have loved to have been with us – but at least I was grateful for all of us, Charlie and George.'

That letter is now a treasured possession, and it forms part of my family archive, a deeply personal document that will be passed on. That I was able to bring such comfort to Aunt Florrie is both humbling and heartwarming, an honour and a privilege. How I wish that I'd been able to arrange this within the lifetimes of my father and Uncle Charlie. I know how much this would have meant to them both. But, back then, I simply wasn't at a stage in my journey where this would have been possible. Looking back, I can see now that my father's death was at least partly instrumental in bringing this long, painstaking odyssey to fruition. It was part of the formula that drove me on, influencing the sequence of events that came to pass, so any regrets that I have are tempered with the knowledge that these thoughts are imponderable and that one might have been the consequence of the other.

My grandfather was a hero on two counts: clearly, as a decorated war hero, but also as a husband, father, provider, and role model for his family. The achievement of the latter, although not formally recognised as is that of the brave warrior, is no less worthy of praise. Victor Hugo puts this perfectly: 'Life, adversity, isolation, abandonment, poverty are battlefields that have their heroes, the obscure sometimes greater than the illustrious.'

William qualified as both an obscure and an illustrious hero. His life was an epic struggle as a civilian and as a soldier; from his humble beginnings in the back streets of Bethnal Green, growing up amongst the poverty and privation of the East End, surviving war, disease, injuries, and wounds whilst serving in the army, to sheltering, feeding and clothing his family in Bermondsey during turbulent economic times, it's truly heroic. Nevertheless, I do not venerate him as a saint. He was a working-class soldier from the East End, familiar with the earthier aspects of life. But his love for his wife and children, reflected in their recollections – particularly significant in the case of his stepchildren – and his deep feeling and care for horses reveal a big, generous heart, that of a humanitarian. He is a role model for succeeding generations. He is what I aspire to be, my lodestar, my touchstone.

Twenty years have passed since I'd begun my search in earnest, that point when the obsession with my grandfather's life became a quest with a defined endgame, had assumed a structure, and forged its own pathway. That was when my thoughts crystallised and I was able to articulate what I would do. My earlier boyish interest developed into a forensic investigation in adulthood to construct a profile of this man. I combed all of the records, sought out the primary and secondary sources, and took fresh evidence from my Aunt Florrie to corroborate the historic evidence gathered from my father and Uncle Charlie.

Had I succeeded in finding him? Both physically and metaphorically, the answer is undoubtedly yes, four times over: I had found his actual remains in Nunhead Cemetery; I had found the schoolboy in Mowlem Street School; I had found the husband, father, and provider in Bermondsey; and I had found the soldier in Belgium and France. And it is the latter to which I will return again and again.

This is not the end of my journey; this is a lifelong relationship. For as long as I am able, I will go back to the battlefields of Ypres and the Somme to connect with the soldier, for it is this version of my grandfather that fired my imagination and that resonates with me still. It is there that I will commune with him, where I feel close to him, where the veil that separates the dead from the living is at its thinnest, at its most porous. Where I will walk with his ghost again.

# EXPLANATORY NOTES AND SOURCES

PAGE 11    **'When you see millions of the mouthless dead'**: Charles Hamilton Sorley, *When you see millions of the mouthless dead* in Andrew Motion (ed.), *First World War Poems*, Faber and Faber, London, 2003, p.23.

PAGE 12    **'Life, for the majority of the population'**: Siegfried Sassoon, *Memoirs of an Infantry Officer*, Folio Society, London, 1974, p.156. © Siegfried Sassoon 1930 by kind permission of the Estate of George Sassoon.

PAGE 15    **'Strange Hells'**: Ivor Gurney, *Strange Hells* in Kenneth Baker (ed.), *The Faber Book of War Poetry*, Faber and Faber, London, 1996, p.447.

PAGE 15    **particularly Field Marshal Douglas Haig**: For a range of views on the personality and character traits of Douglas Haig, see Gary Sheffield and John Bourne (eds), *Douglas Haig: War Diaries and Letters 1914-1918*, Weidenfeld and Nicolson, London, 2005, pp.10–17; Gary Mead, *The Good Soldier*, Atlantic Books, London, 2007, pp.1–12; and Robin Prior and Trevor Wilson, *The Somme*, (Yale University Press, New Haven and London, 2005), pp.305–7.

PAGE 16    **Lessons learned at the Battle of Loos in 1915**: Regarding the failings at Loos, see David Stevenson, *1914-1918: The History of the First World War*, (Allen Lane, London, 2004), pp.159–60.

PAGE 16    **at the Somme in 1916 and at Passchendaele in 1917**: Regarding the failings at the Somme, see Peter Hart, *The Somme*, Weidenfeld and Nicolson, London, 2005, pp.532–3; and at Passchendaele, see David Stevenson, *1914-1918 The History of the First World War*, (Allen Lane, London, 2004), pp.333–7.

PAGE 16    **The casualty rates were appalling**: Many reasons have been posited by historians and commentators as factors contributing to the high casualty rates suffered by the British army across the battles of Loos, Somme and Passchendaele. The most valid of these are that of overambitious and unrealistic objectives, inextricably linked with that of insufficient artillery cover – either in terms of quantity or quality. Guns were spread too thinly across too broad or too deep a front or they were inaccurately targeted. In tandem with inadequately primed shells (duds), this resulted in a failure to cut the wire or destroy dugouts and strategically placed machine gun nests, often resulting in a catastrophic outcome for the infantry. (For more on the shortcomings of the artillery, see David Stevenson, *1914-1918 The History of the First World War*, Allen Lane, London, 2004, pp.184–6, and Robin Prior and Trevor Wilson, *The Somme*, Yale University Press, New Haven and London, 2005, p.32, pp.52–3 and pp.62–3.) As far as Haig was concerned, he also had an outdated belief in the ability of the cavalry to decisively influence or exploit any potential breakthrough – a real anachronism in an era of technological advances that included the increasing use of air support and tank warfare. After the example of Loos, although subsequent battleplans were formulated that supposedly accounted for the shortcomings of that action, the issues caused by over-ambition and inadequate artillery cover resurface in both the Somme and Passchendaele battles. In each instance, an over-optimistic groupthink that came to possess the British high command had prevailed over the need to effectively implement the lessons learned at Loos. It is difficult not to conclude that these failings resulted in a greater loss of life than would otherwise have been the case.

PAGE 16 **I received a reply**: refers to a letter from the MOD Departmental Record Officer to the author dated 7th March 1988.

PAGE 16 **he was awarded the Military Medal for gallantry and devotion to duty in action**: The *London Gazette*, Issue 31405, dated 13 June 1919, p.7685.

PAGE 17 **My uncle wrote**: refers to a letter from Charles William Blumsom to the author dated 21 May 1988.

PAGE 23 **Many labourers were casually hired**: for further discussion of the casual labour system, see Friedrich Engels, *The Condition of the Working Class in England*, Penguin, London, 2005, p.120; and Alan Palmer, *The East End: Four Centuries of London Life*, Rutgers University Press, New Brunswick, New Jersey, 2000, p.66.

PAGE 23 **Trade Union membership of the population of London had shrunk to three and a half per cent**: percentage of membership quoted in Victor Bailey, *Charles Booth's Policemen: Crime, Police and Community in Jack-the-Ripper's London*, Breviary Stuff Publications, London, 2014, p.73.

PAGE 23 **Nationally, on the eve of the new century, only twenty per cent**: percentage of membership of trade unions extrapolated from figure quoted in John Benson, *The Working Class in Britain 1850-1939*, IB Taurus, London, 2003, p.190.

PAGE 24 **'We're none of us the same'**: from the poem *They* in Siegfried Sassoon, *The War Poems*, Faber and Faber, London, 1983, p.57. © Siegfried Sassoon 1983 by kind permission of the Estate of George Sassoon.

PAGE 25 **the whole concept of a 'Lost Generation'**: An interpretation of the 'Lost Generation' appears within the introduction to Alan Bishop and Mark Bostridge (eds), *Letters from a Lost Generation: First World War Letters of Vera Brittain and Four Friends*, Little, Brown and Company, London, 1998, p.7; and in Mark Bostridge's introduction to Vera Brittain's seminal work, *Testament of Youth*, Weidenfeld & Nicolson, London, 2009, p.xvi.

PAGE 25 **'That's what you are'**: Ernest Hemingway, *A Moveable Feast*, Jonathan Cape, London, 2010, p.61. © 1964 by Ernest Hemingway Ltd.

PAGE 27 **'In the two minutes' silence'**: Private John McCauley of the 2nd Border Regiment quoted in Richard Van Emden, *The Soldier's War: The Great War through veterans' eyes*, Bloomsbury Publishing Plc, 2009, p.377. Reproduced with kind permission from © Richard Van Emden 2009.

## CHAPTER TWO – THE SEARCH

PAGE 28 **'Your suggestion that I should write history'**: Betty Radice (Translated by), *The Letters of Pliny the Younger*, Penguin, London, 2003, pp.145–6.

PAGE 28 **'It is well known that working men'** and **'there is very little manuscript material'** and **'indirect evidence to build up a composite picture'**: Richard Price, *An Imperial War and the British Working Class*, Routledge & Kegan Paul, London, 1972, p.5. © Richard Price 1972. Reproduced by permission of Taylor & Francis Group.

PAGE 37 **'Black: Lowest class. Vicious, semi-criminal'**: Jess Steele and Mike Steele (eds), *The Streets of London: The Booth Notebooks – East*, Deptford Forum Publishing Ltd, London, 2018, plate facing p.156. Reproduced by kind permission of Dr Jess Steele OBE and Mike Steele.

PAGE 38 **'You are the bows from which your children'**: Kahlil Gibran, *The Prophet*, in *The Collected Works*, Everyman's Library, London, 2007, p.107.

PAGE 40 **I subsequently discovered that the cemetery had been abandoned**: For a concise history of Nunhead Cemetery, see Tim and Carol Stevenson (eds), *A Short Guide to Nunhead Cemetery*, The Friends of Nunhead Cemetery, London, 2003, pp.7–8.

PAGE 43 **the first truly technological, industrialised, Total War**: Although the term *Total War* predates the First World War, and some historians argue that earlier conflicts such as the American Civil War and the Napoleonic Wars qualify as such, the unprecedented scale and global nature of the Great War, whereby practically the whole civilian populations and all of the state resources of the combatant nations were contributing to their war efforts push it to a whole different level.

## CHAPTER THREE – FAMILY HISTORY: SILK WEAVERS, HUGUENOTS AND BOOTMAKERS

PAGE 45 **'Twas August, and the fierce sun overhead'**: Matthew Arnold, *Sonnet on East London*, quoted in Ed Glinert, *East End Chronicles*, Allen Lane, London, 2005, p.51.

PAGE 46 **'Some had deserted their houses in despair'**: William Page (ed.), *A History of the County of Middlesex: Volume 2, General; Ashford, East Bedfont With Hatton, Feltham, Hampton With Hampton Wick, Hanworth, Laleham, Littleton*, Victoria County History, London, 1911, p.136.

PAGE 46 **In the 1820s, the Jacquard Loom**: For an explanation of the deleterious effects of technological advances (such as the Jacquard Loom) suffered by the 'home' or traditional silk weavers, see Dan Cruickshank, *Spitalfields: The History of a Nation in a Handful of Streets*, Random

House Books, London, 2016, p.267; and John Marriott, *Beyond the Tower: A history of East London*, Yale University Press, New Haven and London, 2011, p.115. The repeal of the Spitalfields Acts in 1824 exacerbated the challenges faced by the weavers. The Acts, dating back to 1773, had been intended to regulate pay and working conditions and protect the home market by restricting imports from abroad. All well and good, but they had unintended consequences. In practice, the legislation had an adverse effect; the Acts were restricted to London and Middlesex, and consequently, the provinces were free to set their own rates. Market forces ensured that the larger employers simply moved their manufacture to the Midlands and the North where costs were at least a third less than those in the capital. The eventual repeal of the Acts was a triumph for the employers and manufacturers, who resented any sort of regulation in the marketplace. Not so for the London weavers, for whom the Acts were still popular, and although they risked pricing themselves out of the market, they hung on to the concept of a fixed rate of pay – effectively a minimum wage –, and therefore, passionately resisted the 1824 Act. This resistance took the form of demonstrations and petitions, but it was to no avail. The Masters' success in repealing these Acts did nothing to improve the lot of the journeymen weavers, and whatever negative effects the legislation had had whilst in force, deregulation was to make things far worse, pushing wages down further to plunge more silk workers below the poverty line. It seems the weavers were damned if they did and damned if they didn't.

PAGE 47    **With the passing of the Poor Law Amendment Act in 1834**: For more detail on the Poor Law Amendment Act 1834 and the workhouse system, see Carl Chinn, *Poverty amidst Prosperity: The urban poor in England, 1834-1914*, Carnegie Publishing Ltd, Lancaster, 2006, pp.81–4.

PAGE 47    **The origins of the workhouse or poorhouse system**: See Peter Higginbotham, *Workhouses of London and the South East*, The History Press, Stroud, Gloucestershire, 2019, p.69.

PAGE 48    **'Ranks of the great army [of unemployed] that goes marching on'**: Margaret Harkness (writing as John Law), *Out of Work*, Swan Sonnenschein & Co., London, 1888, p.120.

PAGE 49    '**The first, following the St Bartholomew's Day massacre of 1572**':
For a comprehensive study of the St Bartholomew's Day Massacre 1572
and the Revocation of the Edict of Nantes 1685, see Robin Gwynn,
*Huguenot Heritage: The history and contribution of the Huguenots in Britain*,
Routledge & Kegan Paul, 1985, pp.14–23. © Robin D. Gwynn 1985.

PAGE 50    '**The houses of the weavers**': Hector Gavin, *Sanitary Ramblings: Being
Sketches and Illustrations of Bethnal Green*, John Churchill, London,
1848, pp.66–7.

PAGE 51    '**Ninety per cent of the largest single monthly influx**': Robin Gwynn,
*Huguenot Heritage: The history and contribution of the Huguenots in
Britain*, p.170.

PAGE 51    **Gwynn details the experience of the de Robillard family's escape**:
For a first-person account of the de Robillard family's escape to
England, see Robin Gwynn, *The Huguenots of London*, The Alpha Press,
Brighton, 1998, postscript. For another contemporaneous account of a
refugee family's ordeal, see Gwynn, *The Huguenots of London*, p.7.

PAGE 53    **Gwynn asserts that the assimilation of an ethnic minority into
a host society**: For more details on the assimilation process, see
Robin Gwynn, *Huguenot Heritage: The history and contribution of the
Huguenots in Britain*, pp.160–175.

PAGE 55    **before I'd looked into the origins of our surname**: For origins of the
surname, see P.H. Reaney, *A Dictionary of British Surnames*, Routledge
and Keegan Paul, 1979, p.39.

PAGE 56    **not to be confused with the 'official' blue plaque**: In contrast to the
City of London's rectangular blue plaque, English Heritage's standard
design is circular with a white border. In recognition of the City's civic
independence from the rest of Greater London, it was agreed in 1879 that
it had the sole responsibility of installing blue plaques within its bounds.

PAGE 60    '**A man came yesterday from Bethnal Green with an account of that
district**': Charles Greville, diary entry dated 17 February 1832, *The
Greville Memoirs, Part 1 (of 3), Volume 2 (of 3)*, Longmans, Green and
Co., London, 1874, pp.261–2.

PAGE 61 **'thousands gathered in the Strand, mostly East Enders especially half-famished Spitalfields weavers'**: Iorwerth Prothero, *Artisans and Politics in Early Nineteenth Century London*, Routledge Revivals, Abingdon, 2013, p.279. © 1979 I.J. Prothero. Reproduced by kind permission of Taylor & Francis Group. Reproduced with permission of Informa UK Ltd through PLSclear.

PAGE 62 **'The houses built by the French refugees are all several storied'**: Hector Gavin, *Sanitary Ramblings: Being Sketches and Illustrations of Bethnal Green*, John Churchill, London, 1848, p.42.

PAGE 62 **'The gutter in the centre of this court was very filthy'**: Hector Gavin, *Sanitary Ramblings: Being Sketches and Illustrations of Bethnal Green*, pp.44–5.

PAGE 63 **'The Weavers, who comprised the majority'**: Ed Glinert, *East End Chronicles*, Allen Lane, London, 2005, p.43.

PAGE 63 **The writer Sarah Wise observes**: see Sarah Wise, *The Blackest Streets: The Life and Death of a Victorian Slum*, The Bodley Head, London, 2008, p.188.

PAGE 63 **It has to be said that Morrison's depiction**: see Sarah Wise, *The Blackest Streets: The Life and Death of a Victorian Slum*, p.233.

PAGE 64 **Sarah Wise points out that**: see Sarah Wise, *The Blackest Streets: The Life and Death of a Victorian Slum*, p.100 and p.279.

PAGE 65 **'mainly poor dock labourers, poor costermongers, poorer silk weavers'**: John Hollingshead, *Ragged London in 1861*, Dodo Press, Gloucester, reprint of 1861 edition, p.30.

PAGE 65 **'of greater height, with a close, black, uneven staircase'**: John Hollingshead, *Ragged London in 1861*, p.34.

PAGE 66 **'The statistics of silk weaving show'**: John Hollingshead, *Ragged London in 1861*, pp.34–35.

PAGE 66 **Hollingshead details a letter dated the 2 February**: The complete letter appears in the appendices within John Hollingshead, *Ragged London in 1861*, pp.151–154.

PAGES 67–8 'It may be remarked that the worst parts of Bethnal Green': Thomas Archer, *The Pauper, The Thief and the Convict; Sketches of some of their Homes, Haunts and Habits*, Groombridge and Sons, London, 1865, pp.9–10.

PAGE 68 'Huguenots brought a distinct culture to East London': John Marriott, *Beyond the Tower: a History of East London,* Yale University Press, New Haven and London, 2011, p.54. © John Marriott 2011. Reproduced with kind permission of Yale Representation Limited through PLSclear.

PAGE 68 'a quiet, respectable set of people': Police Inspector Pearn quoted in Jess Steele and Mike Steele (eds), *The Streets of London: The Booth Notebooks – East*, p.144. Reproduced by kind permission of Dr Jess Steele OBE and Mike Steele.

PAGE 69 'I took it up because my wife's father was in the trade': Henry Mayhew (eds E.P. Thompson and Eileen Yeo), *The Unknown Mayhew: Selections from the Morning Chronicle 1849-50*, Pelican Books, Penguin Books Ltd, London, 1973, p.318.

PAGE 69 'About two years ago I travelled from Thomas Street, Bethnal Green': Henry Mayhew, *The Unknown Mayhew: Selections from the Morning Chronicle 1849-50*, pp.318–9.

PAGE 70 'An out worker...his wife and daughter were closers': Alan Fox, *A History of the National Union of Boot and Shoe Operatives,* Blackwell, Oxford, 1958, p.17. © Alan Fox 1958. Reproduced with kind permission of John Wiley and Sons Limited through PLSclear.

## CHAPTER FOUR – THE LIE

PAGE 71 'He told a lie': Eva Dobell, *In a soldiers hospital 1: Pluck*, in Fiona Waters (ed), *A Corner of a Foreign Field: The Illustrated Poetry of the First World War*, Transatlantic Press, Croxley Green, Hertfordshire, 2007, p.156.

PAGE 72 'We had so many addresses': T. Lummis and P. Thompson. (2009). *Family Life and Work Experience Before 1918, 1870-1973.* 7th Edition. UK Data Service. [data collection]. DOI: http://doi.org/10.5255/UKDA-SN-2000-1

PAGE 72 **'A family who have lived'**: Maud Pember Reeves, *Round About a Pound a Week*, Persephone Books, London, 1913, p.34.

PAGE 73 **'There was a neighbourliness'**: Gilda O'Neill, *My East End*, Viking, London, 1999, p.84.

PAGE 73 **'We all lived within'**: Gilda O'Neill, *My East End*, p.148.

PAGE 73 **'great family parties'**: Inspector Pearn in Jess Steele and Mike Steele (eds.), *The Streets of London: The Booth Notebooks – East*, p.144.

PAGE 74 **'When a person has relatives'**: Michael Young and Peter Wilmott, *'Family and Kinship in East London'*, Penguin Modern Classics, London, 2007, p.104.

PAGE 76 **'I John Doyle do hereby declare'**: Dan Cruickshank, *Spitalfields: The History of a Nation in a Handful of Streets*, Random House Books, London, 2016, p.276.

PAGE 77 **'middle height, moustache, squash black felt hat'**: George Duckworth in Jess Steele and Mike Steele (eds), *The Streets of London: The Booth Notebooks – East*, p.172.

PAGE 77 **'all two storey'**: Jess Steele and Mike Steele (eds), *The Streets of London: The Booth Notebooks – East*, p.171.

PAGES **'very mixed road, some pink'**: Jess Steele and Mike Steele (eds), *The 77–8 Streets of London: The Booth Notebooks – East*, p.170.

PAGE 78 **'two-storey houses, two families in each'**: Jess Steele and Mike Steele (eds), *The Streets of London: The Booth Notebooks – East*, p.152.

PAGE 79 **'two-storey cottages, flush with street'**: and **'respectable and purple at the north end'**: Jess Steele and Mike Steele (eds), *The Streets of London: The Booth Notebooks – East*, p.152.

PAGE 82 **'The importance attached to the earnings'**: Benjamin Seebohm Rowntree, *Poverty, A Study of Town Life,* London, 1901, p.60.

PAGE 82 **'a law of direct compulsion'**: Matthew Arnold, *Annual Reports of the Committee of Council on Education – Parliamentary Paper 1870*, xxii, p.298.

PAGES **'It was Jack the Ripper'**: Compton Mackenzie, *My Life and Times:*
83–4 *Octave One 1883-1891,* Chatto and Windus, London, 1963, pp.164–5.

PAGE 85 **'We would go along Hackney Road'**: Gilda O'Neill, *My East End*,
p.115.

PAGE 86 **'when visiting our elementary schools'**: Leo George Chiozza Money,
*Things That Matter,* Methuen & Co, London, 1912, pp.209–10.

PAGE 86 **'And then comes the great stampede'**: Leo George Chiozza Money,
*Things That Matter*, p.211.

PAGE 87 **including oysters, hot eels, pea soup, fried fish, pies and puddings**:
see Henry Mayhew, *London Labour and the London Poor*, Oxford
University Press, Oxford, 2010, pp.9–10.

PAGE 87 **'[Fish] Ni-ew Mackerel, 6 a shilling'**: Henry Mayhew, *London Labour
and the London Poor*, p.39.

PAGE 88 **'Wherever a man of vigour'**: Jack London, *The People of the Abyss*,
Tangerine Press, Tooting, 2014, p.170.

PAGE 89 **'pack twelve months dinners in my belly'**: Frank Richards, *Old
Soldier Sahib*, Parthian Library of Wales, Cardigan, 2016, p.10. This
and all subsequent quotes © Frank Richards 1936. Reproduced by
kind permission of Parthian Books.

PAGES **'instead of putting six months on to my age'**: Frank Richards, *Old
89–90 Soldier Sahib*, p.11.

## CHAPTER FIVE – SOUTH AFRICA

PAGE 91 **'What has your country done for you'**: Emily Orr, *A Recruit From
the Slums*, from *A Harvester of Dreams*, Burns, Oates & Washbourne
Ltd, London, 1922, p.36.

PAGES **'We have spent two hundred million pounds'**: Rudyard Kipling,
93–4 from *The Lesson*, in *The Definitive Edition of Rudyard Kipling's Verse*,
Hodder and Stoughton, London, 1989, p.299.

PAGE 96    **'Since I wrote the last page'**: David Verney (ed.), *The Joyous Patriot: The Correspondence of Ralph Verney 1900-1916*, Leo Cooper, London, 1989, p.48.

PAGES      **'not since 1ˢᵗ Army Corps left England'**: *Worcestershire Chronicle*
99–100     dated Saturday 23 March 1901, p.2.

PAGE 100   **'…I shan't be away long'**: Guy du Maurier, letter to his mother dated March 1901, at sea en route to South Africa.

PAGES      **'Well, I've had my baptism of fire'**: Guy du Maurier, letter dated 6
100–1       May 1901, Commando Nek.

PAGE 101   **'But I don't hunger after more than a year of this'**: Guy du Maurier, Letter dated 8 May 1901.

PAGES      **'An exciting day and a sad one'**: Guy du Maurier, letter dated 23
101–2      June 1901, Middlefontein.

PAGE 103   **'We moved off at 9'**: Ibid.

PAGE 105   **'They throw in Drummer Hodge, to rest'**: Thomas Hardy, *Drummer Hodge*, in Kenneth Baker (ed.), *The Faber Book of War Poetry*, Faber and Faber Limited, London, 1996, p.120.

PAGES      **'Mmm…The important thing is that he has a name'**: Alan Bennett, *The*
105–6      *History Boys: The Film*, Faber and Faber, London, 2006, p.60. © Forelake Ltd, 2006. Reproduced with permission from Faber and Faber Ltd.

PAGE 106   **Claire Tomalin, in her biography of Thomas Hardy**: *Thomas Hardy: The Time-Torn Man*, Claire Tomalin, Viking, London, 2006, pp.274–6.

PAGE 106   **'If I should die, think only this of me'**: Rupert Brooke, *The Soldier*, in *The Faber Book of War Poetry*, p.119.

PAGE 107   **'Dulce et decorum est pro patria mori'**: For an authoritative English translation see *Horace: The Complete Odes and Epodes*, Oxford University Press, Oxford, 2008, p.78.

PAGE 108    **'I wish my mother could see me now'**: Rudyard Kipling, from *M.I. (Mounted Infantry of the Line)*, in *The Definitive Edition of Rudyard Kipling's Verse*, pp.463–6.

PAGE 109    **'That is what we are known as'**: Rudyard Kipling, from *M.I. (Mounted Infantry of the Line)*, in *The Definitive Edition of Rudyard Kipling's Verse*, pp.463–6.

PAGE 109    **'We've got in at last for a rest'**: Guy du Maurier, letter dated 12 September 1901, Nylstroom.

PAGE 110    **'...there is no chance of my coming home this year'**: Guy du Maurier, letter dated 17 September 1901, Nylstroom.

PAGE 110    **'Don't think that I have somehow exchanged'**: Ralph Verney, *The Joyous Patriot*, p.44.

PAGE 112    **'We are making great arrangements'**: Guy du Maurier, letter dated 23 December 1901, Nylstroom.

PAGE 112    **'Major du Maurier, who is commanding the 20th MI'**: Ralph Verney, *The Joyous Patriot*, p.49.

PAGES 112–13    **'I'm tired of war and would prefer Sicily.'**: Guy du Maurier, letter dated 9 January 1902, Dyson's Farm, Orange River Colony.

PAGE 113    **'I've just received 7 pipes from the Queen'**: Guy du Maurier, letter dated 24 January 1902.

PAGE 114    **'best MI columns'** and **'they were the elite of the army.'**: Thomas Pakenham, *The Boer War*, Weidenfeld and Nicolson, London, 1979, p.545.

PAGE 116    **'No rest for us and we are off tomorrow morning'**: Guy du Maurier, letter dated 19 March 1902.

PAGE 116    **Many Boers shared the same ancestry**: Estimated figure of 400 Huguenot refugees to South Africa appears in Robin Gwynn, *Huguenot Heritage: The history and contribution of the Huguenots in Britain*, Routledge & Kegan Paul, 1985, p.24.

PAGE 117     **'Today we are resting and tomorrow we have at them again.'**: Guy du Maurier, letter dated 2 April 1902, Karranfontein.

PAGES     **'It's much too early to think yet of plans'**: Guy du Maurier, letter
117–18    dated 16 April 1902.

PAGES     **'I'm very fit except for veldt sores'**: Guy du Maurier, letter dated
118–19    22 April 1902, near Klerksdorp.

PAGES     **'I've just been reading Mr. Broderick's great army reform scheme'**:
119–20    Guy du Maurier, letter dated 27 April 1902.

PAGES     **'Got into the Blockhouse line and are resting.'**: Guy du Maurier,
120–21    letter dated 22 May 1902.

PAGE 121     **'We cannot consent to purchase a shameful peace'**: *The Boer War*, p.563.

PAGE 122     **'You will have heard long before now'**: Ralph Verney, *The Joyous Patriot*, p.55.

PAGES     **'General Oliphant who commands here inspected us on Tuesday.'**:
122–23    Guy du Maurier, letter dated 18 July 1902, Elandsfontein.

PAGE 124     **'I got definite orders about my battalion last night'**: Guy du Maurier, letter dated 1 August 1902.

## CHAPTER SEVEN – INDIA

PAGE 127     **'When the 'arf-made recruity goes out to the East'**: Rudyard Kipling, from *The Young British Soldier*, in *The Definitive Edition of Rudyard Kipling's Verse*, pp.416–8.

PAGE 130     **'the normal routine of the 1st Battalion'**: Charles Allen, *Duel in the Snows*, John Murray, London, 2004, p.178.

PAGE 130     **'it was here that the Raj's imperium'**: Richard Holmes, *Sahib: The British Soldier in India*, Harper Collins, London, 2005, p.87. © Richard Holmes 2005. Reprinted by kind permission of Harper Collins Publishers Ltd.

PAGE 131   'it was the most sociable and one could not gain or lose much at it': Frank Richards, *Old Soldier Sahib*, pp.82–3.

PAGE 131   'Sonny, the soldiers of the old John Company': Frank Richards, *Old Soldier Sahib*, p.63.

PAGES 132–33   'Each girl had a couple of towels': Frank Richards, *Old Soldier Sahib*, p.149.

PAGE 134   '...expert knitters: they bought wool from the Bazaar': Frank Richards, *Old Soldier Sahib*, p.99.

PAGE 134   'Extended his Army Service to complete 8 years with the colours': Ref WO97/4375, Statement of the Services of No. RF7535 Name William Chas. Blumsom, The National Archives.

PAGES 134–35   'To qualify for the top rate of pay': Frank Richards, *Old Soldier Sahib*, p.157.

PAGE 135   'I knew many first-class soldiers who': Frank Richards, *Old Soldier Sahib*, p.157.

PAGE 136   '...so that time-expired men sent to Deolali': Frank Richards, *Old Soldier Sahib*, p.52.

PAGE 138   'By stop-tap most of us had said what utter fools we had been': Frank Richards, *Old Soldier Sahib*, p.262.

## CHAPTER EIGHT – TO FRANCE

PAGE 140   'Quiet night-time over Rouen, and the station full of soldiers': May Wedderburn Cannan, *Rouen*, from *The Tears of War: The Love Story of a Young Poet and a War Hero*, Cavalier Books, Upavon, 2000, pp.40–3. Reproduced by kind permission of Cavalier Books.

PAGE 141   'On arrival at a new station we pre-war soldiers': Frank Richards, *Old Soldiers Never Die*, Parthian Library of Wales, Cardigan, 2016, pp.2–3. This and all subsequent quotes © Frank Richards 1933 reproduced by kind permission of Parthian Books.

PAGE 142   'Whenever I imagined I was beginning to understand them': Richard Lovell, *Churchill's Doctor: A biography of Lord Moran*. ©

1992 Royal Society of Medicine Services Ltd, London, p.41. By permission of the Royal Society of Medicine.

PAGE 142   **'The Germans yelled across to the 1st Royal Fusiliers'**: Francis Clere Hitchcock, *Stand To: A Diary of the Trenches 1915-1918*, The Naval and Military Press, Uckfield, 2009, p.90.

PAGE 142   **'Reinforcement (No.15) of 89 other ranks'**: WO/95/1613/2_1 War Diary 1st Battalion Royal Fusiliers 01/10/1914 to 31/10/1915, The National Archives, p.70 of 75.

PAGES   **'25 other ranks joined battalion'**: WO/95/1613/2_2 War Diary 1st
142–43   Battalion Royal Fusiliers 01/10/1914 to 31/10/1915, The National Archives, p.9 of 67.

PAGE 143   **'of whom 59 were returning sick'**: WO/95/1613/2_2 War Diary 1st Battalion Royal Fusiliers 01/10/1914 to 31/10/1915, The National Archives, p.13 of 67.

PAGE 143   **'were a wonderful generation … let's face it'**: Sergeant W.J. Collins, quoted in Max Arthur, *We Will Remember Them: Voices from the aftermath of the Great War*, Weidenfeld & Nicolson, London, 2009, p.238. © Max Arthur 2009. Reproduced with kind permission of Orion Publishing Group Limited through PLSclear.

PAGE 143   **…'it tells something of the battalion that during the battle there were no sick'**: Richard Lovell, *Churchill's Doctor*, p.48.

PAGE 143   **'it was the unwritten law among the men'**: Lord Moran, *Anatomy of Courage*, Avery Publishing, New York, 1987, p.183. © Lord Moran 1945. This and all subsequent quotes reproduced with kind permission of Little Brown Book Group Limited through PLSclear.

PAGE 143   **'during a gas attack'**: Lord Moran, *Anatomy of Courage,* pp.175–6.

PAGES   **'Likewise in the English professional army'**: Lord Moran, *Anatomy*
143–44   *of Courage*, p.33.

PAGE 144   **'The sentries when they saw an officer approaching'**: Lord Moran, *Anatomy of Courage*, p.77.

PAGE 145 'do not seem to fit into the structure of society' and 'vaguely discontented' and 'all warlike people are a little idle' and 'The cockney soldier has become a legend' and 'by more careful folk' and 'quickness and shrewdness of the non-commissioned officers': Lord Moran, *Anatomy of Courage*, p.155.

PAGE 145 'this gift of humour which encased our cockneys': Lord Moran, *Anatomy of Courage*, p.144.

PAGE 145 'Cockney warrior' and 'infinitely brave without vindictiveness': Donald Hankey, *A Student in Arms*, Andrew Melrose Ltd, London, 1917, p.95.

PAGE 146 'the officers and men of the First Battalion': Lord Moran, *Anatomy of Courage*, Acknowledgements page.

PAGE 146 'At Ypres I was beginning to understand': Lord Moran, *Anatomy of Courage*, p.3.

PAGE 146 'became a legend, as if men could scarcely believe': Lord Moran, *Anatomy of Courage*, p.4.

PAGE 147 'A man's courage is his capital': Lord Moran, *Anatomy of Courage*, p.xii.

PAGES 147–48 'Private W. Thurston of "A" company': WO/95/1613/2_2 War Diary 1st RF, The National Archives, p.6 of 67.

PAGE 148 'About 20 shells landed rear "B" company' and 'Enemy fired about 50 shells' and 'Enemy put 5 shells': WO/95/1613/2_2 War Diary 1st RF, The National Archives, pp.10–11 of 67.

PAGE 150 'Mademoiselle from Armenteers-Parley vous!': John Brophy and Eric Partridge, *The Daily Telegraph Dictionary of Tommies' Songs and Slang 1914-18*, Frontline Books, London, 2008, p.49.

PAGE 152 'a very dirty "low-down" game to play shooting out that damnable "gas"': Sir John French, quoted in Richard Holmes (ed.), *The Little Field Marshal: A Life of Sir John French*, Weidenfeld & Nicolson Ltd, London, 2004, p.300.

PAGE 152 'an offence not only against the rules of war, but "against all humane considerations"': Edward Grey, quoted in Brigadier

General J.E. Edmonds and Captain G.C. Wynne, *Official History of the War Military Operations France and Belgium 1915, Vol. I*, Reprint by Battery Press, Nashville, Tennessee, 1995, originally published 1927, p.193.

PAGE 153 **'all ranks fitted with respirators'** and **'550 goggles issued which completed battalion'**: WO/95/1613/2_2 War Diary 1st RF, The National Archives, p.19 of 67.

PAGE 153 **'the Cockney warrior does not hate the hun'**: Donald Hankey, *A Student in Arms*, p.95.

PAGE 153 **'are not good haters.'**: Lord Moran, *Anatomy of Courage*, p.52.

PAGE 154 **'a German sergeant belonging to 139 Regiment'**: WO/95/1613/2_2 War Diary 1st RF, The National Archives, p.20 of 67.

PAGE 154 **'Hun'** and **'flattened'** and **'great bull neck'** and **'nailed soles of his enormous boots'**: Lord Moran, *Anatomy of Courage*, p.54.

PAGE 155 **'Anyway, mate, that's one bloody Hun less'**: Lord Moran, *Anatomy of Courage*, p.55.

PAGE 155 **'While our guns were giving the Prussians opposite us hell'**: James Churchill Dunn, *The War the Infantry Knew 1914–1919*, Abacus, London, 2004, p.113.

PAGE 155 **'when [we] were opposite the Saxons near Ypres'**: Vera Brittain, *Testament of Youth*, Weidenfeld & Nicolson, London, 2009, p.138. © Mark Bostridge & Timothy Brittain-Catlin, Literary Executors of Vera Brittain, 1970. This and subsequent quotes reproduced with kind permission of Orion Publishing Group Limited through PLSclear.

PAGE 156 **'amusement and tolerance'**: Lord Moran, *Anatomy of Courage*, p.55.

CHAPTER NINE – YPRES

PAGE 157 **'Day dawns in a mist.'**: Stephen Graham, *The Challenge of the Dead*, Cassell and Co Ltd, London, 1921, p.37.

PAGE 157    'well-made and revetted, but the parapets were much lower' and 'everywhere there was the sickly smell of the gas': *Stand To: A Diary of the Trenches 1915-1918*, p.33.

PAGE 157    'we were all greatly astonished at first': *Stand To: A Diary of the Trenches 1915-1918*, p.35.

PAGES 158–59    'at 11:30 Sir John French came to see me': Robert Blake, (ed.), *The Private Papers of Douglas Haig 1914-1919*, Eyre and Spottiswoode, London, 1952, pp.91–2.

PAGES 159–60    'The city was deserted and desolate': *Stand To: A Diary of the Trenches 1915-1918*, p.39.

PAGE 162    'intolerably nameless names' and 'Sepulchre of Crime': from the poem *On Passing the New Menin Gate* in Siegfried Sassoon, *The War Poems*, p.153. © Siegfried Sassoon 1983 by kind permission of the Estate of George Sassoon.

PAGE 163    'Ypres has gained a new monument': extract from newspaper article by Stefan Zweig, in *Berliner Tageblatt*, dated 16 September 1928, quoted by Dominiek Dendooven, *Menin Gate and Last Post: Ypres as Holy Ground*, De Klaproos Editions, Koksijde, Belgium, 2003, p.71.

PAGE 164    'I was shocked by the dead horses and mules': Robert Graves, *Goodbye to All That*, Everyman's Library, London, 2018, p.218. © Trustees of the Robert Graves Copyright Trust. Reproduced with kind permission from Carcanet Press.

PAGE 165    'Hooge had been continually under shellfire': *Stand To: A Diary of the Trenches 1915-1918*, p.66.

PAGE 166    'Attack on enemy's position near Hooge': WO/95/1613/2_2 War Diary 1st RF, The National Archives, p.50 of 67.

PAGES 166–67    'model of how an operation could be conducted': Nigel Cave, *Ypres: Sanctuary Wood and Hooge*, (Battleground Europe series) Leo Cooper, Barnsley, 2002, p.59.

PAGE 167    'we lay there waiting for the order to charge.': Unnamed soldier, quoted in Nigel Cave, *Ypres: Sanctuary Wood and Hooge*, p.71.

PAGE 168 **'connected with the 1st Royal Fusiliers'**: *Stand To: A Diary of the Trenches 1915–1918*, p.63.

PAGE 168 **'Fine day. Enemy shelled Zouave Wood'**: WO/95/1613/2_2 War Diary 1st RF, The National Archives, p.51 of 67.

PAGE 168 **'Everywhere lay the dead.'**: *Stand To: A Diary of the Trenches 1915–1918*, p.64.

PAGE 169 **'A few solitary stakes and strands of barbed wire'**: *Stand To: A Diary of the Trenches 1915–1918*, p.64.

PAGE 169 **'Serving in the Ypres salient'**: *Stand To: A Diary of the Trenches 1915–1918*, p.66.

PAGE 169 **'we could not have been in a worse position'**: *Stand To: A Diary of the Trenches 1915–1918*, p.67.

PAGE 170 **'If this went on much longer'**: *Stand To: A Diary of the Trenches 1915–1918*, p.68.

PAGE 170 **'almost all from shell fire'**: WO/95/1612/2 War Diary 2nd Battalion Leinster Regiment 01/03/1915 to 31/10/1915 The National Archives.

PAGE 172 **'The moon had risen above the blackness of Zouave Wood'**: Lord Moran, *Anatomy of Courage*, pp.193–4.

PAGE 172 **'Information received that the following NCOs and men'**: WO/95/1613/2_2 War Diary 1st RF, The National Archives, p.57 of 67.

PAGE 173 **'was awarded the Russian St. George Medal'**: *The London Gazette, Supplement 29275*, dated 24 August 1915, p.8512.

CHAPTER TEN – WAR PILGRIM

PAGE 174 **'The war pilgrim, paying his due of honour'**: Stephen Graham, *The Challenge of the Dead*, pp.2–3.

PAGE 175 **'most of the cemeteries in the more obscure places'**: Stephen Graham, *The Challenge of the Dead*, p.96.

PAGE 176 'so it will be with us; we shall join the authentic dead': Stephen Graham, *The Challenge of the Dead*, p.97.

PAGE 176 'And I remember, Not the war I fought in': From *The Great War*, in Vernon Scannell, *Collected Poems 1950-1993*, Faber and Faber Ltd, London, 2010, pp.68–9. © Vernon Scannell, 1993. Reproduced with kind permission of Martin Reed, Literary Executor for the estate of Vernon Scannell.

PAGE 177 'In a way, although it's not something they would have wanted': Private Harry Wells, quoted in Max Arthur, *We Will Remember Them: Voices from the aftermath of the Great War*, Weidenfeld & Nicolson, London, 2009, p.253. © Max Arthur 2009. Reproduced with kind permission of Orion Publishing Group Limited through PLSclear.

PAGE 179 'most useful piece of work' Fabian Ware, quoted in David Crane, *Empires of the Dead: How One Man's Vision Led to the Creation of WWI's War Graves*, William Collins, London, 2013, p.41.

PAGE 179 'The biggest single bit of work since any of the Pharaohs': Rudyard Kipling, quoted in Gavin Stamp, *The Memorial to the Missing of the Somme*, Profile Books, London, 2006, p.12.

PAGE 181 'All that is done of structure should be for endurance': Sir Edwin Lutyens, quoted in David Crane, *Empires of the Dead*, p.113.

PAGE 181 'the principle of equality of treatment': Extract from Sir Frederick Kenyon's report to the War Graves Commission, quoted in David Crane, *Empires of the Dead*, p.128.

PAGE 182 'organised religion seems to have been conspicuously absent' and 'the surviving first-hand evidence': David Stevenson, *1914-1918 The History of the First World War*, Allen Lane, London, 2004, p.215.

PAGE 182 'if we happened to be out of the line on a Sunday' and 'John Wesley had a little dog': Frank Richards, *Old Soldiers Never Die*, Parthian Library of Wales, Cardigan, 2016, pp.60–1.

PAGE 183 'says that the great difficulty is the general indifference': Charles Booth, *Life and Labour of the People in London, Volume 1*, Macmillan and Co., London, 1902, p.26.

PAGE 183 **'God heard the embattled nations sing and shout'**: Sir John Collings Squire, *Epigram I: The Dilemma*. Reproduced by kind permission of Roger Squire.

PAGE 184 **'this grave on the top of a mountain'**: Vera Brittain, *Testament of Youth*, p.456.

PAGES **'We found the cemetery, as Edward had described it'**: Vera Brittain,
184–85 *Testament of Youth*, p.463.

PAGE 188 **'He is not missing, he is here'**: Field Marshal Lord Plumer quoted in David Crane, *Empires of the Dead*, p.210.

PAGE 189 **There, the Brigade was broken up and reorganised**: The 17th Brigade was transferred from the 'Old Army' 6th Division to the recently shattered and demoralised 24th Division and reorganised as follows: The old sweats of William's 1st Royal Fusiliers and the 3rd Rifle Brigade were paired with the 'New Army' service battalions of the 8th Buffs (East Kent Regiment) and the 12th Royal Fusiliers in one of the reformed Brigades, (confusingly) retaining the old number – the 17th, while the other two 'Old Army' battalions, the 1st North Staffords and the 2nd Leinsters, joined the remaining 'New Army' units in the 72nd and 73rd Brigades, respectively, thereby transplanting an experienced spine into each of the three brigades. The outgoing 'New Army' 71st Brigade transferring from the 24th in the opposite direction would reorganise likewise and keep their number whilst serving in the 6th Division.

PAGE 191 **'Surely the memorial for all the soldiers of all wars?'** and **'has the gravity and strength of grief'**: Henry Williamson, newspaper article titled 'Return to Hell: Part Four', *Evening Standard*, dated 2nd July 1964. Reproduced by kind permission of the Henry Williamson Literary Estate.

PAGE 191 **'a Cathedral precinct like Canterbury or Winchester'**: Herbert Baker quoted in David Crane, *Empires of the Dead*, p.108.

PAGE 193 **'Many of the ideas which I hold to this day'**: Anthony Eden, *Another World*, Allen Lane, London, 1976, p.81.

PAGE 197 **'We were rushing along in Gillymong'**: Max Arthur, *When This Bloody War is Over*, Piatkus, London, 2002, p.92.

PAGE 198 **'For six weeks, division after division battered up the slope'**: Lyn Macdonald, *The Roses of No Man's Land*, Michael Joseph Ltd, London, 1980, p.178. © Lyn Macdonald 1980.

PAGE 199 **'It's our Goddamned guns. I can't make out what the hell they're up to'**: Lord Moran, *Anatomy of Courage*, p.121.

PAGE 200 **'a terrific noise; everything vanished for a moment'**: Lord Moran, *Anatomy of Courage*, p.121.

PAGE 200 **'The men were angry; they had been let down'**: Lord Moran, *Anatomy of Courage*, p.122.

PAGES 200–1 **'B Company were shelled by our own 9.2s'** and **'Bosch shelled us this afternoon from 3 to 5'**: War Diary 1st RF WO/95/2207/2_1, p.29 of 51. The National Archives.

PAGE 201 **'This perfect unit of the old army has been turned into a labour battalion'**: Lord Moran, *Anatomy of Courage*, p.123.

PAGE 202 **'the men grinned with glee and one big fellow'**: Lord Moran, *Anatomy of Courage*, p.124.

PAGE 202 **'Simultaneously out got a line of forms from the British trenches'**: *Stand To: A Diary of the Trenches 1915-1918*, p.141.

PAGE 203 **'had succeeded in taking Guillemont station'** and **'the best of the men seemed to have gone out'**: Lord Moran, *Anatomy of Courage*, p.125.

PAGE 203 **'Something had happened on the right'**: *Stand To: A Diary of the Trenches 1915-1918*, p.142.

PAGE 204 **'Capt. M.C. Bell took out his two officers and four other ranks'**: War Diary 1st RF WO/95/2207/2_1, pp.34–5 of 51. The National Archives.

PAGE 205    'Them's the First': Lord Moran, *Anatomy of Courage*, p.127.

PAGE 210    'See that little stream – we could walk to it in two minutes': F. Scott Fitzgerald, *Tender is the Night,* Penguin, London, 2010, p.61.

PAGES      '[T]here are places on the Western Front where if you can't feel':
210–11     David Olusoga, speaking on *Desert Island Discs*, broadcast on Radio 4, the 10 January 2021. Reproduced by kind permission of David Olusoga.

## CHAPTER TWELVE – SALONIKA

PAGE 215    'I have watched a thousand days': Rudyard Kipling, *Salonikan Grave*, in *The Definitive Edition of Rudyard Kipling's Verse*, Hodder and Stoughton, London, 1989, p.391.

PAGE 221    'the greatest internment camp in the world': German quote cited in Alan Palmer, *The Gardeners of Salonika*, Andre Deutsch, London, 1965, p.62.

PAGE 222    'The Gardeners of Salonika': Georges Clemenceau, quoted in Alan Palmer, *The Gardeners of Salonika*, p.70.

PAGE 227    'Bulgars discovered our evacuation to right bank of Struma': WO95/4836, 6th Battalion Royal Dublin Fusiliers (RDF) War Diary dated 15/06/17, The National Archives.

## CHAPTER THIRTEEN – EGYPT AND PALESTINE

PAGE 229    'On the rock-strewn hills I heard': from the poem *In Palestine* in Siegfried Sassoon, *Diaries 1915-1918*, Faber and Faber, London 1983, pp.226–7. © Siegfried Sassoon 1983 by kind permission of the Estate of George Sassoon.

PAGE 230    'We have had to read out to the men on parade': Noel Drury in Richard S. Grayson (ed.), *The First World War Diary of Noel Drury, 6th Royal Dublin Fusiliers: Gallipoli, Salonika, The Middle East and the Western Front*, Army Records Society, The Boydell Press, Woodbridge, Suffolk, 2022, pp.185. This and subsequent extracts reproduced with kind permission from the National Army Museum Archive, Accession ref: NAM 1976-07-69.

PAGE 231 **'The 10th Division has landed, with the exception of one battalion':** Letter from Allenby to Robertson dated 26 September 1917 in Matthew Hughes (ed.), *Allenby in Palestine: The Middle East Correspondence of Field Marshal Viscount Allenby,* Army Records Society, Sutton Publishing Ltd, Stroud, Gloucestershire, 2004, p.60.

PAGE 231 **'more resolute leadership':** David Lloyd George, *War Memoirs Volume II,* Odhams Press Limited, London, 1936, p.1087.

PAGES **'I told him in the presence of Sir William Robertson':** David Lloyd
231–32 George, *War Memoirs Volume II,* pp.1089–90.

PAGE 233 **'The Bull'** and **'BBL' – 'Bloody Bull's Loose':** see David R. Woodward, *Forgotten Soldiers of the First World War,* Tempus, Stroud, Gloucestershire, 2006, p.113.

PAGE 236 **'It was the most magnificent sight':** Noel Drury, *The First World War Diary of Noel Drury,* pp.198–9.

PAGE 237 **'employed salvaging enemy war material along Rushdi system':** WO95/4583, 6th RDF War Diary dated 09/11/17, The National Archives.

PAGE 237 **'There is a lot of fever in the 10th Division – some 3,000 cases':** *Allenby in Palestine: The Middle East Correspondence of Field Marshal Viscount Allenby,* p.67.

PAGE 239 **Allenby knew a military genius when he saw one:** A view that Winston Churchill shared. He wrote, 'Lawrence had a full measure of the versatility of genius. He held one of those master keys, which unlock the doors of many kinds of treasure houses. He was a savant as well as a soldier. He was an archaeologist as well as a man of action. He was an accomplished scholar as well as an Arab partisan. He was a mechanic as well as a philosopher': Winston Churchill, *Great Contemporaries,* Odhams Press Ltd, London, 1948, p.129. For quotes reproduced from the speeches, works and writings of Winston S. Churchill: Reproduced with permission of Curtis Brown, London on behalf of The Estate of Winston S. Churchill © The Estate of Winston S. Churchill.

PAGE 240  **a huge bounty payable of £10,000 dead and £20,000 alive on his head**: see Michael Korda, *Hero: The Life and Legend of Lawrence of Arabia*, JR Books, London, 2011, p.358.

PAGE 240  **His activities required that the Ottoman Turks**: The threat posed by Lawrence's Arabs from the desert, to the east of the Ottoman army, caused the Turks to redeploy regiments of experienced troops from the Gaza–Beersheba front to patrol the vital railway supply lines and defend their left flank – estimated to be the equivalent of an extra Army Corps fighting for the British. See Adrian Greaves, *Lawrence of Arabia: Mirage of a Desert War*, Weidenfeld & Nicolson Ltd, London, 2007, pp.226–7.

PAGE 241  **'men show a great improvement in march discipline and turn out'**: WO95/4583, 6th RDF War Diary dated 18/11/17, The National Archives.

PAGE 241  **'Our patrol held up near El Tireh village by about 40 Turks'**: WO95/4583, 6th RDF War Diary dated 05/12/17, The National Archives.

PAGES 241–42  **'During the race north to gain the western approaches to Jerusalem'**: Raymond Savage, *Allenby of Armageddon*, Hodder and Stoughton, London, 1925, pp.219–20.

PAGES 242–3  **'2 representatives sent to join Divisional Party'**: WO95/4583, 6th RDF War Diary dated 10/12/17, The National Archives.

PAGE 243  **'by the evening of the 28th, not only had the enemy failed'**: *Allenby in Palestine: The Middle East Correspondence of Field Marshal Viscount Allenby*, p.149.

PAGES 244–5  **'peculiarly shabby looking fellow mouching along'** and **'He looked such a disgrace that I was on the point'**: Noel Drury, *The First World War Diary of Noel Drury*, p.237.

PAGE 247  **'Events in Europe overtop the little happenings in this theatre'** and **'my own projects have been modified'**: *Allenby in Palestine: The Middle East Correspondence of Field Marshal Viscount Allenby*, p.148.

PAGE 248  'did not expect victory until at least 1919': David Stevenson, *1914–1918 The History of the First World War*, Allen Lane, London, 2004, p.425.

PAGE 249  'we should settle him next year': Lt. Col. Walter Vignoles, 9th Northumberland Fusiliers, quoted in Malcolm Brown, *The Imperial War Museum Book of 1918: Year of Victory,* Sidgwick & Jackson, London, 1998, p.219.

PAGE 249  'the black day of the German Army in the history of the war': General Erich von Ludendorff, quoted in Malcolm Brown, *The Imperial War Museum Book of 1918: Year of Victory,* p.190.

## CHAPTER FOURTEEN – RETURN TO THE WESTERN FRONT

PAGE 251  'Tis not the bit of bronze and metal': Lee Charles McCollum, *The Medal,* from Fiona Waters (Selected by), *A Corner of a Foreign Field: The Illustrated Poetry of the First World War,* Transatlantic Press, Croxley Green, Herts, 2007, p.169.

PAGE 253  'The enemy are now driven into the open country': Noel Drury, *The First World War Diary of Noel Drury,* p.259.

PAGES 253–54  'We were all itching to get on fast': Noel Drury, *The First World War Diary of Noel Drury,* p.260.

PAGE 256  'During the three days' fighting the Division advanced': Brian Bond and Simon Robbins (eds), *Staff Officer: The Diaries of Walter Guinness (First Lord Moyne) 1914–1918,* Leo Cooper, London, 1987, p.234.

PAGES 259–60  'The South African attack went on fast': Noel Drury, *The First World War Diary of Noel Drury,* p.266.

PAGES 260–61  '"A" Company met with considerable opposition from all quarters': WO95/3140, 6th RDF War Diary, Operations 16–17 October 1918, The National Archives.

PAGE 262  'Boys, girls, old men and women lay mangled in heaps': Peter Hodgkinson, *The Battle of the Selle: Fourth Army Operations on the*

*Western Front in the Hundred Days, 9-24 October 1918*, Helion & Company Limited, Solihull, West Midlands, 2017, p.166. © Peter Hodgkinson 2017. Reproduced by kind permission of Helion & Company.

PAGE 262     **'I got down into Le Cateau about 15:00'**: Noel Drury, *The First World War Diary of Noel Drury*, p.267.

PAGE 263     **'The BGC wishes to congratulate the Brigade'**: WO95/3140-3_02, 6th Battalion Lancashire Fusiliers War Diary, Missive dated 21/10/18, p.1 of 130, The National Archives.

PAGE 264     **'thruster in a class of his own'** and **'like quicksilver'**: *Staff Officer: The Diaries of Walter Guinness (First Lord Moyne) 1914-1918*, p.16.

PAGE 264     **when he was accused of losing a document**: *Staff Officer: The Diaries of Walter Guinness (First Lord Moyne) 1914-1918*, p.17.

PAGE 265     **'a wonderful fighting soldier, but a terror to the administration of an army'**: *Staff Officer: The Diaries of Walter Guinness (First Lord Moyne) 1914-1918*, p.17.

PAGE 265     **'the drive, marching and staying power of the men'**, and **'foresight and initiative displayed by junior officers and NCOs'**: WO95/3140/3_02, 6th Battalion Lancashire Fusiliers War Diary, Special Order dated 24/10/18, p.4 of 130, The National Archives.

PAGE 265     **'The 6th RDF of 198th Bde were detailed to mop up Le Cateau'**: WO95/3140/3_02, 6th Battalion Lancashire Fusiliers War Diary, Special Order dated 24/10/18, p.3 of 130, The National Archives.

PAGE 266     **'Well, we stop today'**: Noel Drury, *The First World War Diary of Noel Drury*, p.280.

PAGE 267     **'[T]hey just stared at me and showed no enthusiasm at all'**: Noel Drury, *The First World War Diary of Noel Drury*, p.280.

PAGE 267     **'To it [the 66th Division] fell the honour of retaking Le Cateau'**: WO95/3140/3, 6th Battalion LF War Diary, Special Order dated 17/11/18, The National Archives.

PAGE 273    **'There are strange Hells within the minds War made'**: Ivor Gurney, *Strange Hells*, in Andrew Motion (ed.), *First World War Poems*, Faber and Faber, London, 2003, p.73.

PAGE 274    **'What is our task? To make Britain a fit country for heroes to live in.'**: David Lloyd George (Earl Lloyd-George of Dwyfor) 1863-1945. Speech at Wolverhampton, 23 November 1918, quoted in *The Times*, 25th November 1918. (The Oxford Dictionary of Modern Quotations" by Tony Augarde.)

PAGE 275    **'Where are they now on State-doles, or showing shop patterns'**: Ivor Gurney, *Strange Hells*, in Andrew Motion (ed.), *First World War Poems*, p.73.

PAGE 275    **'Died some, pro patria'**: Ezra Pound, *Hugh Selwyn Mauberley (Life and contacts)*, in Andrew Motion (ed.), *First World War Poems*, Faber and Faber, London, 2003, p.138. Reproduced with permission from Faber and Faber Ltd.

PAGE 276    **'That it is a gigantic problem'**: *Unhealthy Areas Committee paper*, 14 January 1920, Catalogue ref: HLG 101/258B, The National Archives. The Ministry of Health appointed Neville Chamberlain as chair of an Unhealthy Areas Committee, to determine the scale of the housing problem and make recommendations regarding slum clearance and the redevelopment of housing.

PAGE 276    **In Bermondsey alone, 10,000 houses**: figure mentioned in speech by the Bishop of Southwark quoted in Roy Hattersley, *Borrowed Time: The Story of Britain Between the Wars*, p.205.

PAGE 276    **As late as 1935, across the whole of the country**: figure quoted in Roy Hattersley, *Borrowed Time: The Story of Britain Between the Wars*, Little Brown, London, 2007, p.211.

PAGE 278    **'Us fellows, it took us years to get over it. Years!'**: Rifleman Fred White in Max Arthur, *We Will Remember Them: Voices from the aftermath of the Great War*, Weidenfeld & Nicolson, London, 2009, pp.157–8. © Max Arthur 2009. Reproduced with kind permission of Orion Publishing Group Limited through PLSclear.

PAGE 279 **Ramsay Macdonald, relied on the unimaginative economic orthodoxy**: For an in-depth analysis of Ramsay MacDonald's handling of the economic crisis, see Roy Hattersley, *Borrowed Time: The Story of Britain Between the Wars*, pp.159–168.

PAGE 285 **'Which ended with the ambulance outside'**: Michael Longley, *In Memoriam*, in Andrew Motion (ed.), *First World War Poems*, Faber and Faber, London, 2003, p.157.

## CHAPTER SIXTEEN – REMEMBRANCE SUNDAY, 13 NOVEMBER 2005, CHURCH OF ST. SEPULCHRE-WITHOUT-NEWGATE, HOLBORN VIADUCT, LONDON

PAGE 286 **'And you, the soldier: you who are dead'**: Conrad Aiken, *The wars and the unknown soldier*, from Fiona Waters (Selected by), *A Corner of a Foreign Field: The Illustrated Poetry of the First World War*, Transatlantic Press, Croxley Green, Herts, 2007, pp.166–7. © Conrad Aiken. Reproduced with kind permission of Oxford Publishing Limited through PLSclear.

PAGE 286 **O valiant hearts, who to your glory came'**: This hymn is widely used in Remembrance Day services throughout the United Kingdom and the Commonwealth. Originally a poem by Sir John Stanhope Arkwright, it was later set to music.

PAGE 287 **and naught more deadly than the *Storm of Steel***: a reference to Ernst Junger's memoir of the Great War. Incidentally, Junger was deployed at Guillemont a matter of days after William was wounded in action there.

PAGE 291 **'I still look back on the 13th of November as a wonderful day'**: Letter from Florence Maybank (née Blumsom) to the author, dated 5th December 2005.

PAGE 291 **'Life, adversity, isolation, abandonment, poverty, are battlefields'**: Victor Hugo, *Les Misérables*, Penguin Books, London, 2016, p.613.

# BIBLIOGRAPHY

Ahamed, Liaquat, *Lords of Finance*, Windmill Books, London, 2010

Allen, Charles, *Duel in the Snows*, John Murray, London, 2004

Archer, Geoffrey, *The Glorious Dead: Figurative Sculpture of British First World War Memorials*, Frontier Publishing, Kirstead, 2009

Archer, Thomas, *The Pauper, The Thief and the Convict; Sketches of some of their Homes, Haunts and Habits*, Groombridge and Sons, London, 1865

Arthur, Max, *We Will Remember Them: Voices from the aftermath of the Great War*, Weidenfeld & Nicolson, London, 2009

Bailey, Victor, *Charles Booth's Policemen: Crime, Police and Community in Jack-the-Ripper's London*, Breviary Stuff Publications, London, 2014

Baker, Kenneth (ed.), *The Faber Book of War Poetry*, Faber and Faber, London, 1996

Baker, T.F.T. (ed.), *A History of the County of Middlesex: Volume 11, Stepney, Bethnal Green*, Victoria County History, London, 1998

Barr, James, *Setting the Desert on Fire: T.E. Lawrence and Britain's Secret War in Arabia, 1916-18*, Bloomsbury, London, 2006

Begg, Paul, *Jack the Ripper: The Definitive History*, Routledge, London, 2004

Bennett, Alan, *The History Boys: The Film*, Faber & Faber, London, 2006

Benson, John, *The Working Class in Britain 1850-1939*, I.B. Taurus, London, 2003

Birkin, Andrew, *J.M. Barrie & the Lost Boys*, Constable, London, 1979

Bishop, Alan and Bostridge, Mark (eds), *Letters from a Lost Generation: First World War Letters of Vera Brittain and Four Friends*, Little, Brown and Company, London, 1998

Blake, Robert (ed.), *The Private Papers of Douglas Haig 1914-1919*, Eyre and Spottiswoode, London, 1952

Bond, Brian and Simon Robbins (eds), *Staff Officer: The Diaries of Walter Guinness (First Lord Moyne) 1914-1918*, Leo Cooper, London, 1987

Bostridge, Mark, *Vera Brittain and the First World War*, Bloomsbury, London, 2014

Bourke, Joanna (ed.), *The Misfit Soldier: Edward Casey's War Story 1914-1918*, Cork University Press, Cork, 1999

Bowman, Timothy, *Irish Regiments in the Great War: Discipline and Morale*, Manchester University Press, Manchester and New York, 2004

Brice, Beatrice, *The Battle Book of Ypres: A Reference to Military Operations in the Ypres Salient 1914-1918*, Pen and Sword Military, Barnsley, 2014

Brits, Elsabé, *Emily Hobhouse: Feminist, Pacifist, Traitor?* Robinson, London, 2018

Brittain, Vera, *Testament of Youth*, Weidenfeld & Nicolson, London, 2009

Brophy, John and Partridge, Eric, *The Daily Telegraph Dictionary of Tommies' Songs and Slang, 1914-18*, Frontline Books, London, 2008

Brown, Malcolm, *The Imperial War Museum Book of 1918: Year of Victory*, Sidgwick & Jackson, London, 1998

Brown, Malcolm (ed.), *T.E. Lawrence in War and Peace: An Anthology of the Military Writings of Lawrence of Arabia*, Greenhill Books, London, 2005

Cannan, May Wedderburn, *The Tears of War: The Love Story of a Young Poet and a War Hero*, Cavalier Books, Upavon, 2000

Cannon, Richard; Groves, John Percy & Waller, G. H., *Historical Records of the 7th or Royal Regiment of Fusiliers: now known as the Royal Fusiliers (The City of London Regiment), 1685-1903*, Frederick B. Guerin, Guernsey, 1903

Carver, Lord, *The National Army Museum Book of the Turkish Front 1914-1918*, Sidgwick and Jackson, London, 2003

Chinn, Carl, *Poverty amidst Prosperity: The urban poor in England, 1834-1914*, Carnegie Publishing Ltd, Lancaster, 2006

Chiozza Money, L. G, *Things That Matter*, Methuen & Co, London, 1912

Churchill, Winston, *Great Contemporaries*, Odhams Press Ltd, London, 1948

Clark, Alan, *The Donkeys*, Pimlico, London, 1991

Collinson Owen, H, *Salonica and After*, Hodder and Stoughton, London, 1919

Cook, Judith, *Daphne: A Portrait of Daphne Du Maurier*, Bantam Press, London, 1991

Cooper, Bryan, *The Tenth (Irish) Division in Gallipoli*, The Naval and Military Press, Uckfield, 2009

Crane, David, *The Empires of the Dead: How One Man's Vision Led to the Creation of WWI's War Graves*, William Collins, London, 2013

Cruickshank, Dan, *Spitalfields: The History of a Nation in a Handful of Streets*, Random House Books, London, 2016

Dendooven, Dominiek, *Menin Gate and Last Post: Ypres as Holy Ground*, De Klaproos Editions, Koksijde, Belgium, 2003

Dixon, John, *Magnificent But Not War: The Second Battle of Ypres 1915*, Pen and Sword Books Ltd, Barnsley, 2003

Dooner, Mildred G, *The Last Post: a roll of all officers (naval, military or colonial) who gave their lives for their queen, king and country, in the South African War, 1899-1902,* J. B. Hayward & Son, London, 1980

Dudgeon, Piers, *Our East End: Memories of Life in Disappearing Britain,* Headline Review, 2008

Du Maurier, Guy, *An Englishman's Home,* Harper & Brothers, New York and London, 1909

Dungan, Myles, *Irish Voices from the Great War,* Irish Academic Press, Dublin, 1998

Dunn, James Churchill, *The War the Infantry Knew 1914-1919,* Abacus, London, 2004

Dunn, Jane, *Daphne Du Maurier and Her Sisters: The Hidden Lives of Piffy, Bird and Bing,* Harper Press, London, 2013

Eastwood, Stuart, *Lions of England: A pictorial history of the King's Own Royal Regiment (Lancaster) 1680-1980,* Silver Link Publishing Ltd, Kettering, 1991

Eden, Anthony, *Another World,* Allen Lane, London, 1976

Edmonds, Brigadier General, J.E. and Wynne, Captain, G.C. *Official History of the War Military Operations France and Belgium 1915, Vol. I,* Reprint by Battery Press, Nashville, Tennessee, originally published 1927.

Egremont, Max, *Siegfried Sassoon A Biography,* Picador, London, 2005

Engels, Friedrich, *The Condition of the Working Class in England,* Penguin, London, 2005

Englander, David and O'Day, Rosemary, *Retrieved Riches: Social Investigation in Britain, 1840-1914,* Scolar Press, Aldershot, 1995

Falls, Cyril, *History of the Great War: Military Operations Macedonia from the Spring of 1917 to the End of the War,* IWM, London and the Battery Press Nashville, Tennessee, reprint of 1935 edition.

Farrar-Hockley, Anthony, *The Somme: The Death of a Generation,* Cerberus Publishing Limited, Bristol, 2004

Fishman, William. J, *East End 1888: A Year in a London Borough among the labouring poor,* Five Leaves Publications, Nottingham, 2008

Fitzgerald, F. Scott, *Tender is the Night,* Penguin, London, 2000

Foss, Michael, *The Royal Fusiliers,* Hamish Hamilton, London, 1967

Fox, Alan. A, *A History of the National Union of Boot and Shoe Operatives,* Blackwell, Oxford, 1958

Fussell, Paul, *The Great War and Modern Memory,* Oxford University Press, New York, 2013

Fussell, Paul (ed.), *Sassoon's Long Journey: An illustrated selection from Siegfried Sassoon's 'The Complete Memoirs of George Sherston'*, Faber & Faber, London, 1983

Gavin, Hector, *Sanitary Ramblings: Being Sketches and Illustrations of Bethnal Green,* John Churchill, London, 1848

Glinert, Ed, *East End Chronicles,* Allen Lane, London, 2005

Graham, Stephen, *The Challenge of the Dead,* Cassell and Co Ltd, London, 1921

Graves, Robert, *Goodbye to All That,* Everyman's Library, London, 2018

Grayson, Richard, S. (ed.), *The First World War Diary of Noel Drury, 6th Royal Dublin Fusiliers: Gallipoli, Salonika, The Middle East and the Western Front,* Army Records Society, The Boydell Press, Woodbridge, Suffolk, 2022.

Greaves, Adrian, *Lawrence of Arabia: Mirage of a Desert War*, Weidenfeld & Nicolson Ltd, London, 2007

Grierson, Sir James Moncrieff, *Scarlet into Khaki,* Greenhill Books, London, 1988

Griffith, Paddy, *Battle Tactics of the Western Front: The British Army's Art of Attack 1916-18,* Yale University Press, New Haven & London, 1994

Griffith, Paddy (ed.), *British Fighting Methods in the Great War,* Frank Cass, London, 1996

Gwynn, Robin, *The Huguenots of London,* The Alpha Press, Brighton, 1998

Gwynn, Robin, *Huguenot Heritage: The history and contribution of the Huguenots in Britain,* Routledge & Kegan Paul, London, 1985

Hall, Anne, *The Du Mauriers: Just As They Were,* Unicorn, London, 2018

Hankey, Donald, *A Student in Arms,* Andrew Melrose Ltd, London, 1917

Harding, James, *Gerald du Maurier: A Biography,* Hodder & Stoughton, London, 1989

Hart, Peter, *The Somme,* Weidenfeld and Nicolson, London, 2005

Hattersley, Roy, *Borrowed Time: The Story of Britain Between the Wars*, Little Brown, London, 2007

Hattersley, Roy, *David Lloyd George, The Great Outsider*, Little Brown, London, 2010

Hemingway, Ernest, *A Moveable Feast,* Jonathan Cape, London, 2010

Higginbotham, Peter, *Workhouses of London and the South East,* The History Press, Stroud, Gloucestershire, 2019

Hitchcock, F.C, *Stand To: A Diary of the Trenches,* The Naval and Military Press, Uckfield, 2009

Hobsbawm, Eric, *Labouring Men: Studies in the History of Labour*, Weidenfeld & Nicolson Ltd, London, 1964

Hodgkinson, Peter, The Battle of the Selle: *Fourth Army Operations on the Western Front in the Hundred Days, 9-24 October 1918*, Helion & Company Limited, Solihull, West Midlands, 2017

Hollingshead, John, *Ragged London in 1861*, Dodo Press, Gloucester, reprint of 1861 edition

Holmes, Richard, *Sahib: The British Soldier in India*, Harper Collins, London, 2005

Holmes, Richard (ed.), *The Little Field Marshal: A Life of Sir John French*, Weidenfeld & Nicolson Ltd, London, 2004

Holmes, Richard (ed.), *The Oxford Companion to Military History*, Oxford University Press, Oxford, 2001

Hughes, Matthew (ed.), *Allenby in Palestine: The Middle East Correspondence of Field Marshal Viscount Allenby*, Army Records Society, Sutton Publishing Ltd, Stroud, Gloucestershire, 2004

Hugo, Victor, *Les Misérables*, Penguin Books, London, 2016

Hutton, Mike, *1919 A Land Fit for Heroes: Britain at Peace*, Amberley Publishing, Stroud, 2019

Inwood, Stephen, *City of Cities: The Birth of Modern London*, Macmillan, London, 2005

Jackson, Tabitha, *The Boer War*, Channel 4 Books, London, 1999

Johnstone, Tom, *Orange, Green and Khaki: The Story of the Irish Regiments in the Great War 1914-1918*, Gill and Macmillan, Dublin, 1992

Judd, Denis and Surridge, Keith, *The Boer War*, John Murray, London, 2002

Junger, Ernst, *Storm of Steel*, Penguin Modern Classics, London, 2004

Korda, Michael, *Hero: The Life and Legend of Lawrence of Arabia*, JR Books, London, 2011

Law, John (Margaret Harkness), *Out of Work*, Swan Sonnenschein & Co., London, 1888

Lawrence, T.E., *Minorities*, Jonathan Cape, London, 1971

Lawrence, T.E., *Revolt in the Desert*, Wordsworth, Ware, Hertfordshire, 1997

Livermore, Bernard, *Long 'Un: A Damn Bad Soldier*, Harry Hayes, Batley, West Yorkshire, 1974

Lloyd, David. W., *Battlefield Tourism*, Bloomsbury Academic, London, 1998

Lloyd George, David, *War Memoirs, Volume II*, Odhams Press Limited, London, 1936

London, Jack, *The People of the Abyss,* Tangerine Press, Tooting, 2014

Lovell, Richard, *Churchill's Doctor: A biography of Lord Moran,* Royal Society of Medicine Services Ltd, London, 1992

Macdonald, Lyn, *The Roses of No Man's Land,* Michael Joseph Ltd, London, 1980

Macdonald, Lyn, *Somme,* Michael Joseph Ltd, London, 1983

Macdonald, Lyn, *They called it Passchendaele: The Story of the Battle of Ypres and of the men who fought in it,* Michael Joseph Ltd, London, 1988

Macdonald, Lyn, *1915: The Death of Innocence,* Headline Book Publishing, 1993

Macdonald, Lyn, *To the Last Man: Spring 1918,* Viking, 1998

Mackenzie, Compton, *My Life and Times: Octave One 1883-1891,* Chatto and Windus, London, 1963

Mallinson, Allan, *The Making of the British Army: From the English Civil War to the War on Terror,* Bantam Press, London, 2009

Marden, Thomas Owen (ed.), *A Short History of the 6th Division August 1914-March 1919,* Naval and Military Press, Uckfield, Facsimile edition

Marriott, John, *Beyond the Tower: A history of East London,* Yale University Press, New Haven and London, 2011

Marwick, Arthur, *The Deluge: British Society and the First World War,* Macmillan, London, 1978

Maurice, Major-General Sir Frederick, *History of the War in South Africa 1899-1902: Volume IV,* Naval and Military Press Ltd, Uckfield, Facsimile edition

Mayhew, Henry, *London Labour and the London Poor: Selection,* Penguin, London, 1985

Mayhew, Henry, *London Labour and the London Poor,* Wordsworth, Ware, 2008

Mayhew, Henry and Quennell, Peter (ed.), *Mayhew's London,* Spring Books, 1969

McCarthy, Terry, *The Great Dock Strike 1889,* Weidenfeld & Nicolson Ltd, London, 1988

Meacham, Standish, *A Life Apart: The English Working Class 1890-1914,* Thames and Hudson, 1977

Middlebrook, Martin, *The First Day on the Somme: 1 July 1916,* Penguin, London, 2001

Middlebrook, Martin, *The Kaiser's Battle,* Penguin, London, 2000

Mighall, Garry (ed.), *Voice from the Past: The life and letters of Joseph William Blumson 1881 to 1937,* University of South Australia, Adelaide, 2001

Miller, Stephen M, *Volunteers on the Veld: Britain's Citizen-Soldiers and the South African War 1899-1902*, University of Oklahoma Press, Norman, 2007

Moorcroft Wilson, Jean, *Robert Graves: From Great War Poet to Good-bye to All That (1895-1929)*, Bloomsbury, London, 2018

Moran, Lord, *Anatomy of Courage*, Avery Publishing, New York, 1987

Morrison, Arthur, *A Child of the Jago*, Oxford University Press, Oxford, 2012

Motion, Andrew (ed.), *First World War Poems*, Faber & Faber, London, 2003

O'Day, Rosemary and Englander, David, *Mr Charles Booth's Inquiry*, The Hambledon Press, London, 1993

O'Neill, Gilda, *My East End: A History of Cockney London*, Viking, London, 1999

O'Neill, H.C., *The Royal Fusiliers in the Great War*, Naval and Military Press, Uckfield, Facsimile edition

Orr, Emily, *A Harvester of Dreams*, Burns, Oates & Washbourne Ltd, London, 1922

Overy, Richard, *The Morbid Age: Britain Between the Wars*, Allen Lane, London, 2009

Packe, Edmund. C, *An Empire-Building Battalion: Being a History, with Reminiscences, of the 3rd Battalion Royal Fusiliers*, Edgar Backus, Leicester, 1956

Page, William (ed.), *A History of the County of Middlesex: Volume 2, General; Ashford, East Bedfont With Hatton, Feltham, Hampton With Hampton Wick, Hanworth, Laleham, Littleton*, Victoria County History, London, 1911

Pakenham, Thomas, *The Boer War*, Weidenfeld & Nicolson Ltd, London, 1979

Palmer, Alan, *The East End: Four Centuries of London Life*, Rutgers University Press, New Brunswick, New Jersey, 2000

Palmer, Alan, *The Gardeners of Salonika*, Andre Deutsch, London, 1965

Parkhouse, Valerie B., *Memorializing the Anglo-Boer War of 1899-1902: Militarization of the Landscape - Monuments and Memorials in Britain*, Matador, Kibworth Beauchamp, 2015

Pember Reeves, Maud, *Round About a Pound a Week*, Persephone, London, 2008

Pollock, John, *Kitchener*, Constable, London, 2001

Price, Richard, *An Imperial War and the British Working Class*, Routledge & Kegan Paul, London, 1972

Prior, Robin and Wilson, Trevor, *The Somme*, Yale University Press, New Haven and London, 2005

Prothero, Iorwerth, *Artisans and Politics in Early Nineteenth Century London*, Routledge, London, 2014

Radice, Betty (Translated by), *The Letters of Pliny the Younger*, Penguin, London, 2003

Reaney, P.H., *A Dictionary of British Surnames*, Routledge and Keegan Paul, London, 1979

Reed, Paul, *Walking the Salient: A Walker's Guide to the Ypres Salient*, Leo Cooper, Barnsley, 2004

Reese, Peter, *Homecoming Heroes: An Account of the Reassimilation of British Military Personnel into Civilian Life*, Leo Cooper, Barnsley, 1992

Richards, Frank, *Old Soldier Sahib*, Parthian Library of Wales, Cardigan, 2016

Richards, Frank, *Old Soldiers Never Die*, Parthian Library of Wales, Cardigan, 2016

Riello, Giorgio, *A Foot in the Past: Consumers, Producers, and Footwear in the Long Eighteenth Century (Pasold Studies in Textile History)*, OUP, 2006

Rowntree, Benjamin Seebohm, *Poverty, A Study of Town Life*, London, 1901

Rubenhold, Hallie, *The Five: The Untold Lives of the Women Killed by Jack the Ripper*, Doubleday, London, 2019

Rule, Fiona, *The Worst Street in London*, Ian Allan Ltd, Hersham, Surrey, 2008

St Leger, Stratford, *Mounted Infantry at War*, Galago, Alberton, South Africa, 1986

Sandford, Stephen, *Neither Unionist nor Nationalist: The 10th (Irish) Division in the Great War*, Irish Academic Press, Sallins, Ireland, 2015

Sassoon, Siegfried, *Memories of an Infantry Officer*, Folio Society, London, 1974

Sassoon, Siegfried, *Diaries 1915-1918*, Faber and Faber Ltd, London, 1983

Sassoon, Siegfried, *The War Poems*, Faber and Faber Ltd, London, 1983

Savage, Raymond, *Allenby of Armageddon*, Hodder and Stoughton, London, 1925

Schneer, Jonathan, *London 1900: The Imperial Metropolis*, Yale University Press, New Haven and London, 1999

Sims, George. R, *Off the track in London*, Jarrold & Sons, 1911

Smith, Tim. R, *'Just say Sarson's – the vinegar brewery, Tower Bridge Road, Bermondsey'*, in London's Industrial Archaeology, No 10, 2012

Stamp, Gavin, *The Memorial to the Missing of the Somme*, Profile Books, London, 2006

Stanley, Jeremy, *Ireland's Forgotten 10th: A brief history of the 10th (Irish) Division 1914-1918 Turkey, Macedonia and Palestine*, Impact Publishers, Ballycastle and Coleraine, 2003

Steele, Jess (ed.), *The Streets of London: The Booth Notebooks – South East*, Deptford Forum Publishing Ltd, London, 1997

Steele, Jess and Steele, Mike (ed.), *The Streets of London: The Booth Notebooks –*
*East,* Deptford Forum Publishing Ltd, London, 2018

Stevenson, David, *1914-1918 The History of the First World War*, Allen Lane,
London, 2004

Stevenson, Tim and Carol (ed.), *A Short Guide to Nunhead Cemetery*, The Friends
of Nunhead Cemetery, London, 2003

Stirling, John, *Our Regiments in South Africa 1899-1902,* William Blackwood
and Sons, Edinburgh and London, 1903

Sutherland, Gillian, *Elementary Education in the Nineteenth Century,* The
Historical Association, London, 1971

Talbot, Philip. A, '*The Regular Mounted Infantry: The Chronic Ikonas of the*
*Composite Regiment*', Journal of the Society for Army Historical Research,
Vol. 82, No. 332, Winter 2004

Taylor, A.J.P., *The First World War: An Illustrated History*, Penguin, London, 1966

Thompson, E.P. and Yeo, Eileen (eds.), *The Unknown Mayhew: Selections from*
*the Morning Chronicle 1849-50*, Pelican Books, Penguin Books Ltd, London,
1973

Tomalin, Claire, *Thomas Hardy: The Time-Torn Man,* Viking, London, 2006

Treasure, Geoffrey, *The Huguenots,* Yale University Press, New Haven and
London, 2013

Trow, M.J., *Ripper Hunter: Abberline and the Whitechapel Murders,* Pen and
Sword Books Ltd, Barnsley, 2012

Van Emden, Richard, *The Soldier's War: The Great War through veterans' eyes*,
Bloomsbury, London, 2008

Van Wyk Smith, Malvern, *Drummer Hodge: The Poetry of the Anglo-Boer War*
*1899-1902*, Oxford University Press, Oxford, 1978

Verney, David, *The Joyous Patriot: The Correspondence of Ralph Verney 1900-1916,*
Leo Cooper, London, 1989

Walkinton, M.L., *Twice in a Lifetime,* Samson Books, London, 1980

Wakefield, Alan and Moody, Simon, *Under the Devil's Eye: Britain's Forgotten*
*Army at Salonika 1915-1918,* Sutton Publishing Limited, Stroud,
Gloucestershire, 2004

Waters, Fiona (Selected by), *A Corner of a Foreign Field: The Illustrated Poetry of*
*the First World War*, Transatlantic Press, Croxley Green, Herts, 2007

West, David (Translated by), *Horace: The Complete Odes and Epodes*, Oxford
University Press, Oxford, 2008

Wise, Sarah, *The Blackest Streets: The Life and Death of a Victorian Slum*, The Bodley Head, London, 2008

Wood, Evelyn, *From Midshipman to Field Marshal*, Methuen & Co, London, 1906

Woodward, David. R, *Forgotten Soldiers of the First World War: Lost Voices from the Middle Eastern Front*, Tempus, 2006

Young, Michael and Wilmott, Peter, *Family and Kinship in East London*, Penguin, London, 2007

# ARCHIVES

WO/95/1613/2 War Diary 1st Battalion Royal Fusiliers 01/10/1914 to 31/10/1915 TNA

WO/95/2207/2 War Diary 1st Battalion Royal Fusiliers 01/11/1915 to 07/07/1918 TNA

WO/95/2208/1 War Diary 12th Battalion Royal Fusiliers 21/08/1915 to 13/02/1918 TNA

WO/95/1612/2 War Diary 2nd Battalion Leinster Regiment 01/03/1915 to 31/10/1915 TNA

WO/95/2218/1 War Diary 2nd Battalion Leinster Regiment 01/11/1915 to 31/01/1918 TNA

WO/95/4836 War Diary 6th Battalion Royal Dublin Fusiliers 01/01/1917 to 31/08/1917 TNA

WO/95/4583 War Diary 6th Battalion Royal Dublin Fusiliers 01/09/1917 to 30/06/1918 TNA

WO/95/3140/2 War Diary 6th Battalion Royal Dublin Fusiliers 01/07/1918 to 29/04/1918 TNA

WO95/3140/3 War Diary 6th Battalion Lancashire Fusiliers 01/03/1918 to 30/04/1919 TNA

WO/95/2643/4 War Diary 21st Battalion Kings Royal Rifle Corps 05/05/1916 to 31/10/1917 TNA

WO/95/1437/1 War Diary 2nd Battalion Suffolk Regiment 01/11/1915 to 31/08/1918 TNA

WO/95/2586/1 War Diary 16th Battalion Rifle Brigade 01/03/1916 to 30/09/1916 TNA

WO/95/2196/1 War Diary Assistant Director Medical Services 24th Division 21/08/1915 to 30/03/1917 TNA

WO/95/2202/1_3 War Diary 72nd Field Ambulance 24th Div. 26/04/1916 to 31/08/1916 TNA

WO/95/2202/2_1 War Diary 73rd Field Ambulance 24th Div. 21/08/1915 to 30/09/1916 TNA

WO/95/2202/3_2 War Diary 74th Field Ambulance 24th Div. 01/06/1916 to 31/12/1916 TNA

# ACKNOWLEDGEMENTS

First and foremost, I would like to thank my longsuffering wife Kim, who has had to live with this obsession for many years – not just my physical absences roaming the battlefields of Belgium and France but also my frequent and ongoing absences of mind when inhabiting the virtual world of my grandfather's reconstructed life. This would never have come to fruition without you. My gifted daughters, Naomi and Natasha, whose support includes reading the manuscript, advice on marketing, and transcribing Lord Moran's handwritten diary. My friend Andrew Minns, who has travelled much of this journey with me. To Fanny Sercu and Patrick Smart, proprietors of 'Ben's Bar at 28' in Ypres, friendly and welcoming hosts who have kept our touring party fed and watered for the best part of two decades. Relatives from the extended Blumsom clan who generously shared the fruits of their genealogical research: Margaret Blumsom, Sandra Kitchen-Hurle, and from the Canadian branch of the family, Jeff Blumsom. My former tutor at the Open University, Dr John O'Donoghue, poet, teacher, and survivor, whose unceasing support and encouragement gave me the confidence to see this through. Jill Stewart and Eve Wilson of the Western Front Association, who gave up their precious time to read my manuscript and make some invaluable suggestions. Ann Wilmore, bookseller, of Bookends, Fowey, Cornwall, who kindly showed me a rare copy of Guy du Maurier's published Great War letters and provided new leads to follow. To Andrew Birkin, author, screenwriter, and director, who generously went to some lengths to retrieve copies of letters by Guy du Maurier, written whilst he commanded my grandfather's MI battalion in South Africa. David Olusoga, historian, writer, and broadcaster, who kindly gave me permission to quote from his Radio 4 broadcast *Desert Island Discs*, which aired on the 10 January 2021. To the University of South Australia, who generously gifted me a copy of my distant cousin's published letters. To the staff of the Imperial War Museum, the National Archives, the National Army Museum, and the Wellcome Trust Library, all of whom were unfailingly efficient and helpful.

# ABOUT THE AUTHOR

Paul Blumsom is a former detective who completed thirty-one years' service as a police officer and a further seven years as a civilian police investigator. During his police service, he enrolled with the Open University and graduated with a First-Class Honours Degree in Humanities with History in 2012. He has a long-standing interest in the Great War and is a member of the Western Front Association, regularly contributing articles to the WFA website. He is a seasoned traveller and tour guide to the battlefields of Belgium and France, leading groups of serving and retired police officers.

BV - #0009 - 260225 - C8 - 234/156/19 - PB - 9781068311116 - Gloss Lamination